CASES AND PROBLEMS IN POLITICAL ECONOMY

CASES AND PROBLEMS IN POLITICAL ECONOMY

Barry Keating

Virginia Polytechnic Institute
and State University

Dolores Tremewan Martin

The University of Nebraska
Lincoln

McGraw-Hill Book Company

New York St. Louis San Francisco Auckland Bogotá
Düsseldorf Johannesburg London Madrid Mexico
Montreal New Delhi Panama Paris São Paulo
Singapore Sydney Tokyo Toronto

This book was set in Univers by Allen Wayne Technical Corp.
The editors were J. S. Dietrich, Marjorie Singer, and J. W. Maisel;
the designer was Joan O'Connor;
the production supervisor was Dennis J. Conroy.
R. R. Donnelley & Sons Company was printer and binder.

CASES AND PROBLEMS IN POLITICAL ECONOMY

2 3 4 5 6 7 8 9 0 DODO 7 8 3 2 1 0 9 8

Library of Congress Cataloging in Publication Data

Keating, Barry.
Cases and problems in political economy.

1. Economics. 2. Economics—Case studies.
I. Martin, Dolores Tremewan, joint author. II. Title.
HB171.5.K38 330 77-27910
ISBN 0-07-045173-7

Contents

To the Instructor

The purpose of *Cases and Problems in Political Economy* is to provide a learning-by-doing approach to economic analysis. This book is designed to be used either in introductory economics classes or "current topics" sequences in economics. Because the book is divided into topics roughly corresponding to those in many principles of economics courses, it can be used as a supplement to such courses or as the primary text for a one-semester introductory economics or current topics course. Since the book concentrates on the application of economic concepts rather than theory, a course built around the book will probably require lectures covering some basic theoretical concepts.

The case method of teaching is the most unique feature of this book; it stems from the authors' belief that only reading sound advice or simply listening to economic statements does little for anyone. The key to grasping and understanding the tools of economic analysis is to practice them. A child learns to walk and talk by trying; college and university students can learn about the tools and methods of economic analysis by applying them. The cases given here will allow students to learn in that they will provoke inquiry rather than relay information in the standard textbook format.

The cases in this book are realistic, and many are rather interesting, but their primary value lies in their ability to stimulate the students' independent constructive thinking. They are descriptions of specific instances or situations. Each description is an abstraction, but some are less abstract than others. The descriptions are the raw materials of economic analysis.

The authors recognize that each instructor will wish to cover some topics and not others; therefore, the book is designed so that each chapter is self-contained. Each chapter includes an introduction to the student that briefly explains any background needed for analyzing the case. A list of the key concepts and definitions relevant to the case at hand are also included in each chapter. The questions directly following each of the cases are designed to guide the student accurately to the most important economic considerations in the case. The "Test Yourself" section of each of the chapters and the answers which appear at the end of this book are designed as aids to students in that they will furnish a simple and rapid method of reinforcement for the materials included in the chapter.

The use of a textbook in a first course in economics does not preclude the use of the case method. Although a textbook's accomplishments cannot be overstated (e.g., economy in presentation of facts), there ought to be some consolidation of substantive knowledge in economic analysis. The case method provides this consolidation in a setting where all members of the group (both the students and the instructor) are given the same basic set of facts on which analyses are to be made and decisions obtained. Each individual has an identical opportunity to contribute to the economic analysis.

In order to give the instructor an idea of what we were aiming at in posing each of the questions following the cases, we have provided detailed answers (available from us) to each of these questions. These *suggested guidelines* are designed not to be definitive answers to each of the questions but to represent the authors' view of at least one correct application of economic analysis.

The instructor will note that there is a chart on the following page keying the chapters of this book to some of the leading economics texts. This is designed to aid the instructor in deciding when to assign given chapters from this book with those of a textbook.

Barry Keating
Dolores Tremewan Martin

CROSS TABULATION WITH SELECTED PRINCIPLES OF ECONOMICS TEXTBOOKS

Text and Pertinent Chapters	Casebook Chapters: Microeconomics 1	2	3	4	5	6	7	8	9	10	11	12	13	14	15	16	Macroeconomics 17	18	19	20	21	22	23	24	25	26	27	28
McKenzie and Tullock	1	2	3	4	5	6	7 8	7 8	9	10	11	12	13	14	15	16 17	18 19	20	21	22	24 25	26	27	28 29	30	32	33	34
Spencer (3d ed.) (hardcover version)	1	1	3 4 20	20 22			23	23		24		29	29	26 27	26 27	33 34 35	2 6	4 31			12 13 14	8 16	8 9	8 9 10 11	9 10 11	38	32	19
Samuelson (10th ed.)	1	1	4 20 21 22	4 23 24			23 24 25	23 24 25	21	25 26	20	8		7 29	7 29	33 34 35 36	8	40			15 16 17	15	18 19	11 12 13 18 19	11 12 13 18 19	43	40	40
Gwartney	1	2	16	17 2	4 28 29	4	18	18	30	20 21 19	15	22 30	27 30	24 25	24 25	31 32	28 29	26	4 29	29	11 12	7 15	7 15	8 9 12 13 14 15	8 9 12 13 14 15	33 22 4	30	5
Mansfield (2d ed.)	1	2	20 21	22 23			24	24	5	25	4 16	5		27	27	31 32 33	5	29	5		13 14 15	8	8	9 10 11	9 10 11	35 3	19	19
McConnell (7th ed.)	1 2	1 2	4 23 24	4 25			22 26 33	22 26 23	35	27 34	31 32	6 7	6 7	30 31 32	30 31 32	41 43 44	5 6 7 8	37			14 15 16 17	10 18	10 18	11 12 13 18	12 13	45	36	42
Dolan	1	1 7 19 20	3 18	1 3 18 22 23			24	24	25	26 27	28	28	29	29		36 37	4 20	32			11 12	14 16		8 9 10	8 9 10	38 39	33	

To the Student

This book has been written in part as a response to repeated complaints from hundreds of students that the economic principles that instructors make them learn have no application in the real world. Regardless of how conscientiously an author of an economics textbook or an instructor in a class tries to tie theory to everyday experiences, this is always done in the face of a time constraint. With only 15 weeks in a semester or 10 weeks in a quarter, how are instructors to combine teaching you theoretical tools and giving you practice in the application of those tools to real-world situations? Many times it appears that when the combination is made, the choice is weighted heavily for theory on the grounds that you must learn theory and can learn to apply it on your own. We are not sure about this approach. For example, we would not feel entirely comfortable being one of the first patients of a physician who had studied a complex brain operation for 10 years but had never practiced on a human.

Cases and Problems in Political Economy attempts to add interest to the theory-only approach to introductory economics. In each of the chapters in this book, it provides you with the means to learn how to evaluate complex real-world problems by applying the tools of economic theory. We hope that you will use this book in a variety of ways to make your study of economics more meaningful. The cases and discussions of important economic and noneconomic issues affect all individuals who make up society. These issues can provide topics for debate in class or over coffee. If you read a chapter in this book in conjunction with your textbook, we are confident that the theory explained in your text will be more understandable. The introductions to each chapter in this book and the selection of self-test questions will give you review materials that are useful in checking your progress in economics.

You may find the *case method* to be a new learning experience. You no doubt have heard the phrase "there is no substitute for experience" or "the best way to learn is by doing." You will be taking the analytical tools of economics and applying them to real situations. To illustrate how the case should be tackled, we have given you a sample case immediately following this introduction and have worked through the mechanics of analyzing the case. It can be used as a model for the cases that you will work on in the book. Remember that there is no "right" answer in the case method. You will be evaluated on the way you analyze a particular case and on the chain of logic that causes you to arrive at your solution. No doubt your position on a particular issue will influence your response or solution. This is perfectly acceptable as long as your reasoning is sound.

We hope that this book will help you to "think like an economist," that is, that it will give you the tools to develop alternative solutions to a problem. And we hope that this method of viewing the world will enable you to apply the concepts you've learned to all manner of problems.

The true test of a learning device is if it makes the process of mastering the skills easier. Only you can judge if we have done the job. We welcome all your comments, positive and negative, and promise given the trade-offs involved to seriously consider any alterations you suggest. Send us your ideas.

Barry Keating
Dolores Tremewan Martin

How to Analyze a Case

The purpose of case study is to help you develop analytical problem-solving skills, not simply accumulate economic facts. The key to grasping and understanding the method of economic analysis is to practice the technique. The first difficulty you will encounter has to do with your knowing little about economic problem solving. These skills will be developed as you learn to use more tools; your level of analysis should therefore improve with the number of cases you study.

Cases are not intended merely to make learning different or interesting. They are presented in the belief that the mind is an instrument to be developed rather than a receptacle to be filled. The cases presented here *may* be realistic and interesting but their primary value lies in their ability to stimulate independent, constructive thinking on your part. Cases are descriptions of specific instances or situations. These descriptions, or cases, are the raw material of the case method. There is a distinction to be made between cases and the case method. The cases in this book may be used in many different ways, but only one technique should properly be described as the case method.

The case method is a technique whereby you are placed in an active role as exchanges develop in three directions: instructor to student; student to instructor; student to student. Students and instructors are encouraged to note the following guidelines for a case method:

1) Read the case until you are thoroughly familiar with all the facts. This may, at first, involve reading the case several times. (It is our intent to confine the content of each case to factual materials.)

2) Identify the problem(s) or question(s) that the case presents. It is critical to locate the basic issue of the case. For example, it is not sufficient to state that individuals are buying fewer goods in a market; this is only a symptom of some change in underlying conditions. Are people buying fewer goods because tastes and preferences changed, because production costs increased, or because incomes have declined?

3) Draw on all your education and experiences as the case is evaluated.

4) Actively participate in the class discussions. Ideas are better grasped and developed when participation is open and encouraged.

The case method represents a technique for allowing you to learn by provoking inquiry rather than simply relaying information from instructor to student via lecture. With these basic rules in mind, read the sample case and follow the analysis of the case questions.

SAMPLE CASE:
Shut the Door on Crime[1]

After 18 months of study and the consultation of 28 specialists in the field of crime prevention, the Omaha-Douglas County Criminal Justice Commission has released (at a public hearing) one phase of their crime prevention package, a home-security law. The law, if adopted, would require Omahans to submit their homes to inspection by city employees before any sale of a home could be completed. The inspection would be conducted to ascertain if the home was equipped with dead-bolt locks on all exterior doors, solid-core exterior doors, peepholes, and other security devices. The estimated cost of bringing the average home up to the security standards of the proposed law is $200 or more. A spokesperson for the Commission estimated that the ordinance, if passed, would significantly reduce burglaries and the associated crimes of assault, murder, and rape that sometimes accompany these types of crimes. Thirty-five homeowners were present to speak against the ordinance.

QUESTIONS

1. Individuals take measures to avoid being victims of crimes, both against person and property; however, there appears to be a contradiction in behavior on the part of individuals who attended the meeting to speak *against* the proposed ordinance. How would you explain this apparent contradiction?

2. The change in the property rights system in Omaha could be expected to affect different individuals differently. What particular group of individuals within Omaha would you expect to receive the largest net benefits from the passage of this ordinance (rich property owners, low-income homeowners, individuals who live in high-crime areas, individuals involved in the sale and manufacture of security devices)? Why?

3. The burden of the ordinance, the additional cost that must be incurred prior to selling residential property, could be expected to fall more heavily on the very poor homeowners in high-crime areas than on the very wealthy homeowners in the most exclusive neighborhoods. Why?

[1] Facts in this case are reprinted with permission from "Door Is Slammed on Security Plan," *Omaha World Herald,* February 2, 1976, © 1976. All Rights Reserved.

SUGGESTED GUIDELINES FOR REASONING TO QUESTIONS ON SAMPLE CASE

1. One of the most important tools that economics can offer the student in understanding social order is the notion of limits to human behavior. To begin, economics is the study of individuals, not organizations, and assumes that individuals are rational. Rationality means only that you as an individual know the goods, services, or activities that you prefer (you like to go skiing better than you like to go bowling) and that when given a choice will select your most preferred good, service, or activity. From this very simple beginning, it is possible to develop the notion of additional (marginal) benefit and additional (marginal) cost and see how individuals choose to limit the scope of any given activity.

If you prefer skiing to bowling, does that mean that you will always choose skiing over bowling? A moment's reflection should indicate that you would not; your choice would depend on the costs involved. You would go skiing as long as the satisfaction you expect to receive is at least equal to the cost of undertaking that activity *and* at least equal to the satisfaction you would receive from undertaking any other activity of equal cost. Individuals do not know what the actual costs and the actual benefits of any activity will be for the simple reason that the events occur in the future. For example, you go skiing and as a result fall and break your leg. You had not planned to break your leg. In your calculations, you had not anticipated the cost incurred from breaking a leg. Had you done so, you would have chosen some other activity. Thus, our behaviorial rule must be expressed in terms of expectations. We will argue that any individual will engage in any activity up until the point that the expected marginal benefits are equal to the expected marginal costs.

When the 35 homeowners spoke out against the proposed ordinance, they were expressing their personal cost/benefit calculations. They must have expected that the $200 additional cost of the security devices would generate *less* than $200 in expected benefits. Or, expressed in another way, these individuals felt that spending the $200 on other goods and services would generate more expected benefits than spending that money on the security devices.

2. The group of individuals that we would expect to receive the largest *net* benefits from the passage of the proposed ordinance would be individuals involved in the manufacture and sale of security devices. The ordinance makes the purchase of such devices mandatory before the sale of a home can be completed. Therefore, sellers of such devices are "given" an automatic increase in the demand for their products. In the absence of the ordinance, a buyer of a solid-core door, for example, would weight the expected benefits and expected costs of the door and make a decision on this basis. If the ordinance passes, the individual who wishes to sell a $40,000 home must have solid-core exterior doors. Thus, by the time he makes the decision about whether or not to purchase the doors, the expected benefits from the purchase have substantially increased (the expected revenue from the sale of the house). An equally correct way to reason is to argue that the cost of not having solid-core doors has increased substantially (the loss of the expected income from the sale of the house).

3. Returning to the reasoning presented in the solution to question 1, we would expect that individuals who had much to lose from burglaries and crimes against their property would act to minimize the expected losses. Thus, we would find that individuals with expensive homes, fabulous art treasures, and relatively high priced antiques, act to protect such valuables in the *absence* of any ordinance. Security devices are expected to yield benefits to these individuals greater than the benefits from spending the money on some other goods. On the other hand, individuals in low-income, high-crime neighborhoods may find that the presence of a locked door is taken as a sign that the individual has something worth stealing. Thus, locks *increase* the incidence of crime rather than reduce it. If this is true, then these individuals would be differentially harmed by the passage of the ordinance. If individuals are free to make their individual subjective cost/benefit calculations, then it is possible to assume that when an individual spends funds for security devices, he expects the benefits to outweigh the costs. One of the problems, of course, is that the action of individual *A* may have a negative effect on others in his neighborhood. For example, if you leave your property unguarded, then you reduce the cost of crime to the burglar and increase the incidence of neighborhood crime.

CASES AND PROBLEMS IN POLITICAL ECONOMY

1

A Way of Understanding the Social Order

Since the beginning of time, humans have been subject to the forces of nature and have had to adapt to survive and to make their lives more pleasant. As people became more sophisticated, they began to study the world around them and attempt to make the cruelties of nature more manageable. In medicine, for example, scientists studied microbes in laboratory environments and were able to use the knowledge obtained in limited experiments to develop vaccines to lessen the effects of disease. Similar examples can be found in every field of science—in each case people are trying to find out more about the world around them by devising models of reality to increase their understanding of the real world.

Like doctors, physicists, chemists, and other physical scientists, economists try to build models to describe real world conditions. Economics often is classified as a behavioral science, like psychology or sociology, because the subject of the economist is the behavior of individuals. To see how individuals behave, economists develop models of the real world (like the physical scientists) so that only the conditions relevant to the problem are analyzed. If experiments or models were not used in science, scientists would have to sift through an enormous number of facts, some relevant and some not relevant to the problem at hand. To make a model more useful, only those conditions that affect the problem are used in the experimental case. Models are sometimes criticized for lacking reality, because only ideal conditions are used to analyze a particular problem. For example, we can examine a market situation with only one buyer and one seller. This situation would not exist in the real world, but once we know how one buyer and one seller react to changes in prices and quantities, we can extend this knowledge to markets with many buyers and many sellers, which do exist in the real world.

Once a model has been proved to accurately sum up behavior in nearly all cases, scientists (and economists) will develop a theory. Although theories, too, tend to simplify real world events, they do enable us to predict or describe behavior—whether it is the behavior of molecules or buyers and sellers in the marketplace. For example, you do not need to know the complexities of price levels to understand that individuals will buy fewer tennis balls if the price increases from, say, $0.50 per ball to $9.00 per ball. (This is one facet of the law of demand which we'll explore later in this book.)

As you expand your knowledge of economics, you will see that the models and theories that you study enable you to understand human behavior. In fact, economics is a "window on the world" through which you can see the enormously complex order in modern society. Our particular focus will be on the individual as an actor in the social system, and in the chapters that follow, we'll describe individual and group behavior, using particular cases to see how economic theories work.

KEY CONCEPTS

Economic theory A statement describing the real world that predicts human behavior when individuals are confronted by a choice.

Economic model A representation of reality emphasizing key points, whether expressed as words, graphs, or mathematical equations.

Economics The study of human behavior in situations where choices must be made and resources are scarce.

CASE 1
The Force of Gravity

The force of gravity is a phenomenon which most of us have been observing since early childhood. However, it is not an easy phenomenon to explain to a young child. In fact, the force of gravity has been generally misunderstood for most of recorded history. The force of gravity was explained by Isaac Newton in 1687; however, a few experiments by other scientists paved the way for his discovery. One of these, by Galileo in 1604, examined the rate of falling bodies. Until Galileo's famous experiment from the Leaning Tower of Pisa, most people believed that heavier bodies fell faster than light ones. Galileo demonstrated that a small ball and a large one would strike the ground at the same time if dropped from the same height.

Today we know that the force of gravity will cause bodies to fall at the same rate in a vacuum regardless of their respective weights. When physicists conduct experiments in a vacuum (a container with no air or other matter), they are using a model to simplify conditions found in the real world. Using a vacuum enables the physicist to concentrate on studying the force of gravity by removing the complicating and, for centuries, confounding influence of air resistance. It may, however, be difficult to explain the force of gravity to children since they can observe that a rock and a feather will not fall at the same rate of speed. Furthermore, you could argue that vacuums are useless since the conditions in a vacuum are not found in the real world. By using this simplifying assumption, however, theories could be developed about gravity and the rate of falling bodies. Once the theories are developed and proved accurate, the events of the real world can be introduced into the model.

People were unable to understand the force of gravity until Galileo's experiments because they were observing too much information at once.

QUESTIONS

1 A frequent criticism of scientific theories is exemplified by the statement ". . .it works in theory but not in practice. . .". In Galileo's experiment, what were some factors which could have changed his observed result? For example, suppose the two balls were dropped from the tower on a windy day. Would this mean that the two balls did not fall at the same rate? Why?

2 From Galileo's experiment, scientists were able to develop theories about falling bodies and gravity. What was the purpose of developing these theories? What determines whether a theory is useful to a scientist?

3 We noted that vacuums do not naturally exist on earth. Does Galileo's theory become invalid because of this fact? Do you think it is valid to criticize theories solely because some aspects of the model may appear unrealistic? Explain.

TEST YOURSELF

1 Economics is considered a behavioral science because (**a**) it is studied by psychologists, (**b**) it studies human behavior, (**c**) it relies on theories and models.

2 Which of the following best describes models? (**a**) Models are collections of all data on a particular situation. (**b**) In models scientists ignore reality. (**c**) Only essential facts are used in models.

3 A theory is judged most useful if (**a**) it contains more data than competing theories, (**b**) it predicts better than competing theories, (**c**) it is more realistic than competing theories.

4 Models of aircraft used in wind-tunnel tests often contain no internal working parts (instruments, hatches, etc.) and are thus unrealistic. These models are (**a**) useless because of their lack of realism, (**b**) probably just as useful as if they had contained internal working parts, (**c**) less than adequate representations of reality.

5 Which of the following is *not* a reason why economists use models: (**a**) to predict real world events, (**b**) to simplify reality for better understanding, (**c**) to create exact replicas of reality?

2

The Framework of Analysis

In order for economists to make some predictions about human behavior, they must start with some basic premise about human behavior before they can develop models and theories. In beginning their study of the real world, economists recognize that people are confronted by limited supplies of goods and services that are necessary for life, whether one lives at a subsistence level or in luxury. Therefore, people must choose some courses of action or some physical goods over other activities or goods. Economists explain this by saying people have wants and that they are most likely to attempt to satisfy first those wants which are most pressing.

Individuals are confronted by a range of choices for almost all events that take place in their daily lives. The selections individuals make are determined by their wants. For example, if you have $5, you can go to a movie and have a hot dog, spend the entire $5 on a nice lunch, stay home and save the $5, etc. Choosing one alternative eliminates the others because the $5 and the time you have for any choice are limited. If you do not like movies and are not hungry, then the last alternative may seem most appealing.

Economists base their theory of behavior on the way individuals choose among alternatives. Rational individuals will select the choices that benefit them the most, or, in the language of economists, *maximize their utility.* The cost to a particular individual of any selection equals the most attractive alternative that is not chosen;

this is called the *opportunity cost* of the choice. In many cases, the *information* you have about the choices influences your selection. If the movie in our example has received critical acclaim or if the star is one of your favorites, you may be more inclined to see the movie than to have a nice lunch. If it is a movie you have already seen or one that you know will be on TV next week, then you may feel that saving the $5 is a better choice. In any case, the additional amount of information you have will alter your selection to some degree.

Individuals often make mistakes in predicting outcomes, and in retrospect their choices may seem irrational. "Monday morning quarterbacks" often delight in hashing over each play of the previous Saturday's game and with perfect hindsight will tell you precisely which plays were bad calls. They imply that the coach or quarterback should have known better than to call such and such a play, and the implication is that the coach or quarterback was irrational. The movie you choose to see may also turn out to be a very bad choice indeed, and with perfect hindsight you may say your choice was irrational—it did not maximize your satisfaction. Both of these choices, however, (the quarterback's call and your movie) were rational ones given the outcomes expected before the event. The economist's assumption of rationality does not assume people will never make mistakes.

KEY CONCEPTS

Wants The needs or desires of an individual. There are some things that each individual wants more than others, and in economics it is assumed that the individual can define his or her field of wants and can consistently order his or her wants from most preferred to least preferred.

Utility maximization Choosing among alternative actions so that the wants which are satisfied are the ones which will increase an individual's satisfaction (utility) the most.

Opportunity cost The loss of value an individual suffers by choosing one alternative over another. Each alternative has a value, and the cost of choosing one alternative is the value the individual places on the most favored alternative not taken. A rational individual will choose alternative actions for which the benefits exceed the costs.

Rational If an individual is said to be rational by an economist, it is assumed that he or she is continually making the choices which will achieve maximum satisfaction.

CASE 2
Choosing College Courses

Each semester or quarter you must select the courses in which you will enroll. Once you have chosen a major or have decided to pursue a particular degree, many of the courses that you will take are "required," leaving you with few electives. However, even if you must take many required courses in order to earn, say, a bachelor's degree in accounting, you may still be able to choose the instructor, the time of day, and/or the particular semester or quarter in which you would prefer to take the course.

Although all accounting majors may be required to take a course entitled "Principles of Economics" during the first semester of their sophomore year, you may not individually choose to take the same section of the course as your roommate. Sometimes several professors teach different sections of Principles of Economics at the same time, say 10:00 a.m. on Monday, Wednesday, and Friday; yet the number of students in each section may differ greatly even though each section can accommodate the same number (i.e., the rooms are the same size). Your course selection process under these conditions is an example of what economists call rational behavior.

QUESTIONS

1 Suppose there are five sections of Principles of Economics offered and you are required to take one of them. Although each section uses the same text and gives the same final examination, each section is offered at a different time and is taught by a different instructor. How would the differences affect your choice? Explain in economic terms (i.e., opportunity cost).

2 Suppose all your friends agree that the "best" professor teaches a section at 8:00 a.m. Why might some students choose to enroll in other sections? Is this behavior irrational to the economist?

3 Suppose that you are studying the way in which students choose courses at universities A and B. University A publishes a schedule of sections that includes the time and professor for each course. University B lists only the time each section is offered. How might the information provided in the schedules affect the relative numbers of students who change sections? Would you expect more changes at university A or university B?

4 There are numerous cola-type drinks on the market today (e.g., Coca Cola, Pepsi Cola, Royal Crown Cola, etc.). Each cola is similar to the others, and the producers spend large amounts of money advertising their particular brand. This advertising could be considered information provision by the companies to affect your choice. In terms of wants and opportunity costs, how do producers try to advertise their products to appeal to different customers?

TEST YOURSELF

1 The basic assumption of human behavior in economics is (**a**) individuals always purchase items with low prices, (**b**) individuals are rational, (**c**) individuals always choose leisure rather than work.

2 The opportunity cost of taking this class in economics is (**a**) that portion of your tuition which pays your instructor, (**b**) the salary your instructor receives, (**c**) your loss of satisfaction from other ways of spending your time.

3 "I'm going to work in the cafeteria from 7 to 9 each morning instead of taking economics this semester." This statement reflects (**a**) irrational economic behavior, (**b**) the high opportunity costs to this individual of taking economics, (**c**) an inconsistent ordering of wants by this individual.

4 The assumption of rational behavior (**a**) is consistent with incomplete information, (**b**) is uncharacteristic of most people, (**c**) is not widely held among economists.

5 If you buy a record album which you later decide was a poor choice, your action was (**a**) irrational because it did not increase your satisfaction, (**b**) rational because you expected to increase your satisfaction, (**c**) irrelevant because the record company set the price of the album.

3

Demand and Price Elasticity

DEMAND

The rational behavior assumption of economists which was explained in Chapter 2 indicated that individuals would seek to satisfy their wants, satisfying the most pressing wants first. The resources individuals have, however, are almost always less than enough to provide for their wants. You may want a Ferrari automobile, a trip around the world, and 51 weeks of vacation a year, but you may not be able to afford them immediately. Given that you cannot have everything that you want, how do you decide which items to purchase and which to forgo? The assumption of rational behavior provides the basis for explaining your choices.

Rational individuals will spend their limited income on those things which will bring them the most satisfaction (utility). When the price of a particular item increases, this increases the opportunity cost of the item to individuals (because they now have less to spend on other wants); consequently they will buy less of the item. Each individual may not buy less of the item; some will purchase less, others will continue to purchase the same amount. The important point is that, on the whole, the more expensive an item is, the less consumers will buy. This conclusion follows directly from the rational behavior assumption and is such a pervasive characteristic of human behavior that economists call it the *law of demand.*

The law of demand (people will buy less of an item when the price rises) provides a basis for predicting behavior with respect to price changes. We would expect theater attendance to increase after ticket prices have fallen. We would expect gasoline purchases to fall as the price per gallon increases. We would expect more solar heaters to be sold as the price of those heaters declines.

The law of demand can be illustrated by drawing what economists call a demand curve. (See Figure 3-1.)

The demand curve is the *DD* line in the diagram. If this were the demand curve for oranges, it would show the different quantities that would be purchased per week, say, at various prices. For example, if the price of oranges were P_1 dollars per pound, the *DD* curve indicates that people would buy quantity Q_1 pounds per week. If the price were to fall to P_2 dollars per pound, people would purchase Q_2 pounds per week. Notice that when the price fell, the demand curve predicted an increase in sales, just as we would expect from the law of demand. In order to get such a result, the demand curve must be *sloping downward to the right* to be consistent with the law of demand.

ELASTICITY

Elasticity is the economist's term for a measure of the responsiveness of consumers' purchases to a change in price. For any given price change this measure is computed by dividing the percentage change in quantity sold by the percentage change in price.

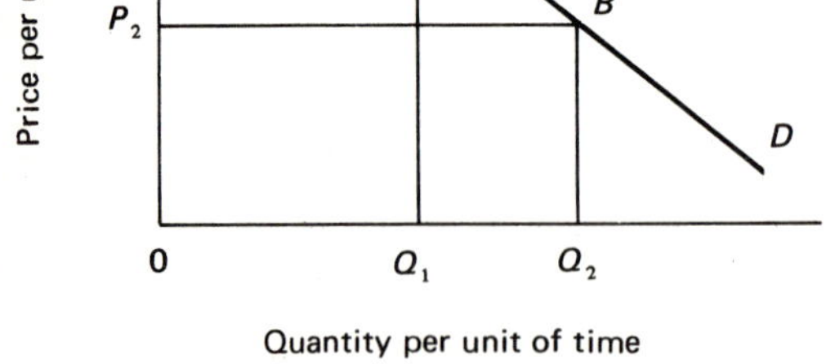

FIGURE 3-1

The price elasticity of demand, often merely called the *elasticity of demand,* measures the responsiveness of quantity demanded to changes in price. If, for instance, the price of oranges were to decrease by 50 percent and the resulting sales were to increase by 100 percent, the price elasticity of demand would be 2 (which is 100%÷50%). The price elasticity of demand provides information of how price changes affect consumer expenditures (or total revenue received by the firm from purchases made by consumers). With a good estimate of price elasticity a firm can accurately predict changes in total revenue (price times quantity sold) produced by price changes.

Economists define three ranges which take into account all the possible numerical values elasticity may cover. If the numerical value of elasticity is more than 1 (as in the case of the oranges where it was 2), the economist calls demand *elastic* at this point. When elasticity is in this range, consumers are said to be relatively sensitive to price changes (small price changes cause large changes in the quantity sold.

If the numerical value of elasticity is less than 1, say ½, the economist calls this *inelastic.* In this range consumers are said to be relatively insensitive to price changes (large price changes cause only small changes in the quantity sold).

If the numerical value of elasticity is computed to be exactly 1, the economist calls this *unitary elasticity.* When elasticity is 1, a 1 percent price decrease will cause a 1 percent quantity-demanded increase. Likewise, with unitary elasticity, a 1 percent price increase would bring about a 1 percent quantity-demanded decrease.

When prices change and the quantities sold either increase or decrease, the total expenditures (total revenue from the company's point of view) of consumers for that item either rise or fall. With a given price change, whether total revenue rises or falls depends upon consumers' reactions to the price change. If oranges increase in price from $0.50 per pound to $1 per pound and sales fall from 200 pounds per week to 100 pounds per week, there will be no change in total revenue. Before the price change the company would have sold 200 pounds of oranges at $0.50 per pound for a total revenue of $100 (which is $0.50 times 200 pounds). After the price change the company would be receiving $1 per pound for the 100 pounds it would sell. Its total revenue would continue to be $100 (which is $1 times 100 pounds).

Economists have found that when elasticity is elastic (numerically greater than 1), total revenue rises when price falls (and falls when price rises). When elasticity is inelastic (numerically less than 1), total revenue falls when price rises (and rises when price falls). When elasticity is unitary, total revenue does not change with a price change (as in the case of oranges when the price changed from $0.50 to $1).

The relationship between elasticity and total revenue can be easily demonstrated with a diagram (Figure 3-2).

The *DD* curve in the upper part of the diagram is the "downward sloping to the right" demand curve. Over part of its range it is elastic (the upper left-hand corner), and over part of its range it is inelastic (the lower right-hand corner). In between these two ranges lies a point where elasticity is 1 (unit elasticity).

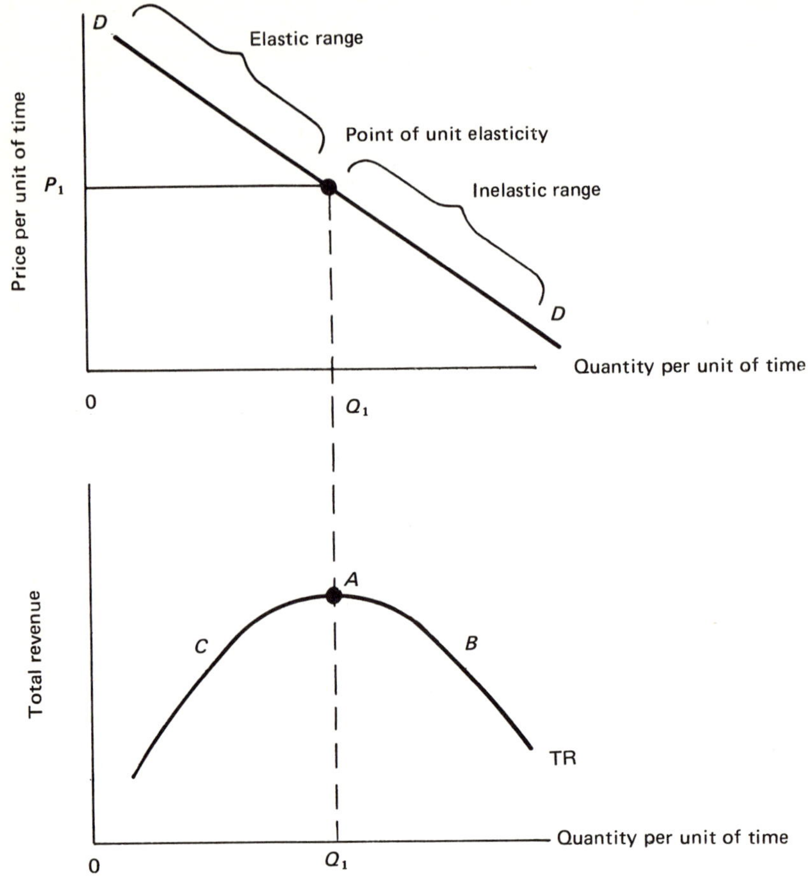

FIGURE 3-2

The lower part of the diagram is the total revenue (TR) curve. It shows total revenue increasing from zero quantity to Q_1 units. At Q_1 units total revenue is at its highest point, and it falls after Q_1 units.

Note that the total revenue curve is at its highest point (maximum) at Q_1, which is precisely where elasticity is equal to 1 (unit elasticity). This is not a coincidence. If price were P_1 and Q_1 units per week were being demanded by people, the company selling oranges could not raise total revenue by either raising or lowering the price from its present position at P_1. If the price were lowered, more units than Q_1 would be demanded, but total revenue would be somewhere to the right of *A*, perhaps at *B*. But at *B* total revenue is lower than at *A*. If the price were to rise, fewer units would be demanded than Q_1, and total revenue would be somewhere to the left of *A*, say at point *C*. But total revenue at *C* is lower than at *A*. Total revenue is clearly at its highest (maximum) when elasticity equals 1.

KEY CONCEPTS

Price elasticity Percentage change in the quantity of a good demanded divided by percentage change in its price.

Elastic A term used to describe a situation corresponding to a measured price elasticity of greater than 1.

Inelastic A term used to describe a situation corresponding to a measured price elasticity of less than 1.

Unit elasticity Situation corresponding to a measured price elasticity of exactly 1.

Law of demand The concept that people buy less of an item when its price rises and more of an item when its price falls.

CASE 3
Seasonal Football Tickets

Virginia Polytechnic Institute (VPI) is the home of the "Fighting Gobblers" (also called the "Hokies") who play football each fall in a league made up largely of Virginia schools and Southern schools. Lane Stadium was constructed on the VPI campus in the 1960s to accommodate the then rising demand for football tickets. For one reason or another, however, the stadium has rarely been filled to capacity. Most football Saturdays find the 40,000-seat stadium occupied by fewer than 30,000 people.

As is the custom at many schools, the university offers faculty and staff members a special season-ticket rate. Regular season tickets available to the general public sell for $37 while the faculty/staff season tickets sell for $25. The price of faculty/staff tickets has risen a number of times in recent years, and the number of faculty and staff purchasing season tickets and attending games has fallen each time the price has increased.

Using data from the athletic department, a VPI economist estimated the price elasticity of demand for faculty/staff tickets to be close to 1 at the $25 price.

QUESTIONS

1 If the economist's estimate of price elasticity at the $25 price is correct (it was estimated to be 1), would the athletic director increase the university's total revenue by raising the price slightly? By lowering the price slightly? Explain. (*Hint:* If price rises, fewer faculty and staff will purchase tickets at the higher price; but if price falls, larger numbers of faculty and staff will purchase tickets at the lower price.)

2 If you were the athletic director, on what basis could you justify the price you had set for faculty/staff tickets? Is your price, in any sense, the "correct" price? Explain.

3 Since there are often empty seats in the stadium, is the university engaging in price discrimination by charging different prices to different people for roughly the same product (i.e., a seat at a football game)? Why?

4 Assume the price elasticity of demand is unity for faculty/staff season tickets at a price of $25. Would you expect this price elasticity to change over time? What conditions would cause it to change?

5 If faculty and staff have a price elasticity of demand of unity for season tickets at a particular price, does it follow that all other groups (e.g., alumni, students, parents of students) have the same price elasticity at that same price? Explain.

6 The changing price of faculty/staff season tickets has caused the quantity demanded to change in recent years. What factors might have caused the demand for faculty/staff season tickets to rise or fall in the same period?

7 Economists agree that there are two conditions necessary for price discrimination: (1) the purchasers must fall into different classes with substantial differences in the price elasticity of demand for the product, and (2) each separate class must be identified and segregated cheaply. Are these conditions met in the case of season football tickets? If so, identify the separate groups. Which groups would have relatively high price elasticities and which would have relatively low ones? Why?

TEST YOURSELF

1 Assume that the demand for a given item is as described in the table below. If you were to graph the data in the first two columns of the table, the result would be a demand curve. Use these data to estimate whether demand is relatively elastic, relatively inelastic, or unit elastic between each of the prices. Use the formula

$$\text{Elasticity} = \frac{(Q_2 - Q_1)/(Q_2 + Q_1)}{(P_2 - P_1)/(P_2 + P_1)}$$

Price	Quantity Demanded		Elasticity Coefficient	Nature of Relationship
$1.00	200		________	________
$0.80	400		________	________
$0.60	600		________	________
$0.40	800	$\frac{(800 - 600)/(800 + 600)}{(40 - 60)/(40 + 60)} =$	(5/7)	(Inelastic)

2 Does the downward-sloping demand curve described above obey the law of demand?

3 Assume that the schedule showing prices and quantities demanded for movie tickets on Saturday night is as follows:

Prices	Quantities Demanded
$1	800
$2	700
$3	600
$4	500
$5	400

What are the price elasticities of demand between $1 and $2, $2 and $3, $4 and $5? (Use the same formula as in question 1.)

4 The demand for a good is relatively elastic if the elasticity is (**a**) 1, (**b**) less than 1, (**c**) greater than 1.

5 Total revenue is at its highest where elasticity is (**a**) greater than 1, (**b**) less than 1, (**c**) equal to 1.

6 A demand curve shows (**a**) how much of an item consumers will purchase at various prices, (**b**) how much producers are willing to sell at various prices, (**c**) how total revenue changes at various quantities demanded.

7 The law of demand states that (**a**) as price increases, quantities demanded increase, (**b**) as price falls, quantities demanded increase, (**c**) as price changes, total revenue remains constant.

8 Cigarettes tend to be relatively price inelastic. This means that (**a**) people who buy cigarettes are not interested in the price, (**b**) small change in the price of cigarettes will cause the quantity demanded to change by a relatively large amount, (**c**) a small change in the price of cigarettes will cause the quantity demanded to change by a relatively small amount.

4

The Law of Supply and Costs

COSTS

What determines the quantity of goods and services that producers offer for sale in the open market? One of the major factors is the cost of producing these goods and services. A second factor is the demand for the good or service from consumers. (Note that goods and services not demanded will not be produced regardless of cost.) The law of demand (see Chapter 3) and the law of supply, which is based on costs, are like the two blades of a scissors for determining which items are produced, in what quantity they are produced, and at what prices they are sold. Without both the law of demand *and* the law of supply, little could be said about which goods would be produced, in what quantities, or at what prices.

Cost is a fundamental concept in economics. Not only is it the basis for determining the supply of goods, but it is important in any decision among several alternatives. Whenever a decision is made, an economist thinks of the cost of the decision in terms of the opportunity cost (the value of the best alternative course of action foregone). In calculating the opportunity cost of any decision, economists include both explicit and implicit costs.

Explicit costs are obvious, out-of-pocket expenditures such as cash outlays required to obtain goods or services (e.g., wages paid for work done, interest paid to bondholders for the loan of their money, payments made to suppliers for raw materials). *Implicit costs* associated with any decision are more difficult to identify because they do not involve cash expenditures. The wages a self-employed farmer could earn working for someone else or the interest you could earn on your money if it were not tied up in a car are examples of implicit costs.

Total cost to an economist is the entire cost (including both explicit and implicit costs) of any decision. Imagine that you and a friend are each given the opportunity of opening a McDonald's franchise near the college campus. The franchise will cost $15,000, but an additional $5000 will be needed for day-to-day expenses. You are lucky and have $20,000 in your savings account. Your friend, on the other hand, must borrow the $20,000 at 10 percent ($2000 per year) from a bank to make the purchase. If both you and your friend are equally capable of operating the franchise, whose total costs are higher? An economist would say the total cost for you is the implicit cost of what interest you could earn on your $20,000 in the next best alternative (which may mean leaving it in your savings account). The total cost for your friend who must borrow the money is the explicit $2000 per year interest charge. It is quite possible that the total costs of purchasing the McDonald's franchise are the same for each of you (if your implicit costs were to equal $2000). Your costs would be implicit, but your friend's costs would be explicit.

MARGINAL COST AND DIMINISHING RETURNS

While total cost is the entire cost (explicit and implicit) involved in any decision, *marginal cost* is the cost of producing only one additional unit of a good or service. Marginal cost is the change in total cost brought about by one-unit change in output. The marginal cost of producing the 2001st hamburger at a McDonald's would be the difference between the total cost of producing 2000 hamburgers and the total cost of producing 2001 hamburgers. The marginal (additional) cost of successive units of any product or service may be constant, increasing, or decreasing according to the particular situation. One thing is certain, however: as more and more units of a good are produced in the short run (a period of time during which a firm cannot change the size of its plant), the marginal cost will begin to rise at some point. This is equivalent to saying that marginal cost curves will have the U shape shown in Figure 4-1.

As more and more hamburgers are produced in a single franchise, the marginal cost (change in total cost resulting from the production of one additional unit) of hamburgers falls. This is not too surprising since it takes almost the same time for a McDonald's franchise to make one hamburger as it does to make two—thus the opportunity cost for each extra hamburger will decline, reducing the marginal cost of hamburgers. But does the marginal cost continue declining forever as more and more units are produced? No.

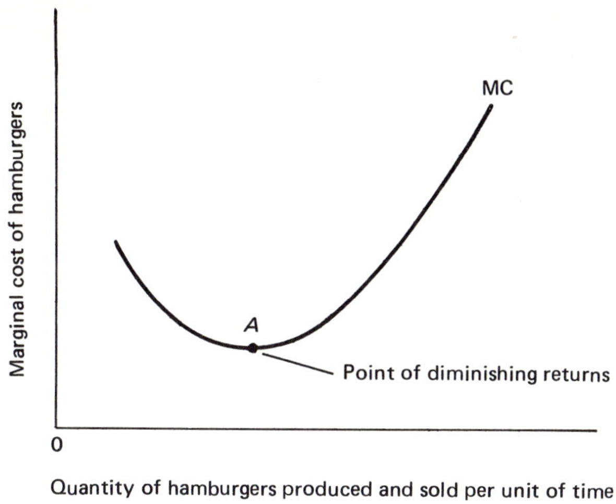

FIGURE 4-1

Consider the following situation. A particular McDonald's franchise has ten employees working today and normally expects to make and sell about 2000 hamburgers at lunchtime. On this particular day, however, eighteen tour buses arrive at lunchtime along with three nursery school classes which decided to give the kids a break today. As the franchise increases the number of hamburgers cooked to meet the orders they have, we might expect the marginal cost of hamburgers to begin rising. With only ten employees and limited work space, cooking and preparation areas would become crowded and chaotic and costly delays would result.

The economist has a term for why marginal cost must sooner or later begin to rise—*the law of diminishing returns.* This law states that as more and more units of a variable factor (say, hamburger components—meat, rolls, etc.) are combined with fixed amounts of other resources (say, the ten employees and the limited work space), eventually output will increase by smaller and smaller amounts. In terms of cost (marginal cost), each additional unit will cost more and more. Thus, carrying hamburger production beyond point *A* in the diagram would mean each additional hamburger adds more and more to total costs.

SUPPLY

Now we are in a position to answer our original question: What determines the quantity of goods and services offered for sale? The upward-sloping section of the marginal curve (that part to the right of point *A*) is the firm's supply curve—it shows the number of units the firm would be willing to supply at each price that might be offered in the market. As marginal cost rises, the firm would have to be paid more and more for each extra unit to make it worthwhile to continue production. If, at some point, the firm is offered a price less than the marginal cost of the unit, it would be foolish to accept the offer—the firm would be spending more to produce the item than it could receive for selling the item. Higher and higher prices induce more and more output in the short run, and so the supply curve slopes upward and to the right. The relationship between the price of an item and the amount of the item that a firm is willing to produce in the short run is called the *law of supply.*

KEY CONCEPTS

Implicit cost Noncash costs which are often hidden costs.

Explicit cost Outlays of money made by firms or individuals for the purchase of goods and services.

Marginal cost The change in total cost brought about with a one-unit change in output.

Total cost All costs attributable to a decision. These will include explicit as well as implicit costs.

Law of diminishing returns The concept that as more and more of an input is used in production, all other things being equal, eventually output will increase by smaller and smaller amounts.

Law of supply The concept that firms produce more of an item when its price rises and less of an item when its price falls.

CASE 4

The 55 Mile Per Hour Speed Limit[1]

In November 1973, President Nixon proposed limiting the speed at which vehicles would be allowed to travel on the nation's highways to a maximum of 50 miles per hour. The proposal was met with much public opposition, but in early 1974 a compromise measure limiting the speed at which vehicles could travel to 55 mph was passed. Prior to this legislation, a maximum of 55 miles per hour was proposed by President Nixon on a voluntary basis. Public compliance with the voluntary speed limit was poor.

The stated objective of the 55 mile per hour speed limit was clearly to reduce fuel consumption. Although estimates varied, all groups agreed that a significant savings in the number of barrels of oil used by Americans per day could be achieved.

There have been a number of developments since the 55 mile per hour speed limit was introduced. First, as might be expected, people are driving more slowly. A news magazine stated that people are driving 6.4 miles per hour slower since the imposition of the 55 mile per hour speed limit. Secondly, the expected saving in oil has occurred. Lower speeds are saving an estimated 100,000 barrels of oil per day. Third, and perhaps most important, there were more than 11,000 fewer traffic deaths in 1974 than in 1973 (44,500 as against 55,600). In addition, the death rate from automobile accidents dropped from 4.3 to 3.5 per 100 million miles driven.

The link between traffic deaths and slower speeds has provoked a number of arguments. Many individuals feel that the reduced number of traffic deaths is merely the result of individuals driving shorter distances on the average. The Department of Economics at San Jose State University, however, has calculated that the drop in deaths which is attributable to the 55 mile per hour speed limit is 53 percent of the total.[2] That is, just over 5500 fewer traffic fatalities are directly attributable to the 55 mile per hour speed limit rather than the shorter distances being driven.

In spite of the benefits in favor of the 55 mile per hour speed limit, there is significant protest against it. Some individuals say that it violates their rights; others find it a bore. Many experts also question the official reports that the lower speed limit really saves lives.

[1] Facts in this case are reprinted with permission from "Rising Chorus against 55 mph Speed Limit," *U.S. News & World Report,* March 17, 1975, © *1975 U.S. News & World Report,* Inc.

[2] B. Chu and G. Nunn, "Causes and Valuation of Traffic Fatalities under the 1974 Energy Crisis: A Case Study of California," presented at the 1975 Western Economics Association Meetings in San Diego, California.

QUESTIONS

1 List some explicit and some implicit costs of imposing the 55 mile per hour speed limit.

2 The voluntary 55 mile per hour speed limit was suggested by the President before the law was imposed. Could you have predicted that the voluntary energy conservation scheme was likely to be ineffective? Why?

3 One of the latest fads to sweep the United States has been Citizens Band radios. Four out of five Citizens Band radios are installed in vehicles. The fad has become so pervasive that the Federal Communications Commission has expanded the number of channels from 23 to 40. One of the uses of Citizens Band radios is to warn other drivers of impending speed traps. Once the 55 mile per hour speed limit became law, how would you evaluate the cost of the Citizens Band radio to an individual?

4 A number of individuals have pointed out the gas-saving advantages of permitting a right turn at a red light, provided the red light is treated as a stop sign. Federal legislation has been introduced that requires every state to allow motorists to make right turns at red lights in order to save gasoline. Can you think of any explicit or implicit costs to the right-turn-on-red laws?

5 One of the responses to the 55 mile per hour speed limit has been for state governments to increase the weight that trucks are allowed to carry (*note:* heavy trucks wear down roads rather quickly). Weighing stations for trucks in each state are normally located near the borders of each state on the major truck routes. These weighing stations ensure that trucks do not exceed the maximum weight limits. Should the increased weight permits in any way be considered a cost of the 55 mile per hour speed limit?

6 Would a change in the market price of gasoline (say a 50 percent drop in price) alter the implicit costs of the 55 mile per hour speed limit?

TEST YOURSELF

1 Assume that an automobile firm's costs are as shown here:

Output (Number of Cars)	Total Costs
0	$ 500*
1	550
2	590
3	640
4	700
5	770
6	850
7	950
8	1100

*Total costs would be positive even with zero output. The firm must still pay rent, lights, etc.

Graph the firm's total cost function below:

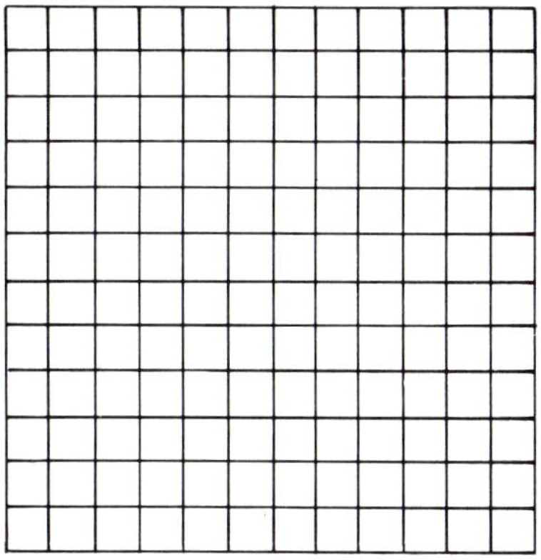

Graph the firm's marginal cost function below:

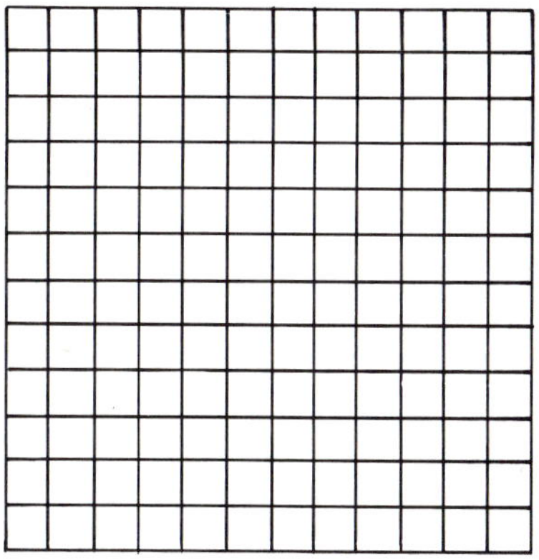

Identify the point on the marginal cost curve where "diminishing returns" set in. Explain why diminishing returns occur in any production process.

2 The supply curve of the firm in question 1 would be the relevant portion of its (**a**) marginal cost curve, (**b**) total cost curve, (**c**) demand curve.

3 The marginal cost curve of a firm eventually begins to rise (slopes upward and to the right) because of (**a**) the law of supply, (**b**) the law of demand, (**c**) the law of diminishing returns.

4 The law of diminishing returns explains why (**a**) the total cost curve will eventually decline as output is increased in the short run, (**b**) the marginal cost curve will eventually rise as output is increased in the short run, (**c**) the demand curve is sloping downward to the right.

5 By the term *short run* an economist means (**a**) a time period too short for the firm to change its output, (**b**) a time period of less than 3 months, (**c**) a time period too short for the firm to change its plant size.

6 When you decide to purchase a car and examine the costs of owning and operating it, which of the following implicit costs should be included: (**a**) the interest you could have earned on the cash you paid for the car, (**b**) the cash outlays you make for gasoline and oil, (**c**) the cash outlays you make for automobile insurance?

7 The most important determinant of the quantity of goods and services that producers offer for sale is (**a**) quantity, (**b**) cost, (**c**) utility.

8 When output per unit of input begins to decrease, this is the result of (**a**) the law of demand, (**b**) the law of supply, (**c**) the law of diminishing returns.

5

Property Rights and Social Order

Suppose that you own your own car. What does that right of ownership mean? You have the right to drive it on public roads, wash it, paint it, sell its use to someone else, or rent its use to your neighbor. In other words, you own the *right* to control your automobile. However, this ownership right is not unlimited; you do not have the right to paint your automobile black and white, install blinking lights and sirens, and letter the word *Police* on the sides. You do not have the right to set back your speedometer before you sell the ownership right, nor can you drive your car at 90 miles per hour through a school zone. Why can't you do these things when it is your car? Who makes the rules? Why should you agree to them?

You limit your ownership rights in agreement with other members of the society in order to have a stable society. You give up your right to turn back your speedometer in return for an agreement from others that they will do the same. By giving up some of your rights for the sake of others, you are assured of maintaining your own rights on an equal basis. The limits of behavior that are mutually agreed upon by the members of society with respect to goods, services, or resources are called *property rights.* Property rights may be constitutionally or legislatively defined by the members of society (for example, the U.S. Constitution states that all members of our society have the *right* to life, liberty, and the pursuit of happiness), or these rights may develop from the customs, habits, or informal rules that govern human interaction. An example of property rights defined by informal rule might be the practice of primogeniture, where by custom the eldest son inherits the right to all the family wealth.

The ability or right to control a resource, good, or service is not always defined in the same comprehensive manner. For example, suppose you want to take your date on a picnic. You get in your car and drive into the country until you find a suitable spot; there you stop, unload your gear, and build a fire to roast hot dogs. Do you have a right to use the picnic area? Maybe and maybe not—it depends on the ownership right. Suppose the picnic area is part of farmer Jones's front yard. Unless you have first received permission to use the property, you have *no* right of use. However, if the picnic spot is part of a state park, then you *may* have the right of use. This would depend upon whether you were the first person to arrive at the picnic spot. Why? The right use of the park is owned *equally* by all the members of the society.

Suppose that the right to the picnic spot had never been defined by the members of the society and you were the first one to discover it. Then you might have the right of ownership by virtue of being first. This is sometimes called a "squatter's right." Of course, the other members of the society must be willing to recognize your right. If no agreement has been reached as to the acceptable limits of behavior, that is, no rights to property established, then the society has anarchy. One purpose for having a government is to provide a means to carry out the agreements of individuals with respect to the control of goods, services, and resources in the society.

The right of ownership gives you an exclusive right but not an unrestricted right to use the good, service, or resource. In exercising your exclusive right of ownership, you may force others unwillingly to bear a cost from your action. For example, when you drive your car during rush hour on a downtown street, you add to the traffic congestion and cause others to bear a cost. Thus, the cost of your private decision to drive your car is borne in part by you and in part by the other affected members of the society. We term these interdependencies of action *external effects,* or *externalities.* External effects are present when other members of the society either benefit or lose from your use of your exclusive right of ownership. The presence of external effects may be a signal to the members of society that a redefinition of property rights is necessary. For example, for decades individuals and firms living along the Great Lakes had the communal right to dump waste into the waters. This practice did not seem to severely affect the marine ecosystem of the lakes. However, as the population grew, this practice caused the virtual elimination of all marine life in many parts of the lake system. In response to the external effects of the polluters exercising their communal right of use, society redefined the "right to dump." This right was severely limited in an attempt to reverse the adverse effects of the past.

As the definition of rights of ownership emerges because of the interaction of individuals within a society, these rules of behavior are subject to differing opinions as to the limits of such ownership. For example, the "right to bear arms" in the society today means generally that any adult who does not have a criminal record has the right to own a gun. Many individuals are working to change this rights structure, so that the right to bear arms would be more severely restricted in the society. Changes in the law would affect the conditions of ownership within the society.

KEY CONCEPTS

Property rights or behavioral rules The rules, laws, or customs that define the limits of social behavior by establishing the permissible use of goods, services, and resources.

Communal rights to property A situation in which every member of society has equal rights to use all resources, goods, and services.

Anarchy A social system in which there is the complete absence of specified rights to property.

Social costs The total of all costs generated from a given economic transaction.

External effects The effects that are unwillingly borne by individuals not involved in a given decision-making process. The general term for such interdependencies of action is *externalities.* If you purchase a horse from farmer Jones, you reach a mutually beneficial agreement. If when you are riding the horse home, it kicks a pedestrian, the pedestrian has unwillingly become a party to your transaction.

Right of ownership The bundle of exclusive controls which include the right of use; the right to receive returns from a good, service, or resource; and the right to change the form of the good or resource.

CASE 5
The Changing Rights Structure for Predator Control[1]

In the United States the rights to wildlife have been held communally since explorers came to this continent. The right to wildlife is distributed to all members of society on a first-come, first-served basis. For centuries, some forms of wildlife have been considered harmful to the well-being of the society, and their removal has been vigorously pursued. Predatory animals as well as "pests" fall into this classification. Billions of public and private dollars have been devoted to ridding the countryside of mountain lions, bobcats, wolves, eagles, bears, foxes, coyotes, and other predators. In general, the eradication programs have been a success. Many of these predators have become virtually extinct. The notable exception is the coyote. The coyote is especially difficult to control because of its natural adaptability to changing environments.

Private and public programs to eradicate predators most often have worked as a loose partnership. The aim of such programs is a reduction in the number of animal losses incurred by private livestock producers as a result of predation. To this end, $3.6 million of federal funds and $4.6 million in state and private funds were spent in 1972. Most spending went for coyote eradication. Private individuals who operate livestock firms in the vast American West bear the negative effects of the communally owned predators. The National Woolgrowers Association, a private group of livestock owners, estimates that the loss of sheep to predators in 1971 averaged 5.3 percent of the total sheep inventory. When translated into dollar terms, the estimated value of sheep lost in the Western United States in 1971 totaled $17 million. Although a good deal of controversy surrounds the accuracy of such estimates, since they were made by the affected livestock owners, there is no doubt that individual producers face economic loss at the mouths of predators.

Coyotes and other predators benefit the society by providing a balanced ecosystem. The predators limit population growth of rodents and other animals. In particular, rodent control, which is costly when produced privately, is performed by the predators as a normal function of their life cycle. Further, society may receive benefits from the sight or sound of such animals, or from knowing that they are not extinct.

In most of the Western United States, the right to feed privately owned livestock on communally owned lands is sold to private individuals. This right exchange is generally called a *grazing rights contract,* or *grazing rights* for short. When the federal government sells the grazing rights to livestock producers, the predator control rights generally are not specified. However, it has been common practice for

[1] Facts in this case are from material presented to the U.S. Senate Committee on Interior and Insular Affairs, Subcommittee on Public Lands, during public hearings on Problems of Predator Control, June 1-4, 1973.

a century that the lessee of the lands has the right to control predators on the leasehold. Historically, the federal government has assisted the livestock producers in their eradication programs on publicly owned lands.

The fastest, most effective way to rid an area of predators is by the use of poisons, and a number of these have been developed specifically for coyotes, foxes, and wolves. The most common forms of predator control, until 1972, were poisons such as 1080 (sodium monofluocacetate) thallium, strychnine, and cyanide. Other methods of predator control include trapping, shooting, and "denning." All these methods are more costly (less effective) in terms of number of predators killed per dollar spent.

Since the late 1960s many members of society have come to feel differently about property rights with respect to predators. The increased awareness of ecology and the relationships among living things can be credited for some of the changes in attitude. The rights affecting the public ownership of predators were radically altered when former President Nixon issued Executive Order 11643 on February 9, 1972. The order restricted the use of poisons for predator control on federal lands and in federal programs except in emergency situations. Subsequently, the Environmental Protection Agency (EPA) suspended and canceled the registration of 1080, strychnine, thallium sulfate, and cyanide for the purposes of killing predators. Further, while it had long been illegal for a private individual to use poisons on federally owned property, this prohibition was never enforced. Since the issuance of Executive Order 11643, the government is following a policy of strict enforcement of the poison ban.

QUESTIONS

1 The federal government has now banned the use of poisons on lands and removed the major poisons from the market by banning their production. How would you expect this alteration in the boundaries of acceptable behavior to affect the numbers of coyotes killed each year? What would you expect to happen to the costs of producing coyote eradication?

2 One of the most useful functions of predators is rodent control, since rodents are the main source of food for coyotes, wolves, etc. If the number of predators increases at the same time that the cost to the predator of eating domestic livestock decreases, what would you expect to happen to the grain producers' losses to rodents, if coyotes prefer sheep to rabbits? How would this affect the price of grain in the domestic markets and the quantity supplied, assuming that other factors remained constant?

3 Many people who are in favor of laws restricting predator eradication are not unsympathetic to the economic hardship that they cause the individual livestock owners. Thus, several mechanisms have been suggested to compensate livestock producers for the increased probability of loss as a result of the ban on poisons. One such compensation scheme proposed by the Cain Commission is a

mandatory livestock insurance program covering all livestock that graze on federal lands, with the federal government paying a portion of the insurance premium for the private producer. A legal precedent currently exists for this sort of compensation. What would be the probable effect on the incentive system of the sheep grower to protect the herd from predators if such an insurance scheme were adopted?

4 Imagine a system where livestock producers who purchased grazing rights to public lands were allowed to bid in an open market for the right to control predators on that land in any manner they chose. Would you predict that such a system would lead to a change in the current levels of predator eradication? The livestock industry currently spends between $1.5 and $3 million a year on predator eradication. Would you expect this amount to rise or fall, under the above property rights scheme? Explain.

5 Alternatively, consider a property rights scheme where the price of grazing rights was reduced each year, on the basis of the previous year's losses to predation. For example, if the private sheep producer lost five sheep to coyotes in the previous year, then the dollar value of this loss would be deducted from the price of the producer's grazing permit. Would you expect this property rights structure to lead to the same results as in the previous case where predator rights are purchased? Explain. Would private expenditures for eradication rise or fall from the current levels of approximately $2 million? Why?

6 Some estimates of the effect of the ban on poisons suggest that the number of predator losses will increase by upward of 100 percent within the next five years. Assuming that the demand for lamb chops, mutton, and wool remains relatively stable over that period, what would be the expected change in the quantity of sheep marketed and the selling price in this market? Relate these effects to the probable entry or exit of firms in this market. How does the general nature of the elasticity of demand for food products affect your answer?

7 Many colleges and universities charge lower prices to students for admission tickets to athletic events, with the provision that the student has no right to transfer ownership of the ticket to someone else. How does the absence of the right to sell the student ticket affect the value of the ticket? If these institutions altered the property rights structure so that student tickets were transferable without penalty, what would you predict would happen to the price of student tickets?

8 Zoning laws in many communities specify the sizes and kinds of structures that can be built in various areas. Suppose a building lot is currently zoned so that either a single-family home or a multifamily home can be built there. What would you expect to happen to the selling price of the lot today if

(a) The city council suddenly altered the zoning law so that the lot could be used for only a single-family dwelling. Suppose this change was completely *unanticipated.*

(b) The city council altered the zoning law so that the lot could be used for only a single-family dwelling, but the intention to change the zoning law had been announced three years before. Thus, the change had long been *anticipated.*

TEST YOURSELF

Determine whether the following statements are true or false.

T F 1. In the complete absence of mutually agreed upon behavioral rules, a society would exist in a state of anarchy.

T F 2. Property rights are grants for the unrestricted use of a good, service, or resource.

T F 3. When all members of the society have equal ownership rights to the local swimming hole, overuse of the property will necessarily occur.

T F 4. One function of government is to provide a means of establishing and enforcing collectively agreed upon property rights.

T F 5. Your rights to exclude others from the enjoyment of benefits from your goods is a necessary condition for a well-functioning system of private property ownership.

PRIVATE AND SOCIAL BENEFITS: AN ILLUSTRATION

The graph below reflects the private demand and supply of education for an individual Jane Doe. Answer each of the questions below based on the information presented in the graph.

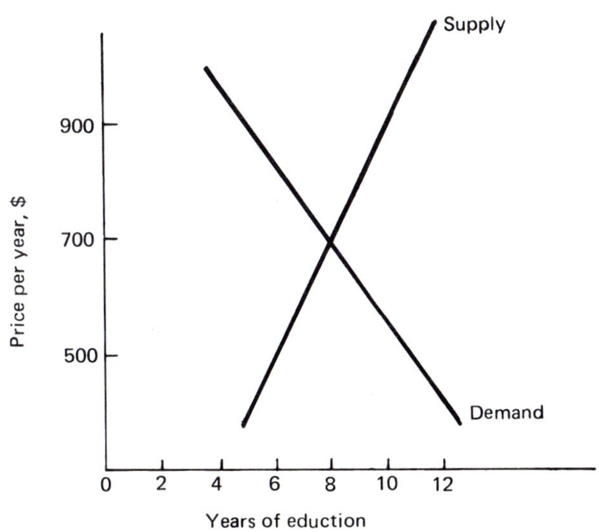

FIGURE 5-1 Jane Doe's marginal costs and benefits of purchasing years of education.

1 By seeking to pursue her own self-interest, Jane Doe will purchase education until she has attended school for

- (a) 4 years
- (b) 10 years
- (c) 8 years
- (d) 2 years
- (e) Indeterminate time

2 If Jane purchased 10 years of education, she would find that in the tenth year

- (a) Her marginal cost was less than her marginal benefit
- (b) Her marginal cost was equal to her marginal benefit
- (c) Her marginal cost was greater than her marginal benefit
- (d) Her well-being could be increased at the margin by purchasing more education at the prevailing price
- (e) None of the above

3 Suppose that all other members of society receive some positive benefit when Jane Doe purchases education in the private market. These benefits may take the form of a reduced probability that Jane will commit serious crimes. Or the benefits may be that because of her educational background, Jane Doe can provide greater services for the community. These benefits are an example of

- (a) Social costs
- (b) Private costs
- (c) Private benefits
- (d) Social benefits
- (e) None of the above

4 Given the information in question 3, suppose that society values the benefits it receives for Jane's purchase of education at $200 per year. The number of years of education for Jane that would be optimal for all members of the society is

- (a) 10 years
- (b) 8 years
- (c) 2 years
- (d) 14 years
- (e) None of the above

5 Given the information in question 3, the optimal amount of education for this society will be produced

- (a) When Jane pursues her own self-interest
- (b) When all individuals are made to attend school for at least 10 years
- (c) When education is produced by the government
- (d) When Jane is made to "internalize the externalities" of her behavior
- (e) (b) and (c) only

6

The Logic of Group Behavior

So far our analysis has focused on the individual as a decision-maker. We have noted that an individual's decisions are influenced by perceptions of cost and benefits associated with available alternatives. In many cases an individual is also a member of a group; i.e., you may belong to an informal group of friends, be a member of a community, be a part of the electorate or the student body, be a member of a family, or at times simply be a part of a crowd. Although you act as an individual in each case, other members of your group have an influence on your perception of the costs or benefits associated with alternative courses of action. Therefore, to move our description closer to reality, we will examine individual behavior in a group setting.

When you are a member of a large group or are in a setting where you are but one of *many* actors, your behavior may be quite different from when you are a member of a small group or are in a setting with a relatively small number of other individuals. For example, you individually might be reluctant to litter the campus while in the company of a few friends, yet when leaving the football stadium in the anonymity of many fans after a big game you may litter with no qualms. The cost of littering to the individual is reduced considerably in the large-number setting. An additional piece of litter in a crowded football stadium will probably go unnoticed; furthermore, the large number of people around you are probably not personal acquaintances, and thus you are less concerned about their possible annoyance. In the small group setting, the litter may be much more noticeable; but, more importantly, the annoyance of friends with whom you have a continuing relationship might constitute a considerable cost.

The number of individuals in a group or in a setting in which you find yourself can also affect the benefits from various courses of action. For example, if your family selects vacation sites by majority vote of the family members, you might be willing to exert a great effort to gather information on the alternative sites. On the other hand, you might be willing to spend very little time studying the issues in a national election because a vote is far less significant in terms of influencing the outcome.

Individuals frequently form groups in order to provide benefits sought by the members of the group. Examples of this range from a group of people getting together on a regular basis to play poker to the creation of a political party, special interest group, or occupational association. The benefits provided by such group activity are in some cases mostly private benefits, such as in the poker playing group, while in other cases the benefits may be of a more public nature, as in a political party organized to pursue certain social goals. In the former case, if any individual member does not participate in the group's activities or "do his or her share," then the individual will not receive the benefits of the activity. However, in the latter case, since the benefits of the group's activities are primarily public, it is possible for the individual to enjoy a "free ride" (or not to do his or her share) and still enjoy the benefits of the group activity.

The problem of an individual member of a group "coasting" comes about for several reasons. The most important reason is that if the benefits of the activity are public, any individual member will be able to enjoy those benefits whether she or he participates in the activity or not. Not all free-riding behavior is the result of deliberate shirking by individuals. In some cases the individual may recognize that whether he or she participates in the activity will have little, if any, effect on the outcome of the group's activity. Therefore, it may be rational to choose to abstain from such activity. This might be the case, for example, in situations where individuals are asked to voluntarily conserve energy by turning back their thermostats during winter months. An individual may honestly believe that energy conservation is a goal worth pursuing; however, he or she may believe that whether an individual turns a thermostat back or not will have little, if any, effect on the overall conservation effort of the nation.

Another reason for the free-rider problem with regard to group behavior involves organizing groups that provide a public good for their members. The benefits to the individuals bearing the costs of organizing the group are no different than those benefits which accrue to the individuals who bear none of these costs. This makes it difficult for many groups to get started or to maintain the provision of an activity for which the benefits are largely public. The following example will serve as a case in point. A college instructor teaches a course in which daily in-class discussions of the reading assignments are required. In order for the students to be able to discuss the readings in class, of course they must read them in advance. The professor tells the students at the beginning of the semester that there will be a surprise quiz on any day that it appears that the students have *not* read the assignment. The way the instructor makes such a determination is on the basis of student responses at the beginning of each class. That is, the professor begins each class by asking several questions. If a number of students are ready and able to answer these questions, the instructor assumes that the class is prepared (the instructor's assumption may be incorrect, but that is irrelevant here). If very few or none of the students are able to answer the questions, a quiz is given.

Obviously, not every student must be prepared every day in order for the entire class to escape the quiz. In fact, in a class of forty students, if ten students are prepared each day, there would probably be sufficient discussion to satisfy this professor. Therefore, if the students could organize and assign ten students to be prepared each day, then any one student would only have to read the assignments for every fourth class. Many students would consider themselves better off under such a group arrangement than they would be if they individually had to prepare for each and every class. In other words, the ten prepared students each day would provide a public good for the rest of the class in that the chosen ten reduce or eliminate the chance of having a pop quiz that day. A particular class of students may feel that everyone in the class would be better off if they organized and provided this public good. However, instructors have observed that with classes of thirty students or larger, such organization for the provision of public goods never takes place over an extended period, such as a month or 6 weeks.

The reason students are never able to maintain organized provision of this public good in the classroom is because of the organizing and enforcing costs and public benefits. At least one student must make up a roster designating which ten students are to be prepared on each day and then must enforce this arrangement. An additional effort is required of this student that is not required of any other student; yet all students in the class receive the same benefits if the public good is provided. Although there may be enough initial enthusiasm in the class to get the group effort started for a class period or two, after a week or so individuals begin to realize that whether or not they are prepared on the day they are assigned makes really very little difference since there still will be nine other students who will be prepared that day. Once individuals begin to free-ride, the group effort quickly deteriorates and no one individual has any incentive to bear the costs of organizing and enforcing the group arrangement. In a class with only ten students, it would be far easier to organize and enforce the organizing agreement because the costs of organization and enforcement would be considerably less with a smaller number of students involved.

A common interest in providing a particular activity among all the individuals in a group, then, will still *not necessarily* ensure that the group will be able to provide this good for its members. This problem will be especially prevalent when the activity for which the group is organized is a public good.

This problem—the costs of organization and enforcement—illustrates the key difference between two alternative theories or explanations of group behavior. The public goods theory of group behavior suggests that individuals, even when they are members of a group, make decisions as rational individuals (see "Key concepts" in Chapter 2) and thus are responsive to costs and benefits at the individual level.

The common interest theory of group behavior holds that individuals with similar or common interests will form groups which act as a separate entity rather than a collection of individual decision makers. This explanation is used when you hear people say, "Congress will override the President's veto" or "General Motors is concerned with energy conservation." If a group does not support an activity, it is because the group chooses not to take that particular course of action. The decision-making unit, in this theory, is the group itself. The proponents of the common interest theory believe that people are rational; but they also contend that when people recognize that they have interests in common (as the students did above) and that they will benefit from collective action, they will develop into organized groups. The costs of organization and enforcement in the provision of public goods are often overlooked by proponents of the common interest theory of group behavior.

KEY CONCEPTS

Social organizers Four means by which the social interactions of individuals can be ordered: (1) voluntary cooperation, (2) exchange of goods and services, (3) government coercion, and (4) violence. A main concern in economies is the market (a system of voluntary exchanges).

Common interest theory of groups The viewpoint of group behavior which states that groups are organized in order to further the common interest of the group. Members of this school believe the group acts as an entity in itself.

Public goods theory of groups The viewpoint of group behavior which suggests that the common interest factor, when it is a public good, is ineffective as the *only* motivator of group behavior. Groups are viewed as being no more than a composite of individuals.

Behavioral rules Principles which guide actions of individuals in order to enhance the collective public good and as such are subject to the same logic as group behavior.

"Free-rider" problem Problem associated with trying to get individual members of a group to "do their share" when the benefits of such action constitute a public good.

Public good A good which when consumed by one individual is also made available to others. One person's consumption of the good does not reduce the amount available for others to consume (e.g., national defense, highways, traffic lights, etc.).

CASE 6
Corporate Contributions[1]

Some social critics argue that today's society demands more from business than simply the efficient production of goods and services. Business, they say, must assume various social responsibilities which are often unspecified but which are said to relate to improving the "quality of life." Corporation presidents these days probably spend hardly a day or a week without receiving some sort of request for money or support. The high profile of most corporations and their large absolute dollar amounts of assets and earnings make them prime targets for many fund-raising efforts (e.g., sponsorship of artistic events, grants to health care facilities, contributions to the United Way, contributions to higher education, etc.). Increased corporate giving or corporate philanthropy is one type of activity which is favored by most social responsibility advocates, and most corporations do make some philanthropic contributions. Corporate contributions as a percentage of total corporate income have increased over the past four decades in the United States.

Luther Hodges, former Secretary of Commerce under Presidents John Kennedy and Lyndon Johnson, describes today's new corporate manager and social responsibility as follows:

> The present day "boss" is generally a college trained specialist with intensive education and skills in business management or finance. The modern manager or chairman president is a professional. Trained either in a collegiate school of business administration or in an executive management form, he has been taught and has learned to see his job as a multifaceted responsibility. He knows his public—especially his local community—and he anticipates and responds to the community's needs. . . .
>
> There seems to be emerging the practical and necessary attitude that business must invest—in its donations and research budgets—in specific programs that seem to have the most potentiality for both short run and long term gains for the good of society and these budgeted investments may be best given in some cases to private institutions and in other instances to public institutions. . . .

The benefits from most corporate giving are rather difficult to estimate accurately because most corporate gifts purchase goods which have some public aspect.

[1] Facts in this case are used with permission from Gerald Keim, "Managerial Behavior and the Social Responsibility Debate: Goals versus Constraints," *Academy of Management Review,* March 1978.

The quote from Luther Hodge's article "The Responsibility of American Business toward the Community" is used by permission of Memphis State University Press from their volume *The Social Conscience of Business,* 1974.

For instance, corporate contributions to business school professorships benefit not only the corporation indirectly because it now has a larger pool of trained individuals to call upon, but also students in general who now have more quality instruction available to them. Its very difficult to think of any contribution which corporations have recently made that does not have some public goods aspects attached to it. Most social responsibility advocates direct their campaigns for increased involvement in social problems toward the very large corporations, presumably because it is thought that large corporations are more likely to commit resources to socially responsible ends than the small corporations. However, contrary to the expectations of the social responsibility advocates, smaller corporations tend to contribute more relatively than the large corporations. If fact, since 1940, the ratio of contributions to net income has been higher for companies with $1 to $5 million worth of assets than for companies with over $250 million worth of assets. Such evidence has prompted some to question the relative stinginess of giant corporations.

QUESTIONS

1 Economic theory assumes that firms are profit-maximizing organizations. Is corporate philanthropy consistent with the assumption of profit maximization? Explain.

2 Individuals are assumed to be utility maximizers. Since corporate executives decide how generous the firm will be, are there any private benefits from philanthropy which may affect their decision making? Explain.

3 Given what you know about the public goods theory of groups, would you suspect that the small corporations give primarily to local charities and philantropic causes or to national or international organizations like CARE or UNESCO? Why?

4 How might you explain the relationship between corporate size (in terms of total dollar value of assets) and corporate giving (in terms of percentage of net income)? In other words, why is it that smaller corporations tend to contribute more relatively than the large corporations? Explain.

5 Explain why three companies X, Y, and Z in a rural area may agree to collectively pay for the construction of a public medical facility in the area.

6 If companies X, Y, and Z were now located in a large metropolitan area, would you expect them to make the same dollar value contributions to improvement of medical facilities? Why or why not?

7 Professor Milton Friedman of the University of Chicago has argued that the law authorizing tax deductions for corporate philanthropy should be repealed. What consequences do you feel might follow the repeal of this law?

8 Assume that you are the president of a large corporation and are in the process of conducting the annual meeting of stockholders. One of the stockholders points out to you at the meeting that the corporation gave $20 million to various

community projects in the last calendar year. The stockholder points out that this $20 million could have been distributed as dividends to the shareholders of the corporation and is irate and demands to know why you have insisted on "throwing away" this money. How would you explain to this stockholder your corporation's point of view?

TEST YOURSELF

T F 1. The common interest theory of groups holds that a group is a collection of individuals whose separate actions appear to be group action.

T F 2. Adherents of the common interest theory of groups believe that groups can more or less be treated as an individual. That is, the difference between a group and an individual is a matter of degree and not form.

T F 3. The public goods theory of groups suggest that in large groups a common interest among members will not be sufficient to ensure that group action is undertaken.

T F 4. The "free rider" is more of a problem for small groups than for large groups.

T F 5. Primary schools (grades 1 to 12) could generally be regarded as an example of a public good.

T F 6. The costs of organization and enforcement for a group are very important in determining whether a particular group will form.

T F 7. An individual who does not turn down the thermostat during the winter months as requested by the President could be considered a free rider.

T F 8. Many goods, such as garbage removal, have both public and private aspects.

T F 9. Since all groups are made up of individuals, economists need only spend their time examining the behavior of individual decision-making units.

T F 10. The size of a particular group has little to do with the decision-making processes of the group.

T F 11. When individuals realize that they can benefit from some sort of collective action, it is reasonable to expect that a group will form. No other considerations in group formation are relevant.

T F 12. A municipality which provides its residents with streets is a group providing a public good.

7

Competition

When an economist talks about a market, the reference is not to a grocery store or an open-air market. Actually, the term *market* does not even refer to a place—it refers, instead, to a process. A *market* is a process by which buyers and sellers interact in order to exchange information about what the participants are willing to buy and/or sell. Some markets, like the market for corporate stock, are located largely in a small geographic area. The New York Stock Exchange (the "Big Board") is located on Wall Street in New York City and handles the major portion of stock bought and sold in the United States. Even the corporate stock market, however, is not located in just one place—the American Stock Exchange (the "Amex"), located only a few blocks from Wall Street, also deals in stocks. There are also a number of smaller exchanges in various cities across the United States (Philadelphia, for example). No one location can bill itself as *the* market for stocks.

So you see, it is *not* the location of the stock markets that is important in defining them as markets. Each of the markets noted is just a place where the *process of exchange* can take place. More formally, the market is the process where the terms of trade (price, quality, amount, etc.) are agreed upon by the participants. In stock markets, buyers and sellers can interact with one another to exchange shares of corporate stock (because trading shares of stock can be complicated, institutions such as stock exchanges were developed as places where buyers and sellers could trade easily).

For the economist, the competitive market is the ideal type of market. In a competitive market, buyers try to outdo other buyers by offering sellers the most attractive terms. Sellers will try to outdo other sellers by offering their goods and services at cheaper prices. Competitive markets exist when there are many buyers and sellers, when entry into the market is not restricted (by government rules, costs of manufacturing, etc.), and when the product being bought and sold is homogeneous (standardized).

Actual examples of the economist's ideal competitive market are a bit difficult to come by; in fact, there may be no situations which *exactly* match these conditions. The market, however, for some agricultural produce (say, tomatoes) tends to be competitive. Many tomato producers often exist in a given market area and sell to many buyers in the same area. The product is more or less standardized (a tomato is a tomato), and any buyer or seller can stop buying or producing at will. Don't be misled, however, into believing that all produce markets are competitive (see Chapter 9).

Recall that in competitive markets the competition does not take place between buyers and sellers. In the market for tomatoes, for instance, the sellers of tomatoes do not compete with the buyers of tomatoes. Rather, the sellers of tomatoes compete with one another by offering lower prices. The buyers compete with other buyers by offering higher prices. This competition is not limited to price competition; it may include variations in quality, information, and so on.

The idealistic or perfectly competitive market has some qualities which make it very desirable. Since there are many sellers of the product in a competitive market, buyers may easily transfer purchases from one seller to another—this ease of transfer encourages sellers to compete with one another by attempting to offer the lowest price, the best service, the highest quality, and so on. If a particular seller refuses to compete with fellow sellers, the buyers may quite rationally transfer their sales to the competition. Any one seller in a competitive market is said to be a *price taker* because he or she cannot refuse to compete with other sellers offering lower prices, for the consequence of doing that would be to lose all one's customers to the other sellers. From the buyer's or consumer's standpoint, this is an ideal situation because he or she is assured that the market will result in the lowest price being offered (that is, the lowest price consistent with the firms not losing money in the long term).

The number or quantity of goods produced in a competitive market is also decided in an ideal manner from the point of view of the consumer. Each seller has the incentive to produce more units and sell them as long as the *extra revenue received is larger than the cost of the additional units.* If one seller fails to produce and sell extra units from which a profit could be earned, another seller (recall that there are many sellers) wlll seize the opportunity. In this way, the consumer will have available as many units as can be produced profitably by the sellers. Recall that in Chapter 4 the supply curve for a competitive industry (the curve which shows how much will be produced at various prices) was shown to be the marginal cost curve for a particular product.

KEY CONCEPTS

Market A process by which buyers and sellers interact in order to exchange goods and services which participants are willing to buy and/or sell and through which terms of trade are determined.

Competitive market A market characterized by many buyers and sellers, a standardized product, and freedom of entry and exit (competitive markets are often called "free markets").

Barriers to entry (or exit) Obstacles which prevent firms from entering (exiting from) a market. Some obstacles would be government restrictions on producing the product (i.e., limitations on the number of banks) or restrictions on exit (i.e., some railroads have been restricted from going out of business).

Homogeneous products Standardized or identical products; ones which cannot be differentiated with respect to source.

CASE 7A
Why Put Oil In Your Car?[1]

It takes gasoline to run an automobile these days, but it is not necessary to use oil! This does not mean that you should drain your crankcase and leave it empty. This does mean that there is a new class of products available today which takes the place of lubricating oil. These products are variously called "synthetic oils" or "synthetic lubricants."

Synthetic oils are getting quite a bit of attention these days because they have some important advantages over conventional mineral oils. They are inherently more stable than currently available motor oils, they don't evaporate out of the crankcase and so require fewer "top-ups," and they naturally have a better viscosity index. (That is, they flow freely at low temperatures and do not thin out as much as mineral oils at high temperature.) Perhaps the most important characteristic of synthetics, however, is their natural detergent and dispersive properties. These properties allow synthetics to keep engines cleaner and cut down on wear from friction; thus engines last longer.

Researchers report amazing results with the new synthetics. After 100,000 miles in a Lincoln Continental with no oil changes and using synthetic oil, the Scientific Laboratory of the Ford Research and Engineering Laboratory found wear "...was fantastically low. Rings and bearings were within factory tolerance—like new parts. We had never seen that in a 100,000-mile engine before."

A number of synthetic oils have recently been introduced: Chevron's Sub Zero Fluid, Mobil Oil Company's Mobil 1, Conoco's Polar Start, Amziol's DN-600 Synthetic Engine Oil, Emery's Frigid Go, and Eon's E-11. While there are actually four distinct categories of synthetic lubricants produced by the various companies, all the new lubricants cost more than mineral oils—four or five times as much at the retail level.

QUESTIONS

1 Competition among market rivals occurs on several levels (price, quality, etc.). In what ways are the oil companies competing with one another? How is this competition a process?

2 Since the synthetic oils are priced at 4 or 5 times the price of mineral oils, is there any price competition between the synthetic producers and mineral oil producers?

3 Why would a company, such as Mobil, which is a major producer of mineral oils, also join in the synthetic oil market?

[1]Facts in this case are reprinted with permission of *Popular Science,* © 1976 by Times Mirror Magazines, Inc. All rights reserved.

4 Given a market demand curve for motor oils in the United States, what would be the likely effect upon this curve of the introduction of synthetic oils?

5 Synthetic oils require heavy molecules similar to those in natural mineral oils, but they are constructed molecule by molecule from various hydrogen-and-carbon-containing light molecules. The processes used in constructing these synthetics are understandably expensive and appear to be the major reason for the high price tag on synthetics. Would you expect the retail prices of this class of products to decrease in the near future? Does your answer depend upon the existence of a "competitive market process"?

6 Each of the new synthetics is apparently different from its competitors in one or more ways. Different claims are made by the various producers of these as yet nonstandardized products. Eon claims 15 to 20 percent better gas mileage when their product is used. Amzoil claims its synthetic oil will run for 25,000 miles. Mobil claims a cleaner engine with less wear will result if 12,000-mile drain intervals are used. Demonstrate that consumers can benefit through this nonprice competition.

7 Synthetic oils are really nothing new. In 1942 during the Battle of Stalingrad, lubricants in German tanks jelled in the extreme cold. The Germans then developed synthetic lubricants for cold-weather use. When jet engines were first introduced, mineral oil lubricants were found to be unsatisfactory in the high heat. Developers used newly created synthetics to solve the problem. Consumer products based on synthetics are relatively new, however. Would you attribute this lag between development and introduction to a lack of competitive process?

CASE 7B
Free the University[2]

Universities in the United States have not always had the characteristics of today's universities. In the nineteenth century, universities fell into two categories. Most important universities were unquestionably church-related schools and were unlike modern universities because they had a specific, clearly defined objective. These schools were usually a means to educate young men and women for careers in the clergy or for preparation to lead "moral" lives. The behavior of trustees and administrators of these church-related institutions was very goal-directed. The responsibility of these individuals was to maximize the religious training purchased with the funds available.

A second important group of schools in American private education was the elitist liberal universities. In these institutions, education was viewed as a kind of a luxury consumption good. They, too, had a clear-cut goal and were designed for training the children of the well-to-do in the humane arts. In each of these two types of institutions, as long as the administrators and the faculty understood the purpose, there was little question about who ran the university and there was little pressure for different types of university organization. The control of these universities clearly rested with the individuals who contributed money to run the institutions and who set the goals of either providing religious education or training individuals in the humanities.

Examples of American universities which began in the church-related tradition would be Harvard, Dartmouth, Antioch, and the University of Chicago. Schools which began as elitist liberal universities are typified by Columbia, William and Mary, Northwestern, Vanderbilt, and Stanford. Often the individuals who contributed to these schools became the trustees of the schools or selected as trustees individuals who would be interested in producing a certain kind of education for a select group of students. These schools covered all costs of tuition for their students and provided their services at a bargain price, that is, below full cost. By subsidizing the students, the donors could continue to control the substance of what was taught.

An abrupt change came about in American higher education in 1862 and 1890 with the passage of the Morrill Acts. The new public universities instituted by these acts had no clear-cut goals comparable to those of the nineteenth century universities. There were government restrictions on religious training; and although liberal arts education was paid lip service, political pressures forced state schools toward the more practical programs—the ones designed to help students earn a living. It is the case even today that the liberal arts and humanities are more painstakingly taught in private universities than in public institutions.

[2]Facts in this case are reprinted with permission of Henry G. Manne from his article "The Political Economy of Modern Universities,"

Recent times have seen a tremendous increase in the amount of government-sponsored research carried on by private universities. In addition, the government provides contributions for their buildings, salaries, and student tuition. Another formidable change from the nineteenth-century private university is the increased amount of outside consulting in which faculty members engage (e.g., working on grants from the National Science Foundation, the Environmental Protection Agency, or the Federal Reserve System).

Such a radical shift has taken place that there is no longer any way for the trustees of public or private universities to keep faculty members in line. As a matter of fact, there is not even a "line" for trustees at all. Today's trustees apparently serve universities only because of status or prestige—they have little power because modern universities have become democratized. Perhaps the most significant characteristic of the modern university trustee is that he or she lacks any real interest in exercising any authority, and most students would agree that the trustees have no real power to determine what views will be taught in most universities. The modern notion of academic freedom has given to the faculty the effective power over subject matter and curriculum in the university.

When students talk about the administration, normally they are referring to the top administrative executive, that is, the president of the university. The character of the university president, like that of the trustees, will reflect the *real power* interests within the university. In other words, the university president will be selected on the basis of characteristics which please or benefit those individuals who actually fund the university. In the nineteenth-century goal-directed, traditional universities, presidents were sympathetic with and had similar qualities to the active and powerful members of the board of trustees. These nineteenth-century presidents displayed qualities of imagination, forcefulness, and innovation. A significant change in the characteristics of college presidents has taken place coincident with the shift in emphasis in universities. University presidents of today are first and foremost fund raisers. They are not supposed to bring their personal influence to bear on issues of educational policy but are primarily to keep the money flowing in from outside sources.

How might the United States gain the benefits of open market competition in university-level education? There are really two types of organizational schemes for the operation of universities: the free market organization and the cooperative system. The university world is presently in the process of operating largely on the cooperative basis, that is, with joint ownership of the universities by a large group of people, namely the taxpayers. It would be possible, however, to change this situation by taking three steps toward a free market organization of higher education services.

First, the government would have to get out of the education business. Thus, state universities would no longer exist, but perhaps state governments would give students tuition chits which could be used at *any* university to pay the student's tuition.

Second, tax exemptions for nonprofit private universities would have to be repealed. These tax exemptions are actually indirect subsidies by the government to private universities.

Finally, and most importantly, the universities might be given (or sold) to the faculties. Actually, except for formal legal purposes, faculty own the institutions now, in that they set university policy on student admissions, faculty hiring, and curriculum. Actually, it is not as necessary to make faculty the formal owners of the university as it is that some form of transferable ownership rights exist. With no subsidies available, universities would find themselves forced to behave more like proprietary institutions; they would cover all their costs from income much as business firms. With faculty members owning shares of stock or other transferable ownership rights in the university, there would be a guarantee of some of the competitive incentive realized in our corporate system.

QUESTIONS

1 If universities actually were given to the faculties and all forms of subsidies were eliminated as the case suggests, what competitive benefits might actually be realized?

2 Why is the existence of shares of stock or some form of transferable interest in the university necessary in order to achieve a competitive outcome? Note that the shareholders of stock in any corporation, whether it is a university or manufacturing corporation, are owners of the firm and as such have a set of rights not unlike those of a single proprietor.

3 If you were operating a firm in a competitive industry in which some of the firms received a subsidy from the government, would you feel that you could effectively compete with the subsidized firms? Would eliminating subsidies foster competition?

4 The cooperative form of management which exists in most universities today means that decision making is inevitably a negotiated compromise of the various conflicting interests within the faculty, the administration and the university's funding agency. If the free market form of universities were chosen in lieu of the cooperative form, whom would the universities seek to please? Explain.

5 If, as the case describes, the free market alternative for universities were implemented, what characteristics of competitive markets would you find in the university situation?

6 It is probably the case that even if the free market alternative were chosen for universities, many universities would charge higher tuition than others. In fact, it would not be unusual to find some institutions charging 10 or 12 times the tuition of other institutions. In competitive markets, however, the firms are usually thought of as price takers. Why do you suspect that it might be possible for some universities to charge higher tuitions than others under a free market system? Would this then be a perfectly competitive market?

7 Many individuals feel that we now have a competitive market in universities. These individuals say that students may now choose from among thousands of universities in the United States that one which they choose to attend. Does our current university system have the characteristics of a competitive market? In what ways, if any, does it differ?

8 What might be some disadvantages of the free market organization of universities? Could these disadvantages be overcome without resorting to an institutional arrangement similar to the one existing now?

TEST YOURSELF

1 In many markets supply is fixed in the short run (i.e., the quantity of agricultural produce for sale on a given day is more or less fixed). Assume the supply of lettuce in a particular market area is limited to 200 heads and that the demand for lettuce is as shown below.

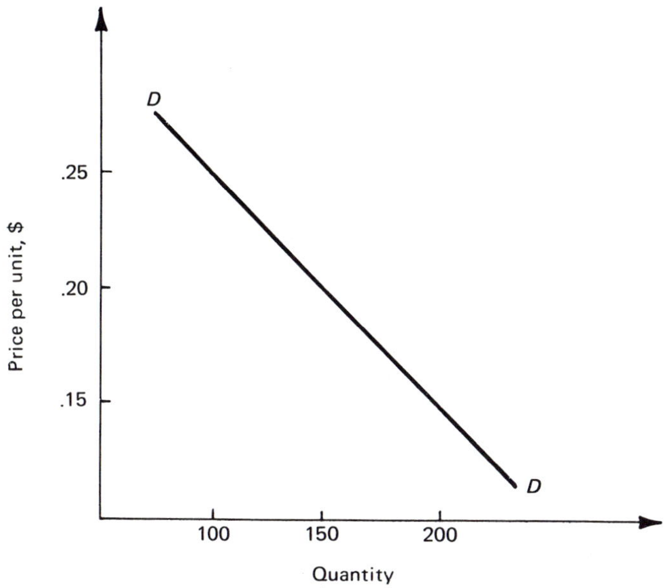

The price which will satisfy both buyers and sellers is (**a**) \$0.15, (**b**) \$0.20, (**c**) \$0.25.

2 Considering the information in question 1, how many heads of lettuce will be sold if the market price is \$0.15? (**a**) 200, (**b**) 150, (**c**) 100.

3 A competitive market is characterized by (**a**) many buyers and few sellers, (**b**) many buyers and many sellers, (**c**) few buyers and many sellers.

4 The dimensions of competition in a competitive market are many. If a seller refuses to meet the low price of competitors or their high quality, (**a**) the market ceases to function, (**b**) the seller loses buyers to other sellers, (**c**) the process of competition fails to operate.

5 In a competitive market (**a**) sellers compete with buyers, (**b**) sellers compete with other sellers, (**c**) sellers and buyers collude to set prices.

6 In a competitive market the quantity produced and sold is (**a**) more than consumers would want at the market price, (**b**) less than producers are willing to sell at the market price, (**c**) precisely what consumers demand at the market price.

7 Examples of truly competitive markets are (**a**) the stock market and the commodity exchanges, (**b**) probably impossible to find, (**c**) the agricultural product markets.

8 A market with barriers to entry for sellers would (**a**) not be truly competitive, (**b**) lead inevitably to collusion between buyers and sellers, (**c**) be more competitive than a market without such barriers.

Read the following statements and determine whether each is true or false.

T F 1. In perfect competition, one producer may not produce a somewhat different good from another producer in that industry.

T F 2. In a situation of perfect competition, one firm can produce too much of the product and ruin the market.

T F 3. Perfect competition assumes a large number of producers all producing roughly the same product.

T F 4. Barriers to entry may limit competitive forces in a market.

T F 5. Buyers compete with sellers in perfectly competitive markets.

T F 6. Because buyers in a competitive market have many alternative sources of supply, sellers must compete with one another to offer the best terms of trade.

T F 7. Buyers in competitive markets are said to be price takers.

T F 8. Sellers will always produce and sell one more unit if the extra revenue received (marginal revenue) is larger than the cost of the additional unit (marginal cost).

8

Competition in Action

In the model of the market that we've developed so far, we have assumed that the price of a given quantity of a good remains fixed. That is, in the market for blue jeans, the price for each pair will be identical. From your experience, you know that this may not be true. In a downtown store in your city, jeans may be $13.50 a pair. If you check the price at a more exclusive shopping center, you may find that they sell for $21.95. When you check the factory outlet store, the price is $7.50. If you compare blue jean prices in other communities, you may find further price differentials for the same commodity. Why don't blue jeans sell for the same price throughout the country, state, city, and neighborhood? Is the market system breaking down? Does competition exist? Let's look at a particular situation to highlight the nature of the competitive exchange process and the relationship between buyers and sellers in the market for a single commodity.

Suppose that you are the owner/manager of the only liquor store in Dry Gulch and you act to maximize your profits. Let us assume that the closest alternative source of liquor for your customers is Watering Hole, a town 10 miles away. Watering Hole takes its name in part from its large number of liquor dealers in operation. One day Sally Smith, a Dry Gulch resident, comes into your store and tells you that a six-pack of Coors beer is selling for $1.20 less in Watering Hole than at your store. You tell Sally that you have to cover costs of operating and your price is as "cheap" as you can sell Coors. Based on the new price information you received, you consider "meeting" the price in Watering Hole, but decide that you need not be concerned with prices that are not in your market.

Sally Smith, acting to maximize her well-being, has to consider the trade-off between paying the higher price for Coors in Dry Gulch or driving the 10 miles to Watering Hole for the cheaper-priced beer. This is an easy decision for Sally since her job is in Watering Hole; she must drive there every day, and luckily her route takes her past many liquor stores. Sally's friends soon find out she goes to the liquor store in Watering Hole for her Coors, and they begin to send their beer orders with her. Soon Sally is transporting 10 cases of Coors a day to Dry Gulch for a small fee of $0.40 a six-pack. This amount more than pays for her time and trouble as well as the gas expense for the trip. Economists have a special name for the function that Sally is performing in the beer market; they call it *arbitrage.* Arbitrage is the simultaneous buying of a good in one market and the selling of it in another market for a higher price. Sally can make a profit (she no longer finds it necessary to pay for the gasoline for her trips to Watering Hole out of her regular income) by buying Coors "cheap" and selling it "dear," and still her friends are better off (each six-pack is $0.80 less) than if they had to purchase Coors in Dry Gulch.

The owner of the Watering Hole liquor store where Sally does business soon begins to wonder why he is letting Sally make all this money transporting Coors between the two towns. He begins to wonder if he could do the job more cheaply. After all, he owns a beer truck and already pays a driver to deliver in Watering Hole. He begins to look into the possibility of delivery to Dry Gulch and also of setting up a branch operation there. Could it be that the prices on all kinds of liquor are significantly higher in Dry Gulch than in Watering Hole? As the owner/manager of the Dry Gulch liquor store, you have noticed that Coor's sales have significantly declined within the last few weeks. At first you may attribute this decline to colder weather or buyers going on vacation or any number of things; you probably will not be very concerned. After all, you are the only liquor store in Dry Gulch.

Sally Smith's independent decision to transport Coors for her own consumption has set off a chain reaction that will continue until the price differential between Coors in Dry Gulch and Coors in Watering Hole reflects only the actual transactions costs. In this example, the transactions costs are the cost of transporting and handling the beer between the two towns. Other than these costs, the price will be *identical.* How can we know this will be the outcome of the competitive exchange process? When sellers in Watering Hole learn of the opportunity to make more money by selling in Dry Gulch, the Dry Gulch store owner finds sales declining at the old price; if he is going to sell any Coors, he must lower (meet) the price offered to consumers by Sally and other Watering Hole operators. The competition of the liquor sellers among themselves forces beer prices in Dry Gulch down.

What is the limit of this downward pressure on prices? When is it no longer advantageous to transport beer between the two towns, prices will stabilize. Thus, the arbitrage process started by Sally has lead to an equilization of prices in the two towns, given the transactions costs. The desire of independent individuals to make themselves as well off as possible has lead to a situation where the commodity produced is provided in the greatest amount at the lowest price consistent with production and transactions costs. This does not mean that prices will be identical for identical goods in all market exchanges, but it does mean that price differentials, when they exist, reflect differential opportunity costs.

KEY CONCEPTS

Excise taxation A levy imposed by government on the sale of a particular commodity. Excise taxes are usually placed on the manufacture of commodities and are paid by the producer of the good.

Tax shifting The notion that the legal incidence of the tax is different from the economic incidence of the tax. For example, an excise tax on leather goods may be shifted to the consumer of leather goods by the manufacturer's raising the price by the amount of the tax.

Arbitrage The act of simultaneously purchasing any commodity in one market and selling it in another market at a higher price. An arbitrageur (a person who engages in arbitrage) can make a profit whenever the price differential between the two markets exceeds the cost of the transactions.

Sales tax A flat percentage levy imposed by government on the selling price of an item. Sales taxes differ from excise taxes in that they are levied on all, or almost all, transactions.

CASE 8

Illegal Competition: Making Crime Pay[1]

New York City imposes an 8-cent per pack excise tax on the sale of cigarettes in addition to the 15-cent excise levy imposed by the state of New York. This compares with an excise tax rate of 2 cents per pack by the state of North Carolina, with no additional city or county taxes. According to statistics compiled by the Tobacco Tax Council,[2] the average price of a pack of cigarettes in New York City in 1976 was 64.8 cents with all federal, state, and city taxes included. The same package of cigarettes had an average price of 36.6 cents in North Carolina. The Tobacco Tax Council estimates that in the absence of all excise and sales taxes a package of cigarettes could have sold for 21 cents in 1976, and this would have covered all the costs (including normal profits) accruing from the farmer who puts the seed into the ground to the person who sells the finished product to the consumer.

The budget director for New York City, in the face of rising deficits and the fear of bankruptcy, has been considering additional taxes as one means to solve the city's financial problems. Cigarette taxes have always been a popular type of tax with government officials, since the demand for cigarettes tends to be rather inelastic. (See the discussion of elasticity in Chapter 3.) Before any change in the tax structure is made, it is important to hypothesize what the probable effects of such changes would be on consumer and producer behavior. We can illustrate some of these effects by focusing on the excise tax on cigarettes in New York City and the local cigarette market.

The Advisory Commission on Intergovernmental Relations estimates that in 1977 half of all cigarettes smoked in New York City were smuggled in from North Carolina.[3] (It is, of course, illegal to sell cigarettes without paying the state and city excise taxes.) The smugglers purchase cigarettes legally in North Carolina at wholesale prices as low as $2.40 a carton, then load up to 60,000 cartons in a single 40-foot trailer, and peddle them in the city via the organized crime network. The untaxed, illegal cigarettes sell for as much as $2.50 per carton *below* legitimate retail. It is estimated that the city and state lost up to $93 million in tax revenues in 1976 as a result of this illegal market. The tax losses to New York State and New York City as a result of bootlegging cigarettes are estimated at over $600 million in the last 10 years. The state of New York currently employs 50 field staff officers who are exclusively assigned to enforce the tax laws. In 1975, nine smugglers were jailed, each for a few months, with the common penalty being $10 or $15.

[1] Facts in this case are reprinted with permission from "The Cigarette Tax Lesson," *Wall Street Journal*, February 5, 1976, ©1976. All rights reserved.

[2] *The Tax Burden on Tobacco,* vol. 11 (Richmond, Va.: Tobacco Tax Council, 1976).

[3] "Millions in Sales Taxes Lost to Cigarette Smugglers," *The New York Times,* September 4, 1977, p. 1.

QUESTIONS

1 The market for legal cigarettes in New York City would appear to be faced with a good substitute commodity in the form of illegal cigarettes. With the aid of supply and demand curves, graphically illustrate what the effect in the New York market (both legal and illegal) is likely to be if the excise tax rate is raised to aid the city's financial crisis.

2 It has been suggested that New York City and New York State should act to lower the total excise tax bill to 10 cents per package, on the grounds that this change would raise the tax revenues accruing to the government units. How would you evaluate the correctness of this suggestion, if the commonly held belief that demand for cigarettes is inelastic is correct? Are these views necessarily inconsistent?

3 An alternative suggestion to stem the tide of illegal cigarettes into the New York City area is to increase the state enforcement field staff to 250 officers and to make a 5-year jail sentence mandatory for anyone caught smuggling 20,000 cartons or more. The estimated cost of increasing the enforcement staff is set at about $5 million annually; however, if this change resulted in recouping a substantial portion of the $93 million annual loss from smuggling, it would be a very profitable investment. Evaluate the probable effects of this policy on the illegal cigarette market with the aid of supply and demand curves.

4 Suppose that the market for cigarettes were similar to markets for most other goods; that is, there was untaxed entry across state lines (for example, Wisconsin apples are distributed throughout the entire United States without obtaining tax stamps). What do you predict would happen to the current selling price of a package of cigarettes in the legal New York City market under this marketing arrangement (you might think of this as abolishing all excise taxes on cigarettes)? To the selling price in North Carolina? After producers, suppliers, and consumers had been given time to adjust to the change in the market for cigarettes, what do you predict would be the relation of cigarette prices between New York City and North Carolina legal markets? What do you predict would happen in the illegal New York City market? You may wish to illustrate your analysis with the aid of supply and demand curves.

5 If the black market price of cigarettes is $2.50 a carton below the selling price in the legal market, why do we not find that *all* New York City's smokers smoke smuggled cigarettes instead of the reported one-half?

6 The Tobacco Tax Council reports that the per capita sales of packages of cigarettes in New York for 1976 were 124.6 packages, and the same figure for North Carolina was 230.2 packages. On the basis of the information in the case, does this figure indicate that people in North Carolina smoke almost twice as many cigarettes per capita as New Yorkers? Does this figure reflect the existing price differential in the two markets? How?

TEST YOURSELF

True—false

T F 1. Rivalry is an apt term to describe the interaction of sellers with sellers in the competitive market process.

T F 2. When prices of a commodity are uniform within a selling area, we call that a competitive market.

T F 3. The desire to produce goods and services that the buyer wants is the primary force behind the working of the competitive process.

T F 4. Arbitrage causes prices to change in a manner that is related to the economic costs of production or exchange.

T F 5. The limit of a seller's willingness to produce an additional unit of his or her commodity is reached in the short run when the marginal cost of production is just equal to the marginal revenue from sales. This is not true for the long-run case under conditions of free entry and exit.

Multiple-choice

Study Figure 8-1; then answer each of the following questions. Assume both markets are classified as competitive.

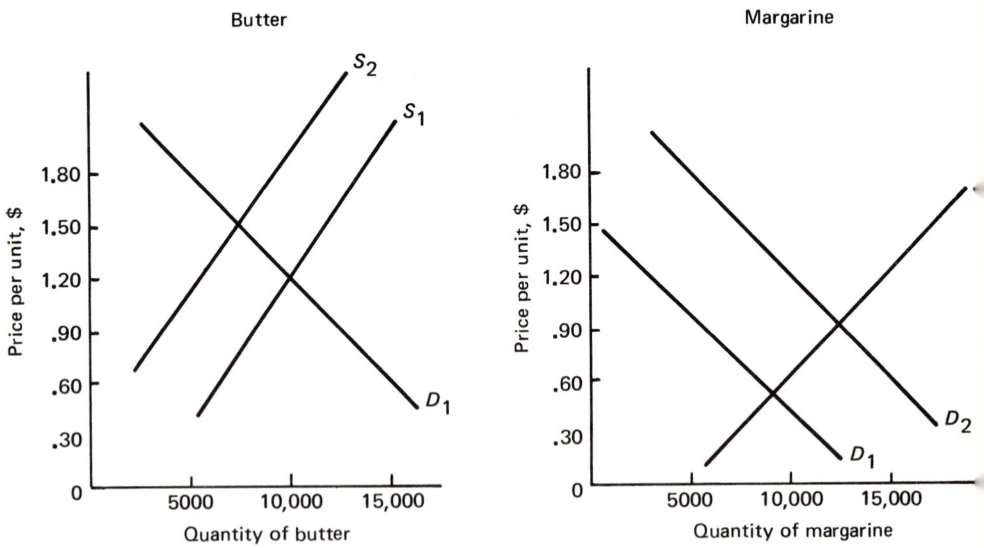

FIGURE 8-1 Market demand and supply curves for butter and for margarine

1 If the present situation in the market for margarine is depicted by demand curve D_1 and supply curve S_1, the price in that market will tend toward

(a) $0.50
(b) $0.20
(c) $0.70
(d) $0.60
(e) None of the above

2 If the present situation in the market for butter is depicted by supply curve S_1 and demand curve D_1, the price in that market will tend toward

(a) $1.50
(b) $1.20
(c) $1.00
(d) $1.40
(e) None of the above

3 We would generally assume that the relationship between the market for margarine and the market for butter was

(a) Unrelated
(b) One in which these goods are purchased together (complements)
(c) One in which these goods substitute for each other
(d) One in which these goods are provided for everyone because they are necessities.
(e) (c) and (d) only

4 Suppose that producers of butter find that milk is more costly because of a disease in the major United States dairy herds that is killing most of the cattle. This consequence would be reflected in the butter market by

(a) An increase in the supply of butter
(b) A leftward shift of the supply curve, such as the movement to S_2
(c) A reduction in the quantity supplied by butter producers, such as a movement along the supply curve S_1
(d) An increase in the supply of margarine
(e) (b) and (d) only

5 As a result of the consequences outlined in question 4, the price of butter

(a) Will rise
(b) Will remain the same
(c) Will fall by 25 percent at least
(d) Will fall by 10 percent
(e) Is not possible to determine

6 As a result of the consequences outlined in question 4, the margarine market will experience

(a) An increase in quantity demanded
(b) An increase in supply of margarine
(c) An increase in the demand for margarine
(d) A shifting outward of the demand curve for margarine, such as a movement to D_2
(e) (c) and (d)

7 When goods are substitutes for one another, it is correct to say that

(a) Conditions in each market are interrelated

(b) Price movements in one market affect the price and quantity in the other market

(c) If supply in market X increases, demand in market Y will decrease

(d) (a) and (c)

(e) (a), (b), and (c)

9

The Market for Food

Prices in agricultural markets (like wheat, lettuce, soybeans, etc.) jump up and down rather rapidly, and so most farmers are in the habit of listening to radio reports every morning or afternoon which give blow-by-blow accounts of price increases and decreases. Many farmers have their money, every cent of it, riding on the line each year because of the heavy investments required by modern farming techniques; and these radio price reports are more than just casual entertainment.

When driving through the Midwest, the breadbasket of the United States, you may have heard these monotonous-sounding descriptions of market activity on the radio and were, no doubt, inclined to switch stations. These reports do, however, suggest to us that agricultural markets are a bit different from the markets we have examined in previous chapters. While these markets are much the same as any other market, there are at least three aspects which set these markets apart. First, weather (hail, rain, drought, etc.) plays an extremely important role in agricultural markets. One 15-minute hailstorm at an inopportune moment can virtually destroy most crops. Second, demand and supply of agricultural commodities tend to be quite inelastic; that is, buyers will buy specific quantities regardless of how high or low the prices, and sellers can do little to produce more or less of a crop once the harvest is complete. Finally, the time between investment (buying seed, fertilizer, farm equipment, etc.) and sales of the final product (sacks of potatoes, bushels of wheat, tons of soybean meal, etc.) tends to be quite long. Although none of these characteristics are unique to agricultural markets, the combination makes the farm market special. Since it is a special market and one that affects everyone, we'll give it a closer look to see how supply and demand theories work and how the government has dealt with farm markets in recent years.

A market for an annual agricultural product like corn may be explained by using Figure 9-1. The demand curve shows, for example, that at a price of $1 per bushel, about 50,000 bushels will be purchased. This supply curve is interpreted a bit differently from those in Chapter 4, however. A farmer of a crop like corn cannot decide on the quantity to grow by observing the current price (it's not available at planting time)—the decision must be based on last year's price. The supply curve, then, shows the various quantities farmers will plant given possible prices of the previous year. For example, the supply curve states that if the price of corn one year were $2 a bushel, the harvest the next year would be 40,000 bushels.

This type of agricultural market tells us predictable price and quantity combinations for future years. Suppose that in a given year (say, year 1) the price of corn was $0.50 per bushel. According to the supply curve, this would mean that farmers would plant and grow 10,000 bushels for sale in year 2. What would be the sale price in year 2? The demand curve shows that if only 10,000 bushels are available, a price of $2.50 will be charged. But if $2.50 is the price in year 2, the supply curve predicts that 50,000 bushels will be planted and grown for sale in year 3, and so on. This type of analysis shows us what often actually occurs in unregulated agricultural markets—the price in one year determines the quantity for sale in the next year, and price and quantity fluctuate considerably from year to year.

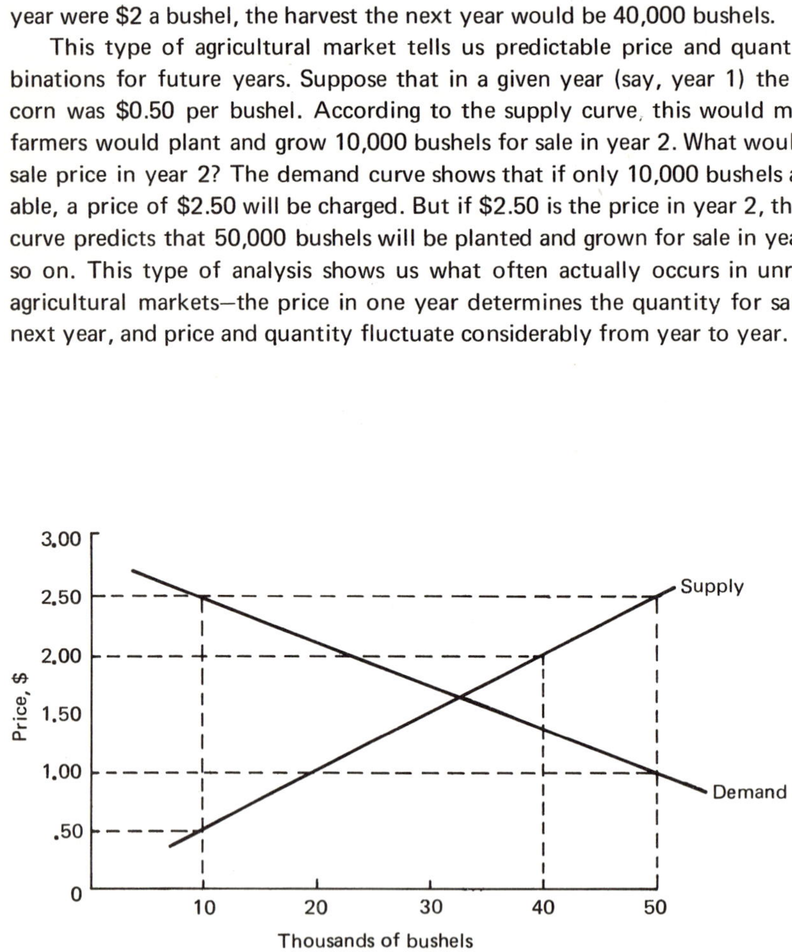

FIGURE 9-1

Most agricultural markets, however, are not free from government involvement and have not been since the 1930s. Most of the government involvement in these markets takes the form of the government actively influencing supply. The price support programs of the federal government and the acreage allotment programs are examples of this influence on supply. The price support programs set a price for particular commodities (say, corn) which the government guaranteed to pay to farmers if they were unable to sell the crop for a higher price in the free market. If the government support price were above the market price (as it is in Figure 9-2), farmers would sell $0Q_2$ units on the private market and $0Q_3$-$0Q_2$ units to the government. In one sense, then, a surplus is produced as a result of the government price setting. The effect of the price support program was to move farmers up the supply curve from *A* to *B* and leave the federal government with gigantic quantities of surplus commodities.

The acreage allotment program allocated a reduced number of acres to farmers of a given crop—that is, farmers could not plant as much of that crop as they wished. The government's intention in acreage allotments was to shift the supply curve from S_1 to S_2 (see Figure 9-3) and thus reduce the quantity of the item brought into market, or the surplus which the government was buying under the price support program. Instead farmers used more sophisticated techniques on the land they were allowed to farm (better fertilizer, more intensive cultivation, etc.) and shifted the supply curve back from S_2 to S_1. Both programs, then, the price support program and the acreage allotment program, had unintended outcomes.

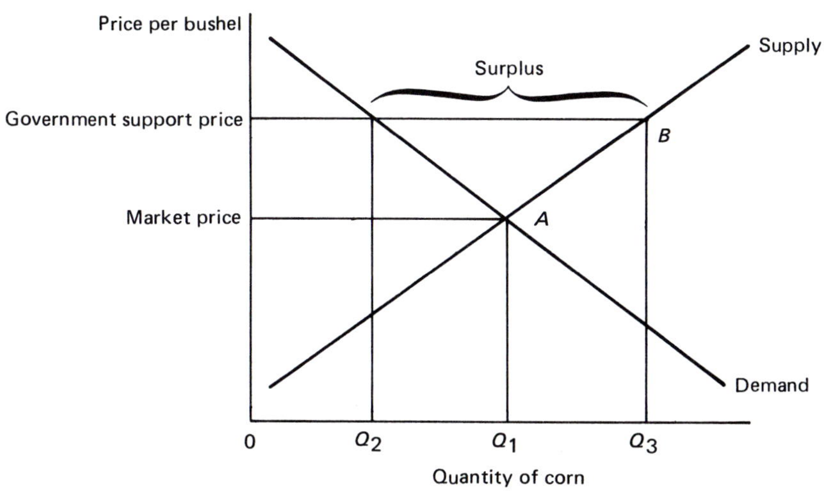

FIGURE 9-2

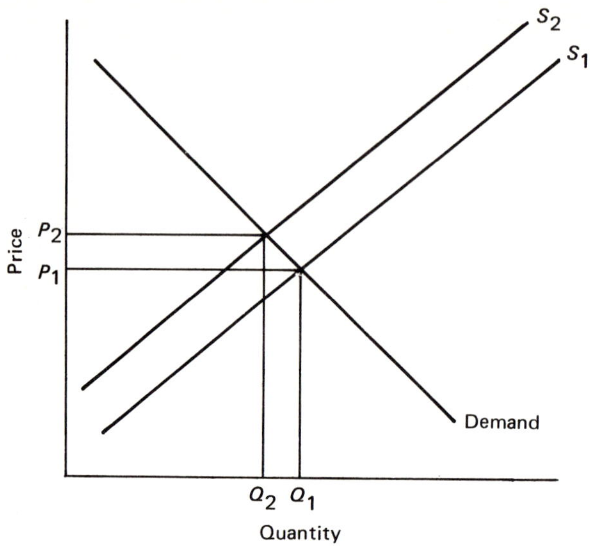

FIGURE 9-3

The most recent development along these lines is the Agricultural and Consumer Protection Act which sets a scheme of target prices for farm products. The government agrees to pay farmers the difference between the target price and the market price for many commodities. If, for example, the target price of corn were \$2.50 per bushel but the market price were only \$2.00 per bushel, the government would pay the farmer \$0.50 for each bushel sold at the \$2.00 price.

Another less recent, but increasingly important, situation in agriculture is the existence of agricultural cooperatives. While most industries are not allowed to set prices or form cartels, the Clayton Act and the Capper-Volstead Act allow such practices in agricultural markets. Large cooperatives with strong price-setting powers and significant supply-limiting capacities are an important entity in agricultural markets.

KEY CONCEPTS

Agricultural and Consumer Protection Act Passed in 1973, this act establishes target prices for many agricultural commodities.

Target price Farmers are paid the difference between a "target price" and the market price if the market price falls below the target price.

Acreage allotment program This system coerces farmers to use only a certain number of acres to produce a given crop. Acreage is distributed among farmers in some fashion.

Clayton Act of 1914 Permits cartels in the farm sector.

Capper-Volstead Act of 1922 Permits price setting by agricultural cooperatives.

Support price A price for a particular commodity which the government guarantees to pay to farmers for their commodities if they are unable to sell their crops for a higher price in the free market.

CASE 9
Money Isn't All That's Green[1]

Cooperatives are a form of organization in the United States controlled by their member-owners on a one-member, one-vote basis. The profits of cooperatives are divided among the members in proportion to the amount of business done with each. It is the case that most Americans come in contact with a cooperative organization fairly frequently. Some telephone utilities and electricity producers are formed as cooperatives; many cable television services are provided cooperatively; consumer services such as day care centers and housing are often provided cooperatively; life insurance and group health care are frequently cooperative enterprises. Among the most important cooperatives, however, are the agricultural marketing and farm supply cooperatives. Their importance stems from a peculiar government regulation which was passed in 1922 and which, with slight modifications, remains in force even today.

Agricultural cooperatives consider the Capper-Volstead Act of 1922 as the Magna Charta of farmer cooperatives. What the act did was to absolve agricultural cooperatives from prohibitions of price fixing as long as the price fixing did not "unduly enhance" farm product prices. Price fixing in other industries is considered a violation of antitrust laws, and while these laws are largely unenforceable, there are from time to time well-publicized legal proceedings. For many years these exemptions for agricultural cooperatives, however, received very little attention and were relatively uncontroversial, since most agricultural cooperatives were so small that they did not possess enough power to affect price levels in any national market. Another reason for the relative unimportance of the special privileges allocated to cooperatives was that the federal government had maintained direct price supports and control programs which had far more significant effects on farm product prices than cooperatives did.

Recently, however, more attention has been paid to agricultural cooperatives because of their large growth and correspondingly greater power in price fixing. In 1976, a lawsuit was filed against the Central California Lettuce Producers Cooperative, which was charged with conspiracy to fix the price of lettuce shipped in interstate commerce from the Salinas Valley in California. The cooperative is organized as a nonprofit agricultural cooperative. Its twenty-two members are engaged in the production of lettuce. The members and the cooperative itself have an agreement which includes the following provisions: (1) members agree to make no discounts or concessions in selling to retailers, and (2) members agree to sell lettuce only within the limits of the ceiling and floor prices established by the cooperative.

Each member of the cooperative has a seat on the board of directors, and the executive committee of the board meets at least once a week to review the supply and demand for lettuce and to determine the current ceiling and floor prices at which the lettuce will be sold.

[1]See James S. Krzyminski, "Update on Antitrust Cases and Legislation," *Federal Regulations and Cooperatives* (Madison, Wisc.: University Center for Cooperatives, 1976).

The court held that the agreement which the cooperative had with its members could not be considered an illegal conspiracy or restraint of trade and that members of such organizations could not be prosecuted under the antitrust laws applicable to most firms for combining to carry out the legitimate objectives of the organization. The Central California Lettuce Producers Cooperative was effectively protected from prosecution by the Capper-Volstead Act.

QUESTIONS

1 Cooperatives often argue that they increase cooperation and coordination among producers and thus reduce prices which consumers must pay in the market for their products. Comment on this argument.

2 Assume the Central California Lettuce Producers Cooperative is able to set a floor price for their product which is above the market price for lettuce. Would economists consider such a floor price as *efficient* in the economic sense of the term? Explain.

3 It is true that most farm commodities are sold in highly competitive markets (that is, markets in which there are many buyers and many sellers); but if lettuce grown in the Salinas Valley must be sold through the Central California Lettuce Producers Cooperative, would you expect consumers to benefit from this form of organization? Explain.

4 While the lettuce cooperative in the Salinas Valley does not have as one of its goals the restriction of lettuce output, what would you expect to be the outcome for both the farmers and the buyers if the cooperative did restrict output? Why?

5 As in most farming situations, lettuce producers are subject to an element of uncertainty in the sense that there is very little that farmers can do at harvest time to alter the available supplies of their crops. In any case where planning and the actual occurrence of costs are separated by a period of time, such an uncertainty will be present. Will such an uncertainty be eliminated by allowing lettuce producers to form cooperatives which engage in price fixing? Explain your answer.

TEST YOURSELF

Multiple-choice

1 Prices for farm products in the United States tend to be **(a)** elastic, **(b)** inelastic, **(c)** unit elastic, **(d)** none of the above.

2 Farm commodities in the United States tend to be sold in **(a)** monopolistic markets, **(b)** oligopolistic markets, **(c)** highly competitive markets, **(d)** unregulated markets.

3 One of the following is *not* a characteristic of American agriculture: (**a**) the demand for farm commodities tends to be inelastic; (**b**) agriculture requires substantial investment in land and equipment; (**c**) revenues in agricultural markets tend to fall rapidly, with relatively small price decreases; (**d**) the government has played no significant role in agricultural markets.

4 One of the following is *not* true of agricultural markets: (**a**) a small change in an expected harvest often leads to significant price fluctuations; (**b**) changes in demand for farm commodities do not significantly affect prices because of the inelasticity of short-run supply; (**c**) the planning and actual occurrence of costs are separated by a relatively long time; (**d**) agricultural commodities have relatively few good substitutes.

5 The Clayton Act of 1914 (**a**) permitted actions in the farm sector which are prohibited in most nonfarm industries, (**b**) permitted nonfarm industries the same actions allowed the farm sector, (**c**) permitted the farm sector the same actions allowed in the nonfarm industries.

6 A support price above the market price for corn will cause (**a**) a shortage of corn at the support price, (**b**) a surplus of corn at the support price, (**c**) just the amount of corn to be produced that consumers demand.

7 By reducing acreage allotments for tobacco (**a**) production will increase, (**b**) production will decrease, (**c**) production may increase or decrease.

8 Prices and quantities demanded of farm products (**a**) are unpredictable, (**b**) change rapidly, (**c**) are relatively stable.

10

Market Performance and Monopoly Power

The output and pricing decisions generated by the market process depend to a very large extent upon the institutional rules that govern the exchange process. We have previously shown (Chapters 7 and 8) that a market in which buyers are forced to compete with other buyers and sellers are forced to compete with other sellers in order to survive will generate the greatest output at the lowest price. But what happens when buyers or sellers are "protected" from competition? What happens to the workings of a market when competitive forces are restricted?

The ability or power to operate in a market without having to face competition from other sellers is termed *monopoly power.* Monopoly power is present when an individual can sell a commodity at a higher price than other sellers in the market. The ultimate in monopoly power is, of course, to be the only seller of a given commodity in the market; we call this situation a *monopoly market.* It should be clear that each of us would prefer to be in this position with respect to the goods, services, or resources that we sell in the market, as we have assumed that each of us seeks to maximize his or her well-being. How then, does one get and keep monopoly power, if everyone is attempting to achieve this same position?

In the short run, monopoly power is generated by being the first to produce a marketable commodity, or the first to change a production process, or the first to see a new and better way of accomplishing some needed task or discovering new uses for old materials, etc., in short, being first to see ways that will make other individuals better off. In the long run, monopoly power is sustained by (somehow) preventing others from following your lead. This can be done by the presence of barriers to entry, natural or artificial. For example, when an individual discovers that her or his natural talent is in great demand by others, that individual can restrict access to her or his talent by not using it. There is only one Alice Cooper, Ringo Starr, or Joe Namath; thus, each has a natural barrier to entry. This barrier prevents an exact replication of the talents by others, but it does not, and cannot, prevent others from attempting to copy the unique feature of the talent.

Artificial barriers to entry are noneconomic constraints that restrict the competitive process. For example, suppose that you were able to get a patent right on the manufacture of a "new and improved" buggy whip in the late 1800s and that individuals found your whip superior in all ways and purchased them in large numbers. This patent right would mean that you could prevent others from duplicating your product for 17 years. With no good alternatives to your product, you could earn higher than normal profits from its production and sale, as long as your whip was in demand. Other individuals, however, have a tremendous incentive to "get on the bandwagon," that is, to make money by providing a still better buggy whip or an alternative to a buggy whip. Thus, alternatives emerge over time to erode the monopoly position even in the presence of barriers. Consider the value of the patent on buggy whips by 1920.

KEY CONCEPTS

Monopoly power The ability of a seller to exercise control over the price at which the good, service, or resource is sold so that his or her price is different than that of other sellers in the market. (*Note:* All sellers can set the price if they have the property rights to their goods. The important point is: can they *sell* their products at a higher price than other sellers?)

Monopoly A market where the firm is the industry—that is, all products are produced and sold by one firm. (*Note:* This is the ultimate in monopoly power; since there are not other sellers, the monopoly has a 100 percent market share.)

Duopoly A market structure where there are only two firms selling the given good, service, or commodity. The behavior of firm A with respect to firm B's price and output decisions is obviously very important; therefore, we would expect to see a high degree of mutual interdependence of action.

Oligopoly A small group of firms that control the vast majority of the market's production of a given good. For example, suppose three firms collectively control 80 percent of a given market. In this market, we would expect that each firm exerts considerable impact on the others when price and/or output decisions are altered.

Monopolistic competition A group of firms operating in a market where each firm has a limited ability to set a price for its products above that of the competitors and still maintain sales.

Cartel A voluntary association of independent producers of a given product that is established for the express purpose of securing increased monopoly power in a given industry.

Natural monopoly An industry in which it is practical to have only one firm producing the product because the industry uses a technology that creates a cost curve on which the minimum average cost is not reached until the firm is producing more than the entire market can absorb.

CASE 10A

The Growing Battle Over NOWs[1]

Although they are privately owned and operated, the financial institutions (commercial banks, savings and loan institutions, mutual savings banks, and credit unions) in the United States play an important role in the economic system as they influence the availability of credit and the size of the money supply. As a consequence of these important impacts, the business practices of financial institutions are regulated by either state or federal levels of government. While these institutions perform broadly overlapping functions (each can make personal or mortgage loans, and each can accept savings accounts), there are some areas where they are differentially regulated. Commercial banks must follow business rules different from those of savings banks. In the past, as a result of these laws and regulations, commercial banks had the monopoly right to hold and create demand deposits (checking accounts), but by a provision of the Banking Act of 1933 they were prevented from paying interest on these accounts.

Under banking regulations in most states, mutual savings banks cannot accept demand deposits; however, savings banks can pay higher rates of interest on time deposits (savings accounts) than commercial banks can. Thus, the regulatory procedure has prevented these comparable financial institutions from competing on an equal basis for the customer's dollars. Savings banks have long sought some means to acquire checking powers so that they could match the one-stop convenience of the commercial banks and thus compete on an equal basis.

Since 1972, Negotiable Orders of Withdrawal (NOWs) have caused increased competition in the banking industry in at least two states, Massachusetts and New Hampshire. NOW accounts provide a bank's customers with the convenience of a checking account while paying interest like a saving account. Since the introduction of NOW accounts in mutual savings banks in Massachusetts and New Hampshire, commercial banks have sought and been granted (in 1974) new regulations that also permit them to offer NOW accounts to their customers. Thus the battle for consumers' funds via the NOW account is vigorously under way in these two New England states.

The increased competition for personal payment accounts can be expected to alter both the market shares of commercial banks with respect to mutual savings banks and the earnings pattern of commercial banks. If the exclusive franchise to create demand deposits held for so many years by the commercial banks were a

[1] Facts in this case are reprinted with permission from Katharine Gibson, "The Early History and Initial Impact of NOW Accounts," *New England Economic Review,* January/February 1975, 17–26; and Ralph C. Kimball, "Impacts of NOW Accounts and Thrift Institution Competition on Selected Small Commercial Banks in Massachusetts and New Hampshire," *New England Economic Review,* January/February 1977, 22–38.

grant of monopoly powers, then we would expect that the profit levels of commercial banks would decline in the face of the increased competition. We would also expect that customers would shift their funds to the banks that could pay the highest rate of interest on NOW accounts. From 1972 until 1974, mutual savings banks had the exclusive power to offer NOW accounts; therefore, we would expect that if increased competition resulted from this change in banking rules, then the market share of the savings banks with respect to the commercial banks would increase.

A survey of the financial institutions in Massachusetts and New Hampshire for 1974 and 1975 estimated that NOW accounts and increased bank competition caused a decline in demand deposits at *commercial banks* of about 3 percent ($400 million). In addition, NOW accounts are estimated to have reduced pretax earnings at all *commercial banks* in the two states by $6.7 million, or 3.4 percent, in 1974 and by $15.9 million, or 11.3 percent, in 1975. This decreased earnings record far exceeded the actual interest cost of the NOW accounts. In March 1976, NOW account powers were extended to all depository institutions in Connecticut, Rhode Island, Vermont, and Maine. Thus the battle of the NOW account appears to be spreading.

QUESTIONS

1 In many states where commercial banks are prohibited from offering interest payments on checking accounts, commercial banks have provided services below cost (for example free checking accounts) and have engaged in other types of nonprice competition such as adding branch facilities for customer convenience. Why might it be argued that *explicit* payments for deposits (in the form of interest) and *explicit* charges for services (fees to cover the cost of providing checking services) would be more desirable from the consumer's viewpoint? Explain.

2 On the basis of the evidence presented, has the average consumer been made better off from the change in the institutional rules that permits interest-bearing checking accounts (NOW accounts) in the New England states? Clearly discuss the process by which you evaluated the empirical evidence to reach your conclusion. What inferences, if any, can be made concerning the establishment of regulatory rules to govern the competitive process that promotes the welfare of the average family?

3 As a result of the declining earnings record for 1974 and 1975 for the commercial banks in the survey, what would you expect to happen to the number and size of commercial banks in the industry? What would you expect to happen to the number and size of the mutual savings banks in New England? Since entry into the banking industry is restricted by state or federal legislation, would you expect your answer to differ from a case of free entry and exit? Why?

4 Within the last few years, the banking industry has been a leader in the adoption of computer technology to speed up the process of fund transfers. Electronic fund transference (EFT) has significantly decreased the time required to process customers' banking transactions, while offering the customer such features as after-hours banking and bank credit cards. How might the introduction of this very expensive electronic hardware have been different if the banking industry was not regulated as to the price it can offer for funds? Would the average bank customer have been better off under this arrangement? Why?

CASE 10B

Competition in the Electric Power Industry[2]

When a market demand for a commodity exists such that a *single producer* can supply the output demanded at a price lower than that which many firms producing in the market would charge, it is said that the firm has a *natural monopoly.* In such a case, competition results in higher costs and excess capacity and is difficult to maintain. Even though the monopoly solution is more efficient (greater output at a lower price) than a competitive one, the monopolist still is earning excess or economic profit. The real world result of this situation in which "competition is unworkable" is the regulation of the price-output decision of the natural monopoly by the government. Local public utilities in most areas are thought to approximate this situation. For example, if your city had five electric companies, each with its own poles, wires, generators, and home meters, costly duplication would result. Thus, government grants a monopoly franchise to one electric power company to serve your city and then controls that company's rate structure.

An additional characteristic of the electric power industry in the recent past has been that high transmission costs severely limited the range of alternative power suppliers available to a given local public utility. Transmission costs have traditionally varied approximately in proportion to distance and inversely with the square of the transmission voltages. Thus, your city power company was forced to purchase extra power when needed from the closest generating source since the transmission costs from more distant sources were prohibitive. Recent technological advances in the generation and transmission of electricity over long distances may make it profitable for a power purchaser (your city's electric company) to choose among several suppliers or even join a power pool to gain access to additional power when needed. For example, it is the use of extra high-voltage transmission lines that has permitted Los Angeles to receive some power from the Four Corners plant in New Mexico, some 600 miles away. The transmission of power via the intertie system from the Columbia River to Los Angeles, a distance of over 800 miles, is another of the examples of long-distance transmission currently in use.

Currently three strategies are being used by local electric utilities to take advantage of the recent technological advances. First, some companies use a system of informal coordination, which involves interconnection of transmission systems, and some limited kinds of agreements such that emergency assistance and other forms of coordination are provided from one utility to another. A second strategy is to formally organize a power pool. Power pools are formed when broad agreements are reached by independent utility companies covering such items as joint dispatch of generation, staggered construction of new plants, sharing of power

[2] Facts in this case are reprinted with permission of Profs. Paul A. Nelson and Leonard W. Weiss from their article "Potential Impact on Competition of Efficiency in Bulk Power Supply," Working Paper, 1974, Michigan Technological University.

reserves, joint ownership of certain facilities, and procedures for compensating each utility for contributions and charging each utility for benefits received. The final strategy, of course, is for a number of utilities to merge, merger being the ultimate form of coordination.

It appears that most regions of the United States would support enough generating plants to permit at least some competition as to the source of power, if such plants were under separate ownership and if they had equal access to transmission and distribution facilities. Existing ownership patterns, however, and government regulatory institutions sharply limit the room for competition in the power supply industry. Even with the current government regulation of the power industry, most companies already engage in some informal cooperation (strategy 1). However, it would be important to know what impact the alternative strategies for adopting the technological advance have upon the cost of power to the customer. Economists Paul Nelson and Leonard Weiss have studied the electric power industry and have examined the differences that might accrue to power consumers if merger (strategy 3) was the more common technique for capturing the large economies of scale brought about by the now feasible low-cost transmission over long distances.

Nelson and Weiss point out that if utilities were to form power pools (strategy 2) as a means of exploiting the economies of coordination, a large enough number of independent power producers would still be left to permit competition in most regions. Merger, of course, would reduce the number of independent producers.

While economists most often would encourage competition, there are a number of reasons why we might expect pools to be less effective than merged utility companies in attaining potential economies of scale. Utilities which are members of pools must make decisions by mutual consent. We could imagine quite readily that differences among members could result in suboptimal decisions or possibly the breakup of the pool itself. A merged utility, on the other hand, settles disputes internally, by arbitrary order if necessary.

The success of the power pool also depends on the characteristics of the member utilities. We could expect that the larger the number of member utilities, the more common and more difficult to settle the disputes would be (recall the discussion in Chapter 6). Likewise, one might expect that with pools the greater the diversity in terms of size and cost among the member utilities, the harder it would be to attain agreement. It is quite possible that large firms might be lax to engage in pooling agreements with much smaller utilities, because they can gain relatively little in economies of scale by pooling while small firms could gain a great deal. Likewise, since various size utilities would face vastly different costs of production, the potential gains from pooling would be greater for high-cost firms than for low-cost firms, and once again agreement might be very hard to reach.

QUESTIONS

1 Regardless of whether individual electric utilities are members of power pools, they would presumably still be monopolies in their local market areas. Would you expect, then, that these monopolies would choose their quantities produced based on a profit-maximizing rule? If an electric utility becomes a member of a power pool, it is now possible for the utility to buy power from a number of different sources. Would you expect this competition in the supply of bulk electric power to affect the individual electric utility's marginal revenue or marginal cost curve? Why?

2 Monopolies have been criticized by economists because of the feeling that they will provide less output at higher cost than a perfectly competitive industry would. If electric utility companies join power pools so that there is competition in the supply of bulk electric power, could this in any way lead to an outcome closer to that which would be achieved under pure competition? Explain your answer.

3 Could you suggest any other technical changes in the electric utility industry which would increase the process of competition and thus reduce the probability of the industry's being treated as a natural monopoly? Explain your answer.

4 While monopoly, the absence of the process of competition, is generally thought to be undesirable, except in instances of natural monopoly, there is at least one category of production in the United States where monopoly is encouraged. The patent laws in the United States permit an inventor the exclusive right to make a certain product or to use a particular process. Patent rights belong to the patent owner for 17 years. On what basis could one justify the absence of competition in this category of production?

5 Most natural monopolies (electric utilities, telephone companies, etc.) are regulated. If technological change transforms the industry into a competitive process, is there further need of government regulation? Why?

TEST YOURSELF

True—false

T F 1. When a firm is able to achieve monopoly powers, it is in the firm's best interest to restrict output relative to the output generated by the competitive market.

T F 2. Price in markets where firms have agreed to fix output (to act as if they were a monopoly) will be higher than in the absence of such an agreement.

T F 3. Barriers to entry mean that a given firm must compete on an equal footing with any other firm willing to produce that output.

T F 4. Monopolists will always make excess or economic profits in the long run.

T F 5. Economies of scale mean that as the output of the firm increases, the per-unit cost also increases.

Multiple-choice

Study Figure 10-1; then answer each of the following questions.

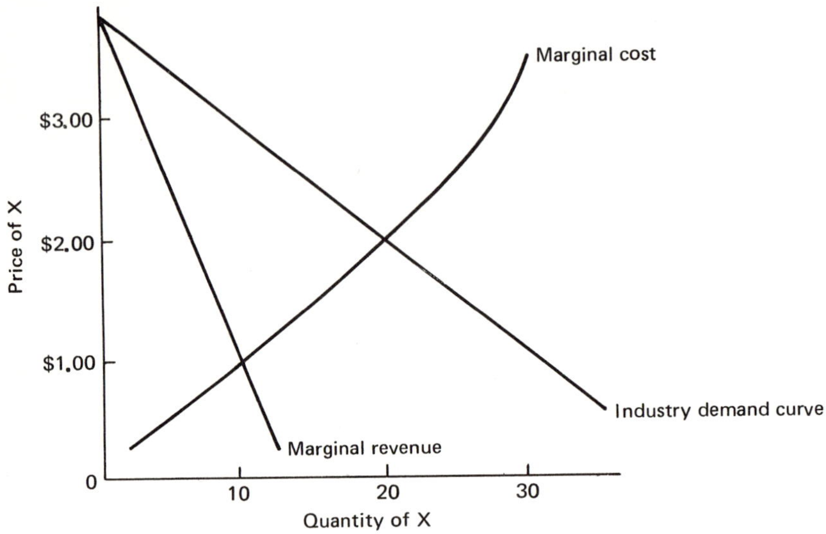

FIGURE 10-1

1 If Figure 10-1 represents the industry demand curve for a competitive industry, output and price tend toward

- **(a)** P = \$1 and Q = 10
- **(b)** P = \$2 and Q = 20
- **(c)** P = \$3 and Q = 30
- **(d)** Not possible to tell

2 If Figure 10-1 represents the industry demand curve for a monopolist (the firm is the industry), output and price would tend toward

- **(a)** P = \$1 and Q = 10
- **(b)** P = \$3 and Q = 10
- **(c)** P = \$3 and Q = 30
- **(d)** Not possible to tell

3 Suppose that Figure 10-1 initially refers to a monopolistic market (such as in question 2) and then because of some change in the market (a change in the regulatory rules, for example) increased competition is introduced. We would expect that output would

- **(a)** Fall
- **(b)** Remain the same
- **(c)** Increase
- **(d)** Not possible to tell

4 The tendency of firms in a competitive market is to provide
- (a) Less output and at a lower price than a monopolist
- (b) Less output but at the same price as the monopoly firm
- (c) More output but at a higher price than a monopolist
- (d) More output and at a lower price than a monopolist

Study Figure 10-2; then answer each of the following questions.

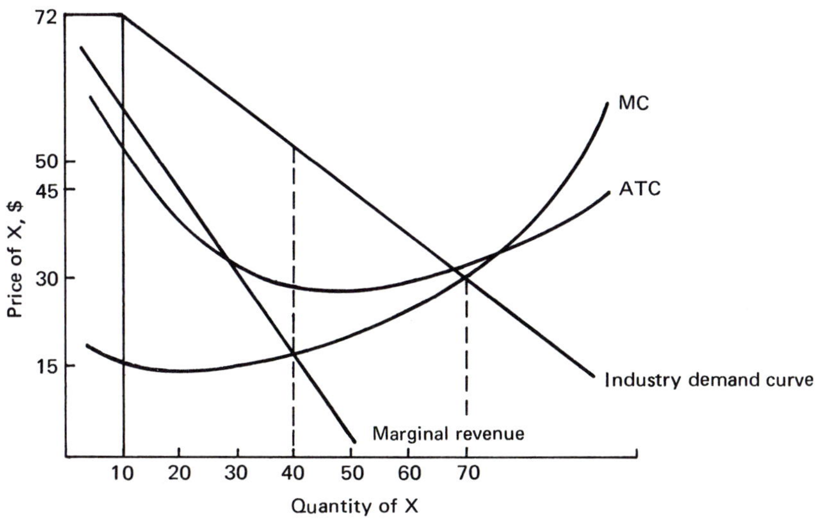

FIGURE 10-2

5 If Figure 10-2 represents the cost and demand curves for product X under conditions of a monopoly supplier, the output will tend toward
- (a) 70 units
- (b) 30 units
- (c) 10 units
- (d) 40 units

6 At profit-maximizing output, the monopolist producer in Figure 10-2 will be in the following positions with respect to profits:
- (a) Profits are zero.
- (b) Profits are positive.
- (c) Profits are negative.
- (d) It is not possible to determine profit level.

7 If Figure 10-2 represents a competitive industry demand and long-run cost curves and if each *firm* in the industry produces 10 units of output, then the market price for product X will be
- (a) $72
- (b) $50

(c) $15

(d) $30

8 If the efficiency condition P = MC were established in the market for product X, producers would

(a) Incur losses and go out of business in the long run

(b) Incur losses only in the short run

(c) Make a normal profit in this industry

(d) Make excess or economic profits even in the long run

11

Prices: What Do They Tell Us?

Prices give vital information to buyers and sellers in a competitive market. A "special" lower price on merchandise offered by a manufacturer is a signal to consumers that the old price for the good was too high relative to prices of other goods in the market. Rational consumers take this new piece of information and examine their expenditure patterns. Price changes enable consumers to determine if a reorganization of their "consumption bundle" will improve their well-being. On the other hand, the lower price offer signals a change in the desires of producers to continue to provide the given good or service at the previous price. When markets have a large number of buyers and sellers and entry is relatively free (i.e., when the market is competitive), the fluctuations of prices provide the market participants with the necessary information for them to benefit from all potential gains from trade.

The competition among all buyers for the available supply of goods in the market and the similar competition among suppliers for the "dollar votes" of the consumer (see Chapter 7) produce a market where individuals can change their possession of goods and services easily. Those persons who place the highest value on any given good (measured in terms of what they will give up to get the good) will end up with that good. Thus, price changes are a mechanism that allows individuals to maximize the value of their personal "bundle of goods" in relation to the quantities of all goods and services available in the market.

When prices are prevented from fluctuating in response to the demand or preference of individuals, then the information carried by the price signal does not get transmitted to the buyers and sellers in the market. For example, assume that the price of natural gas is fixed by government decree at a level below that which would be set by the free interchange of buyers and sellers (that is, below the market price). How is this "below equilibrium" price interpreted by buyers and sellers? Buyers take the price and seek to adjust their goods' holding to include more of this relatively inexpensive good. This situation is depicted in Figure 11-1.

If the maximum price is set at $1 by the government, then buyers will try to purchase 30 units. Sellers, on the other hand, finding the price of natural gas fixed, bring only 10 units into the market. This is an amount consistent with their costs of production at the maximum price. As you can see, a shortage results in this market. This shortage is depicted by the distance between *A* and *B* in Figure 11-1.

With the imposition of a price ceiling, buyers will wish to consume more natural gas at the price of $1 than they find on the market. Therefore, they wish to inform suppliers to produce more. How can they send that message to suppliers? Without controls, prices would be bid up by buyers competing for the available amount, signaling suppliers to increase production. However, when the price is fixed, the suppliers have no way of knowing that buyers want more and would willingly pay more for additional units. This information will not be conveyed to suppliers, and they will continue to supply the same quantity. Thus, when a maximum price is fixed, some device must be adopted to distribute the natural gas to the willing purchasers. One way that might be used by the government is ration coupons. Under this plan, a buyer of natural gas would have to present the seller with a coupon, as well as money, in order to buy the good. By limiting the number of coupons, the amount demanded by buyers could be made equal to the amount supplied by sellers at the fixed price.

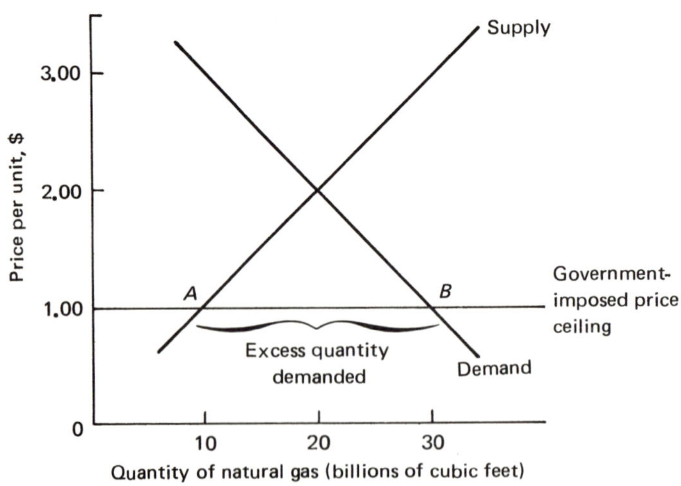

FIGURE 11-1 Market demand and supply curves for natural gas

Another way that individuals might respond to the situation depicted in Figure 11-1 would be to somehow contact a natural gas supplier and offer to pay more than the governmental maximum price. A buyer might attempt to do this to ensure a supply of gas. Under the coupon rationing system the buyer is faced with a lower price but gets the natural gas only if he or she is lucky enough to be allocated a coupon. The buyer may be faced with the situation of choosing between no natural gas at a low price (because of no coupon) or natural gas but at a higher price than the legal maximum. Exchanges between buyers and sellers at prices in excess of the government's maximum are generally illegal, and such trading has come to be called "black marketeering." Black markets are evidence that buyers and sellers have found an alternative market in which to attempt to maximize the value of their personal bundles of goods.

Buyers and sellers also receive important information from examining the differences in price within a given class of goods on the market. Price differences are a means by which the producer can recover some of the costs that result from quantity variations in the production of the product. Price differences for a given good provide the consumer with an expanded set of goods from which to choose. For example, manufacturers commonly run factory outlet stores where slightly damaged merchandise can be purchased at a price below the prevailing retail price. For example, one shopper may be willing to pay an additional $5 for a perfectly round whitewall tire; another consumer prefers to spend the $5 on other goods and purchases a slightly imperfect tire at the outlet store. The existence of a wide range of prices for varying goods' characteristics gives shoppers a better chance to buy the goods they prefer for any given income.

KEY CONCEPTS

Price controls The establishment of price levels that are different from those that would be determined by the interaction of buyers and sellers in the free market.

Price ceiling, or maximum price A price established *below* the price determined by the interaction of buyers and sellers that is designated the maximum allowable price for the commodity. The authority that established the price ceiling must stand ready to take action to enforce this policy.

Price floor, or minimum price A price established *above* the price determined by the interaction of buyers and sellers that is designated the minimum allowable price in the market for the commodity. The authority that establishes the price floor must stand ready to take action to remove the surplus generated by this policy.

Shortage The amount of any commodity that buyers would be willing and able to purchase at a prevailing price but are not able to obtain.

Surplus The amount of any commodity that suppliers would be willing and able to supply at the prevailing price but are not able to sell.

Ration coupons A mechanism that can be used by the agency administering price controls to align the available quantities supplied and demanded at the fixed price.

Black market Transactions involving the trading of goods and services in violation of the rationing or price control mechanism.

Administered prices The notion that prices are set by the interaction of big business and big unions, and *not* by the interaction of buyers and sellers.

Price expectations The perceptions that individuals form with respect to the future availability of goods and services, and hence their prices.

CASE 11

No-Shows, Overbooking, and Uniform Ticket Prices[1]

United States' airline companies operate under the regulatory control of the Civil Aeronautics Board (CAB). The CAB is a federal agency that controls the number of airline companies in the industry, the route schedule of each airline, and the level of ticket prices that each company can charge. Ticket prices for seats on all regularly scheduled flights can vary only on the basis of first- or second-class seating. Tickets may not be differentially priced on the basis of reserved and nonreserved status. All tickets sold are for reserved seats (except for the case of stand-by status for military personnel). This means that the airline guarantees you a seat when you purchase a ticket on a specified flight.

Under current CAB regulations, the airline passengers are not required to make full or partial payment to the airlines at the time they reserve space on a scheduled flight. The price of a ticket includes a reserved seat. Because there is no additional cost to reserve a seat, many travelers make reservations on several flights for a given day. By doing this they then can take the flight that turns out to be most convenient. The traveler, of course, pays for only the flight he or she ends up taking. Thus the current system provides the traveler with a seemingly costless hedge against uncertainty with respect to changes in his or her travel plans. However, the cost of the "no-shows" is borne by all travelers in both direct and indirect ways. When passengers reserve more seats than they can possibly occupy, other travelers are prevented from reserving the same seats, which affects their travel plans. In addition, because the airline has no way of knowing who will fail to show up for a reserved seat until just before the plane takes off, the number of seats occupied on the average airplane is reduced. The reduction in average occupancy increases the cost of air transportation and the price of air tickets.

To combat the problem of no-shows, the airline companies commonly follow a practice of overbooking passengers on flights. *Overbooking* means that more travelers are guaranteed seats on a given flight than there are aircraft seats. How is this done? For example, suppose a United 727 aircraft holds a maximum of 200 people. When making reservations for the plane, United might guarantee seats to 225 people, thus overbooking by 25 seats. United overbooks on the expectation that there will be 25 no-shows for the flight. Obviously, if an airline sells more seats than it has available, then occasionally more passengers will try to board a plane than can be accommodated. Everyone has a reserved seat, but not everyone can board the plane; thus someone is "bumped."

In the real world, how does the practice of no-shows and overbooking balance out? Do most airlines fly with many unoccupied seats because of no-shows, or are

[1] Facts in this case are reprinted with permission from Richard J. Ferris' article, "Ideally, No-shows Balance Out Overbookings," *Mainliner Magazine,* carried aboard United Airlines (September, 1976, page 4), East/West Network, Inc.

many travelers bumped when they hold reserved seat tickets because of overbooking? The records of United Airlines for the 12-month period ending June 30, 1976, are illustrative. Following their practice of overbooking, United made 1,082,082 seats beyond capacity available for double-booking. Of this number, 842,637 were actually used by passengers. These passengers were accommodated because other travelers holding tickets failed to appear for takeoff. For the same period, 16,545 passengers on United flights were denied their reserved space. (Of this number, 5828 arrived at their destination with less than a 2-hour delay after being bumped.) According to United's figures, then, for every traveler that was denied confirmed space (bumped), 51 were given seats by the practice of overbooking.

QUESTIONS

1 The primary reason that airlines have adopted the current practice of overbooking appears to be that the airline travelers are not made to bear the full cost of their actions when they reserve a seat under the current system. In other words, there are external effects. One of the ways that is often mentioned to "internalize" these externalities is to make the airline passengers appear at the airport gate 1 or 2 hours before the plane is scheduled to depart upon penalty of losing their reserved status. Another alternative might be to require passengers to pick up and pay for tickets 24 hours in advance of any flight. What would be some of the costs of "internalizing the external effects" under each of these alternative proposals?

2 What possible recourse should the passenger holding a reserved ticket on an airline flight have when he or she has been bumped because of the practice of overbooking? How would the various legal remedies affect the willingness of the airlines to engage in this practice?

3 When Ralph Nader, the consumer advocate, was bumped from a flight a number of years ago, he sued the airlines in question and recovered damages. Since that time, many consumer groups have been lobbying for the Civil Aeronautics Board (CAB) to change its regulation policies and outlaw overbooking by airlines. These groups argue that if passengers buy reserved seat tickets, then they should have those reserved seats when they arrive at the airport to board; the only way that this can be guaranteed is if the airline sells only as many tickets as there are seats. What would be some of the explicit and implicit costs of a ban on the practice of overbooking?

4 Suppose that the CAB, rather than outlawing the practice of overbooking, allowed the airlines to offer different classes of tickets with respect to reserved status. For example, suppose the airline was allowed to offer three kinds of tickets: Class A, for payment in advance, would carry the right to be guaranteed a seat regardless of pickup or arrival time at the airport prior to takeoff (if you don't show for a class A seat, that seat is unoccupied for the flight); class B would carry the right to be guaranteed a seat if you arrive at the gate and check in with the ticket attendant 2 hours before scheduled departure time; class C would be sold

on a first-come, first-served basis (that is, holders of class C tickets would be seated if they arrived at the airport to claim a seat and there were still class C seats available, or if a class B ticket holder had failed to show. What sort of price structure would you expect to be employed by the airlines under such a ticket system? Contrast the impact of this scheme on the cost of airline tickets with the policy rule that would outlaw overbooking.

5 Recently the Supreme Court ruled that bumped passengers may sue the airline for damages. This reverses a trend of lower courts that had previously held that the CAB must first decide whether overbooking is a deceptive trade practice before passengers who were bumped could sue. Take a position, pro or con, with respect to the practice of overbooking as a deceptive trade practice, and briefly state your arguments.

6 Many states and localities have laws that make it illegal to resell tickets to athletic or theatrical events at a price above the prevailing price at the ticket counter. For example, the California Code, chapter 2, section 18710, reads:

> All tickets of admission to any boxing contest, sparring or wrestling match, or wrestling exhibition shall have printed clearly upon the face thereof the purchase price of the ticket and no such tickets shall be sold for more than that price.

The practice of selling tickets for a price above the prevailing ticket price is known as "scalping" and is very common practice when an event is sold out. Such pieces of legislation impose mandatory price ceilings on the sale of tickets; yet it is very common to observe tickets being sold in excess of the maximum price. What are the differential effects of legal price ceilings on tickets? That is, which individuals would benefit from and which individuals would be harmed by the removal of these legal constraints?

TEST YOURSELF

True—false

T F 1. Price ceilings above the free-market price generate an excess quantity demanded at that price.

T F 2. Buyers and sellers interact in a market to exchange information about desired amounts of the good they wish to buy and sell via fluctuations in the level of prices.

T F 3. A period of rising prices in the market for a given commodity is always a signal that the quantity supplied is restricted relative to the quantity demanded.

T F 4. When the government froze the price of commodities and wages in the 1970s, all individuals were better off because then they could get the goods they desired at a price they could afford.

T F 5. A surplus in the market for wheat refers to the conditions where buyers wish to purchase more goods than are available at the prevailing price.

T F 6. In the absence of administered prices, the market price acts to ration the goods available.

T F 7. Coupon rationing is often used when administered prices are below the free-market or equilibrium prices.

T F 8. Price ceilings rarely lead to shortages or surpluses in real world markets.

T F 9. The free-market or equilibrium price occurs where suppliers are willing to supply the amount demanded by consumers at that price.

Multiple-choice

Study Figure 11-2; then answer each of the following questions.

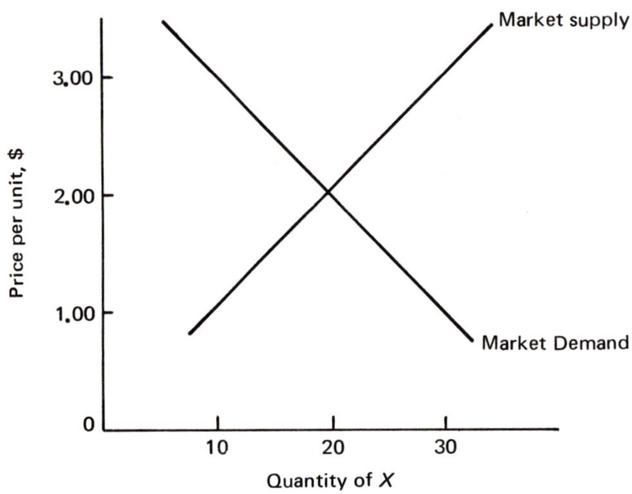

FIGURE 11-2 Market demand and supply curves for commodity *X*

1 At the price of $1 per unit, there exists a
(a) Shortage
(b) Surplus
(c) Condition of equality between buyers and sellers with respect to their desires to hold the good
(d) None of the above

2 At the price of $2 per unit, there exists a
(a) Shortage
(b) Surplus
(c) Condition of equality between buyers and sellers with respect to their desires to hold the good
(d) None of the above

3 Suppose that the government imposed a price ceiling on commodity *X* at the price of $3 per unit. This policy would result in

(a) A shortage of commodity *X*
(b) A surplus of commodity *X*
(c) No change in the free-market price and quantity exchanged
(d) Long lines as people sought to get more of the good
(e) None of the above

4 Suppose that the government imposed a price control in the market for commodity *X* which stated that price could not go below $3 per unit. This would be termed

(a) An administered price
(b) A ceiling price
(c) A price floor
(d) A price expectation
(e) All of the above

5 We might expect that the government would turn to rationing good *X* (since many goods were actually rationed with coupons in World War II)

(a) If the government-imposed price ceiling were at a price of $1 per unit
(b) If the government-imposed price ceiling were at a price of $2 per unit
(c) If the government-imposed price ceiling were at a price of $3 per unit
(d) None of the above

6 If we find that the price of good *X* is fixed by the government (or some other unit) *and* we also observe that there is a shortage of good *X* in the market, this means that

(a) No transactions for good *X* will take place
(b) The government fixed price is below what the free-market or equilibrium price would be
(c) No black market could conceivably exist in such a situation
(d) The government will most likely not issue ration coupons

7 In the absence of administered prices for good *X*, each unit of the good will be rationed by

(a) Price
(b) Demand
(c) Supply
(d) None of the above

12

Government Regulation of Private Markets

If you own a business, generally you have the right to make decisions on prices, output, new investment, hiring and firing of employees, and many of the other questions that arise in the day-to-day operation of your firm. If you are a buyer in a market, generally you have the right to select or withhold your patronage from any of the firms doing business. It is this interchange of buyers and sellers, each making many interrelated but *independent* decisions, that is termed *free-market exchange.* When we turn our attention to a study of market economy, we see that many private markets are not left "free" to operate. The price/output decisions of some firms come under the direct control of government regulatory agencies. Examples of this are the rate-setting policies of the Civil Aeronautics Board (CAB) for the airline industry, the pricing decisions of oil producers that are subject to Federal Energy Office (FEO) approval, and the necessity for private firms to obtain approval of the Department of State to sell farm implements to certain foreign purchasers. Other market transactions may be indirectly affected by the establishment of public policies. Laws designed to prevent discrimination in hiring (equal opportunity guidelines) place limits on the hiring practices of United States corporations, for example.

Why is it necessary and/or desirable for government to intervene in the operation of the private market? Why can't the airlines and the oil companies set their own prices? Why can't business people hire whomever they please? Why can't buyers choose among all available sellers? The obvious answer to these questions is that sometimes, for some reasons, the outcome provided by markets does not turn out to be the outcome that society finds most preferred. In these cases, an alternative mechanism is sought. Government may be able to do a better job than that done by the unregulated interaction of buyers and sellers. The lack of market response to the wishes of the members of society has come to be termed *market failure.*

We have provided the reason for government involvement in the operation of the markets, but we have yet to explain *why* markets fail. One reason that markets may fail to provide the most preferred bundle of goods for the consumer is that the protective function of competition may not work. For example, suppose you are the only lemonade vendor (seller) operating on a crowded beach on a hot summer day. As the only vendor, you are in a position to exercise some monopoly power. We know from our previous analysis of monopoly power that if you wish to maximize profits, you will restrict output, will charge higher than competitive prices, and may earn economic profits in the long run. Your presence as a single producer is an example of market failure because you are able to sell your lemonade at prices above those that would prevail in a competitive market.

Should the city government that owns the beach step in and "correct" the market failure? The necessity for government intervention clearly depends on the prospect of competition emerging in this market. You are the only seller today, but will you be able to maintain that monopoly position? That is the critical question. The mere fact that a firm, at one point, is the sole producer is not sufficient reason for assuming that the market cannot correct itself. Will other sellers appear on the beach tomorrow, next week, or next year? Will competition emerge to force sellers' prices down and eliminate monopoly profits? Of course, the answer depends on the ease of entry and the costs of production relative to the demand for lemonade on the beach. The adjustment process takes time, producers have to learn of profitable opportunities, and consumers have to learn of new sellers.

Under conditions of easy entry, suppose that you remain the only seller of lemonade on the beach for 5 years. This may be taken as a demonstration that the competitive process of markets in the production of lemonade is not operating. The city council may wish to either reduce drink prices by regulating the price or subsidize a new seller to set up business on the beach. The underlying hypothesis, while not generally stated, is that in intervening in the lemonade market the city council is providing consumers with a *less costly alternative* than the continued presence of the monopoly seller. The assumption must be that the cost of government intervention into the private market is less than the inefficiencies that the uncontrolled market would generate. From this very simple illustration you can see that it is an extremely difficult problem to assess market failure in a dynamic (changing) market.

In addition to regulation to reduce or eliminate monopoly power, collective action is often introduced into market transactions as a means of *internalizing externalities.* The production or exchange of many kinds of goods creates external effects for individuals not directly involved in the production/consumption process. An example of this type of problem is found in the controversy surrounding the U.S. Department of Commerce ban on killing spinner porpoises and the establishment of quotas on other kinds of porpoises killed as well as the strike of the United States tuna fleet. Tuna fishers kill thousands of porpoises each year in the process of casting their nets to catch the tuna that swim beneath these mammals. The porpoises are communal property. They are owned equally by everyone in society. The tuna fishers do not pay damages to society for the destruction of this communal property; thus, their costs of production are reduced.

The Marine Mammal Protection Act passed in 1972 reaffirmed the communal ownership rights of all individuals to the porpoises. The government intervention in the tuna market is an attempt to force firms that generate negative effects to bear the cost of their actions. The tuna industry is strongly opposed to the new ban and the quotas since they severely restrict the producers' ability to catch the tuna and thus to survive. The rights of society to the porpoises and the rights of the tuna fishers to earn their livelihood are obviously in conflict. Government regulation of the tuna fishing market is sought as a means to resolve this rights conflict. Of course, the external effects can be positive as well as negative. In another case, the private firms would underproduce the good, resource, or service. For example, the production of hydroelectric power leads in many cases to the creation of reservoirs that have recreation potential; however, these benefits were not considered when the decision was made to produce electric power.

The fact that regulation of the private market by government is very common in the United States today is not sufficient evidence that government has been able to alter the behavior of markets to provide a *more preferred goods bundle* for society than would have been provided in the absence of intervention. The success of government controls aimed at making markets more efficient must be evaluated by looking at actual experiences; that is, it must be judged by the actual performance of the market and not by what government controls are *intended* to do.

Economists have only recently begun to study the performance differences in regulated and unregulated industries. Although the evidence is not conclusive, two hypotheses have been developed to show that regulation does not always give society the bundle of goods deemed most desirable. First, if the industry that is currently regulated was a natural monopoly prior to regulation, then regulation has *no significant effect* on the industry's performance.[1] Second, if the market was generally competitive prior to government interference, then regulation *reduced competition* and made the industry more like a monopoly.[2] In addition to the direct effects of regulation on industrial performance in the United States, it is important to remember that the costs of government regulation are not borne by

[1] See G. J. Stigler and C. Friedland, "What Can Regulators Regulate? The Case of Electricity," *Journal of Law and Economics,* vol. 5, pp. 4–11, October 1962.

[2] See W. A. Jordan, *Airline Regulation in America* (Baltimore: The Johns Hopkins Press, 1970).

the industry alone. The consumer who is being "protected" from big business also pays through the inefficiencies generated by regulation. The costs of regulation have pervasive effects throughout the economy as output/pricing decisions are altered. Before government is chosen as the mechanism to provide society with its most desired goods bundle, the alternatives should be carefully weighed. The cost of regulation should be contrasted with the ability of the market to respond to the wishes of society.

KEY CONCEPTS

Nonmarket regulation The control (either direct or indirect) of price and/or output decisions of firms by other than market forces. Term generally used to describe government intervention.

Countervailing power A concept which suggests that the government should use its size to thwart the monopoly power of large corporations. The term is associated with the economist J. K. Galbraith.

Regulatory anarchy The state or condition in which all productive effort is devoted to gaining regulatory safeguards against competition.

Regulatory lags The time necessary for a regulatory body to adjust policies in the face of changing economic conditions for the regulated industry.

Market failure The condition where the exchange of goods, services, or resources in the market does not lead to the preferred output.

CASE 12A:

The Investment Adviser[3]

The Securities and Exchange Commission (SEC) was authorized by Congress in 1934 in response to a growing number of fraudulent stock cases and the sharp decline in stock prices in the early 1930s. The SEC has the power to police stock exchanges, license brokers, supervise the issuance of new corporate stocks and bonds, and regulate the fees received by stock brokers. In addition, under the Investment Advisors Act of 1940, the SEC is empowered to register securities advisers who sell investment advice to the public.

The adviser's registration process is currently very simple. The applicant pays a $150 registration fee and is merely required to keep records of all transactions. The SEC has very limited power to refuse to register individuals; these limits apply to those with securities violations or criminal records. Also, the SEC can fine registered advisers who attempt to defraud investors. The SEC claims that as a result of the current nonrestrictive registration practices, many ill-equipped advisers are being registered and then they are using the fact that they are registered to generate confidence in their advice. For example, they say, "Buy your stock information from a U.S. government registered adviser." The SEC has stated that several teen-agers have applied for and been granted registration status, and are in the market selling securities advice.

To prevent advisers from generating trade on the basis of registration, the Securities and Exchange Commission has requested that Congress take action by strengthening the statutory mandate of the SEC to control the registration process. To this end, Representative John M. Murphy (Democrat, New York), chairman of the House Commerce Committee's Subcommittee on Consumer Protection and Finance, has introduced H.R. 13737 which would amend the Investment Advisers Act of 1940 to authorize the SEC to prescribe standards of qualification and financial responsibility for investment advisers and to study the feasibility of establishing a self-regulatory organization (composed of representatives of all currently registered investment advisers) to ". . . adopt rules, establish standards of conduct, take appropriate disciplinary action, establish and administer tests, and perform such other functions with respect to the regulation of their members as are consistent with the purpose of this title."[4]

A variety of alternative policies exist that could be pursued by the SEC rather than increased regulation of advisers. For example, if registration generates false and misleading information in the market for advice as to the reliability of any

[3] Facts in this case are from "Government 'Powerless' over Investment Advisors," *Lincoln Star,* August 18, 1976; and U.S. Congress, House of Representatives, 92d Cong., 2d Sess., H.R. 13737, a bill introduced May 12, 1976.

[4] 94th Cong., 2d Sess., H.R. 13737, a bill, page 6, lines 17–24, May 12, 1976.

given adviser, then the registration of advisers could be abolished. This would remove the bias that appears to be present in the current system and "deregulate" the market for advice. Under such a scheme, any individuals who wished to enter the market and sell advice would be free to do so: their success would be linked to the correctness of their advice, not to the fact that they are registered advisers.

QUESTIONS

1 The Securities and Exchange Commission controls not only the registration of investment advisers but also the selling and buying of securities by licensing brokers. Stock brokers, registered by the SEC, are also in the business of selling advice to investors; therefore, they compete to a limited extent with the securities advisers. (Security advisers cannot buy and sell stock as a broker can, however.) Would you expect that stock brokers as a group would favor increasing regulation of advisers or the deregulation of the market for advice? Why?

2 Suppose that the legislation, as drafted, is passed by Congress and that the SEC established a new regulatory department to police the admission and performance of securities advisers. How would you expect this body to act with respect to the numbers of securities advisers licensed in terms of the current procedure? Would you expect this department to adopt barriers to entry, education standards, apprenticeship requirements, etc.?

3 As a potential buyer of stocks and bonds, would you prefer to have the market for advice regulated or deregulated? As a potential securities adviser who meets all the registration criteria, would your preferences toward regulation be different from your answer to question 1? Why?

4 In a famous study of the stock market in the 1960s, economist George J. Stigler concluded that the SEC's attempt to provide investors with a "better, more informed" market by regulation of the securities market has had little or no effect on the profitability of purchasers of new issues. Further researchers have suggested that investors can, on the average, do just as well by picking stocks at random as by following the advice of paid investment advisers. Suppose that it is true that investment advisers *cannot* predict future stock movements based on past behavior of the stocks in the market, and that the variance of any given stock issue over time tends to be a random phenomenon. Then who are the primary beneficiaries of the current legislation to strengthen registration standards? Explain your answer.

CASE 12B:

The 15-Second Match[5]

On April 1, 1976, the Consumer Product Safety Commission (a federal regulatory agency) announced that in an attempt to "eliminate or reduce unreasonable risks of death or injury" from the use of cardboard matchbooks, it was seeking to impose regulations on the matchbook industry that would require paper matches to extinguish themselves within 15 seconds and burn no longer than 1 inch. The safety agency noted that in 1975 alone, some 9500 persons were treated in hospital emergency rooms for match-related injuries. The Council on Wage and Price Stability (also a federal government agency) estimates that the new regulations will add $68 million to the *annual* cost of matchbook production in the United States. Further, the council noted that over 97 percent of those treated in hospitals for burns were released after minor treatment, and only 7.4 percent of those treated were children under 5 years old.

In addition to shortening the burning time of paper matches, the Consumer Product Safety Commission (CPSC) wants to ban all mail-in coupons (for home-study courses, premiums, and goods) from matchbook covers. The CPSC argues that people tear off the coupons and continue to use the matches uncovered, which is very hazardous. One-eighth of the cover would have to be used to give a safety message and the striking surface would have to be placed on the bottom back, if the new regulations go into effect.

QUESTIONS

1 The potential of bodily harm exists given the current manner in which book matches are produced and sold, and it is now technologically possible to produce a self-extinguishing match. Why, then, would you hypothesize that it is necessary for a government agency to mandate the production of such a clearly superior product? Why wouldn't the matchbook industry voluntarily seek to market this product innovation?

2 You are to select the pro or con position with respect to this proposed piece of regulatory law and develop a defense of your selected point of view. You should address both the explicit and the implicit (opportunity) costs and benefits in your defense.

3 The Council on Wage and Price Stability's estimate of the annual cost of the new regulation is $68 million. Discuss how, if you were a member of the council, you would develop such an estimate. What factors would and/or should go into the calculation?

[5] Facts for this case were taken from press releases of both government agencies.

TEST YOURSELF

True—false

T F 1. If property rights are not clearly definable, such as in the case of fish in the ocean, government intervention in the private market may improve the allocation of resources.

T F 2. Firms may seek regulation to protect themselves from competitive pressures.

T F 3. When selecting the correct price and output policy, the regulatory agency gets cost figures from the firms that it regulates.

T F 4. The public interest is always best served by regulating monopoly producers of goods and services.

T F 5. Government has the ability to correct all market failures.

T F 6. John K. Galbraith feels that the government should use its countervailing power to balance the power achieved by monopoly industries.

T F 7. Government agencies alter the free-market supplies of goods and services by making rules that change the price and output of different goods and by changing the requirements for entry into a particular market.

T F 8. A regulatory lag is the time needed for the regulatory agency to adjust to changing economic conditions for the regulated industry.

T F 9. The government is the best judge of the goods bundle preferred by society, so it should make private firms produce goods at prices all can afford to pay.

T F 10. If average cost is declining when it cuts the demand curve, we can assume that in the long run this firm will emerge as a natural monopoly.

Multiple-choice

Study Figure 12-1; then answer each of the following questions.

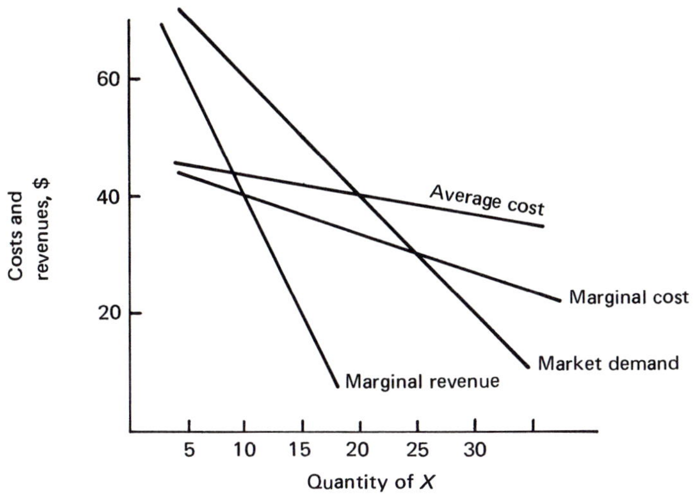

FIGURE 12-1 Market demand and cost conditions for commodity *X*

1 The firm will expand output up to the point where MR = MC if it wishes to maximize profits or minimize loss. Output at this level is

(a) 10
(b) 20
(c) 30
(d) 25
(e) None of the above

2 When the firm is maximizing profit or minimizing loss,

(a) Average cost is greater than marginal cost
(b) Average cost is equal to marginal cost
(c) Average cost is less than marginal cost
(d) Average cost is equal to marginal revenue

3 At the efficient competitive output, the value of the last unit produced is exactly equal to the value of the resources that go into the production of the last unit. The competitive output level in the above Figure 12-1 is

(a) 10 units
(b) 40 units
(c) 20 units
(d) 30 units
(e) None of the above

4 Suppose that society sought to regulate this firm's price so that it was forced to produce at the efficient output level. The owner of the firm would

(a) Still earn an economic profit
(b) Continue to produce at the previous output level
(c) Incur a loss
(d) Be happy to comply for this would be the profit-maximizing output anyway
(e) None of the above

13

Government Protection for the Consumer

The United States economic system is most often described as a *mixed economy.* This means that neither private industries nor the government has complete control over the production of goods and services. In a *free-market economy* all the goods and services provided are produced by the private sector, with private individuals determining the output level and the prices. In a *command economy,* government makes all the production decisions and determines what will be provided, how much will be produced, and who will receive the goods. In our economy, private firms provide most of the goods and services produced, but the government also provides many public goods (national defense, police and fire protection) that are not provided by the private sector. In addition, the government steps in to limit the action of private firms. One such example of government intervention in the market is consumer protection. From what must the consumer be protected? Consumers must be protected from the business sector. Why? Business people are thought by many to be in a superior position when dealing with consumers and thus are able to take advantage of them. Consumer protection legislation is aimed at reversing this position by establishing standards of business conduct with respect to output quality, quantity, and prices.

How does this notion of "producer supremacy" fit in with the ideas on the workings of markets we have previously discussed (see Chapters 7, 8, and 10)? We have argued that the free market (or competitive market) should serve as the principle coordinator of economic activity since it is the mechanism that best responds to the individual preferences of consumers. The operation of the free market protects the consumer by making the consumer's preferences dominant. If producers wish to survive in a free exchange economy, they do so by producing what buyers want to purchase. This notion has come to be called *consumer sovereignty.* These two views of the outcomes generated by the working of an exchange economy lead to quite different conclusions as to the role of government. We can distinguish two types of government regulation of the voluntary exchange mechanism. *Market-supporting regulation* is government intervention that enables the market to work more smoothly. *Market-supplanting regulation* substitutes government activity for the operation of the free market. Let us consider how government regulation can protect the consumer.

The market for tobacco products such as cigarettes, cigars, and pipe tobacco is large, and many private firms have found profitable opportunities in manufacturing and selling for this market. There is substantial evidence that the smoking of cigars, pipes, and cigarettes imposes high risks of injury to the smoker's health and increases the chance of premature death. In addition, the health of nonsmokers is damaged because they must breathe the polluted air. This seems to be a clear case of external effects. When they put smoke into the air, smokers do not pay nonsmokers for the right to change the quality of the air they both breathe. That is, smokers are not bearing the full costs of their actions. In this case smokers receive the benefit from smoking, but nonsmokers bear some of the costs in the form of reduced air quality.

Will a voluntary exchange economy internalize these external costs or is government intervention needed to protect the consumer? Will the tobacco industry voluntarily provide members of society with information on the health hazards related to use of its product? Will smokers take into consideration the harm they inflict on others by smoking? If government intervenes in the working of the voluntary exchange process, what kinds of actions are called for? Should government place an outright ban on tobacco smoking, limit smoking to those individuals already in bad health or old enough to understand the risks involved, distribute information to the consumer as to the harmful effects of tobacco, or establish property rights to the airspace and develop a mechanism to settle competing claims? Your own view of the hazards of cigarette smoking will affect your response to these questions.

To demonstrate that there exists a need for regulation of the tobacco market by government requires very difficult cost-benefit judgments. Clearly a change in working rules of this market will affect different individuals quite differently. When individuals are left free to choose among the many competing goods and services on the market, then they must rely on their own individual initiative to protect their own interest. If individuals are free to purchase tobacco products, then some individuals will accept the risk of lung cancer and smoke. When information on the danger of tobacco is readily available, then the costs of smoking can be weighed against the benefits received for a given individual. The nonsmoker's rights could be protected by the provision of a legal, institutional framework that sets out the property rights to the common airspace.

Government provision of information on the effects of tobacco use is an example of a market-supporting intervention because that information enables market participants to better assess benefits and costs. Why might government step in and provide such information? The tobacco producers will willingly provide this information only if they are held liable for the damages incurred from the use of their product. The problem comes, of course, in establishing the casual relationship between use of tobacco and lung cancer *in a particular case.* (Why? Consider that nonsmokers also get lung cancer.)

The least costly method may be for government to disseminate the information to the public. This type of government intervention in the market does not restrict the choices available to individuals, but rather makes them more aware of the costs involved in a given choice. Consumer protection by government intervention in the market can take the more direct form of regulation, as we have discussed previously (see Chapter 12). The ability of the government to protect the interests of the consumer in the market exchange process must be judged on the basis of the expected consequences of the intervention and not on what the intervention in the market seeks to accomplish. The decision to let government protect consumers must be evaluated by comparing the costs of intervention with the costs borne by society when private markets operate imperfectly.

KEY CONCEPTS

Product liability Laws enacted that establish the legal responsibility for the specific quality or quantity of a given good.

Consumer sovereignty The concept that the dollar votes of the purchaser in the market determine the goods bundle that producers supply.

Externalities Costs or benefits that affect people other than the parties to a given transaction.

Caveat emptor The implied liability rule of the marketplace states that buyers of goods have to take care of themselves with respect to the good purchased.

Caveat vendidor The implied liability rule of the marketplace which states that sellers of goods must be responsible for how the goods they sell are used.

CASE 13:

What Price Prices?[1]

On November 3, 1975, the U.S. Senate Commerce Committee's Subcommittee for Consumers opened hearings on Senate bill S. 997, the Price Disclosure Act, whose major facets include the requirement that most individual items in grocery stores have the price marked on the package. Testimony before the subcommittee revealed that vastly divergent views were held by the grocery industry and the representatives of consumer interest groups as to the desirability of such legislation. The source of the controversy centered on the introduction of the Universal Product Code (UPC) and the subsequent computerization of the check-out process in many United States supermarkets. This case will briefly present the factors leading to the introduction of the proposed legislation and then summarize the positions for and against passage of the Price Disclosure Act.

Computer-assisted check-out, where purchases are processed by means of an electronic scanner, became a viable alternative to traditional cash register procedures with the development and industrywide adoption of a standard means of product identification, the Universal Product Code (UPC) symbol. The UPC is a rectangular array of lines, bars, and numbers which, when scanned by a laser beam, allows a computer to identify the product. The symbol given identifies a 303 can of Del Monte green beans. The first five digits (24000) specify a Del Monte product, and the second five digits (01391) represent the specific item and size; the zero on the left side denotes a grocery item. (Of course the laser does not read the numbers; it reads the vertical lines.) When the checker passes the item with the UPC symbol over the scanner, the symbol is read by the laser and transmitted to the computer, which matches the item to the current price and then flashes the price on the register screen. The computer keeps track of each item's price, and the customer is presented with an itemized sales receipt at the conclusion of the transaction. Since the prices of all items are stored in the central store computer,

[1] Facts in this case are based on testimony and materials presented before the Subcommittee for Consumers of the Committee on Commerce of the United States Senate, 94th Congress, 1st Session, in Hearings on S. 997, the Price Disclosure Act.

it is no longer necessary for the checker to have a visual record of the price of each item checked. That is, the price of each item is not marked on the can or package. Therefore, the system permits the elimination of price markings on each individual item in the store. The customer knows the price on any item by looking at the price label on the shelf directly beneath the product. The potential removal of item pricing by supermarkets has led to "the battle at the supermarket counter."[2] Consumer groups have objected vigorously to the notion that food stores may not continue to price-mark individual items, relying instead on shelf rail marking and cash register receipts that list the price of each item by name to convey price information. The grocery industry has responded to consumer interests by pointing out that the expected savings of the new system will be passed on to the purchaser in the form of decreased prices and faster check-out time. Let us now look at these positions in slightly more detail.

GROCERY INDUSTRY POSITION

The industry position with respect to point-of-sale scanning equipment is that adoption of this technological innovation will have the following desirable effects on the food selling industry and the consumer.

1 It will appreciably reduce the cost of labor—fewer individuals will be needed to stock, price, and reprice since individual item pricing will have been eliminated.

2 It will reduce price-marking error—there is no chance of a checker punching the wrong keys for an item.

3 It will improve merchandise control—the supermarket will now have an up-to-the-minute record of every item in the store.

4 It will reduce the number of times a product is sold out—with an accurate record of sales the reordering process can be handled automatically.

5 It will improve tax collections—by computing the taxable items and the tax rate automatically, the chance of human error is reduced.

6 It will improve customer information—the purchaser will receive an itemized record of each purchase, thus allowing customers to make price comparisons among stores and over time without packing around the item.

How much will the new system save? According to industry estimates, when the system is working, the introduction of computer point-of-sale scanning will result in total *annual* savings in food distribution costs of $149 million.[3] A portion of the annual savings would be lost if supermarkets were forced to mark each individual item. What is the price of individual item pricing? The industry estimates that it costs $1 per 1000 items marked and $3 per 1000 items if goods must be repriced (at 1973 wage rates); therefore, current pricing practices add between

[2] See *Fortune,* vol. 92, no. 3, September 1975.

[3] $384 million as the cost of the computer facilities and labeling changes and $533 million as the savings in check-out labor, training, pricing, repricing, recapping, misrings, and reorders.

$250 and $300 million annually to the cost of food in the United States. These costs are ultimately borne by the final consumer via higher food prices. The new retailing system provides the consumer with prices via the shelf label and a new type of cash register receipt which itemizes each purchase by name and price (for example, Campbell's soup—$0.47).

In speaking out against S. 997, which requires that each article have a marked price, the industry argues that the ultimate test of the advisability of removing item pricing is in the marketplace. If purchasers are willing to patronize a supermarket that removes prices, then that firm will survive and prosper; if not, the supermarkets that still have itemized pricing will remain in business, and the other firms will be forced out. As long as the market for retail food is highly competitive, as the industry claims, the consumer will be protected by the competition of supermarkets for the food dollars of the consumer.

CONSUMER PROTECTION POSITION

The organized consumer groups in the United States have raised serious objections to the widespread implementation of unit price removal. Opponents of a complete switch to the point-of-sale scanning system believe that it will have the following undesirable effects on the consumer.

1 It will prevent (or reduce) the consumer's ability to compare price marks on newly purchased items with price marks on previously purchased items.

2 It will be much more difficult to compare the prices of items in different parts of the store, i.e., canned corn versus frozen corn.

3 Since the consumer has no visual check of prices, the computer system can make a mistake and the consumer has no easy way of checking.

4 The consumer will pay the expected cost of the computerized system (between $1 and $5 billion) in the form of higher food prices.

5 It will not appreciably reduce the cost of labor since most supermarket chains are covered by union agreements for workers.

6 Unless the supermarkets introduce massive changes in their order transmission, buying, and logistics systems, there would be little effect on inventory control.

7 It will allow supermarkets to automatically keep records of individual purchases and also credit information on the buyer by storing this information in its central computer.

Consumer spokespeople speaking in favor of passage of S. 997 and the House companion bill, H.R. 3126, argue that the retail grocery industry is not competitive as the industry representatives suggest. As a result of the noncompetitive nature of this market, any savings that might be generated by the system will benefit the industry only in the form of higher profits and not benefit the consumer by lowering prices. For example, consumer groups point to the possibility that much of the purported savings in faster check-out time for the shopper will be eroded by the supermarket's simply reducing the number of check-out lanes. The shopper would wait just as long as before, and the store would save the labor costs of the checkers. The consumer groups seem willing to bear the cost of higher food prices (there seems to be no major disagreement on the part of consumer advocates that mandatory unit price marking will eliminate some of the savings associated with the computerized check-out system) rather than be faced with packages without prices.[4] They see the real danger as the diminution of price consciousness on the part of the purchaser. This would allow supermarkets to raise food prices over time, and the consumer would not be able to detect this effect.

QUESTIONS

1 Under what market conditions would you expect the retail food industry to pass on the estimated reductions in operating costs to the purchaser in the form of reduced grocery prices? Explain.

2 What would you expect the position of a labor union such as the Retail Clerks International to be with regard to the installation of computerized check-out machines? Why? How consistent would their position be with that of consumer groups advocating pricing of all merchandise in supermarkets?

3 Should Senate Bill S. 997 be adopted, how would you predict that supermarkets would react with respect to further development and use of computer technology? Even if the Price Disclosure Act does not pass Congress, how would you expect the uncertainty of passage to affect business managers' decisions to purchase computer equipment?

4 In many parts of the United States, "wholesale markets" have sprung up as a means by which individuals can stretch their food dollar by giving up some of the amenities of the retail food store. Shoppers in such markets mark their own purchases with grease pencils, bag and carry their own groceries, and shop in un-air-conditioned comfort. The passage of the Price Disclosure Act would force such wholesale markets to mark the price on each item, the same as the more conventional food store. What group of individuals is likely to bear the greatest burden by the reduction of the cost advantages of such wholesale markets?

TEST YOURSELF

True—false

T F 1. Increases in information about product hazards are one very effective way for the government to provide consumer protection.

T F 2. Increased safety features in automobiles can be viewed as a characteristic of that good in the same way as bucket seats. Therefore, if individuals are interested in safety, they would be willing to pay for it in automobiles.

[4] "A New Supermarket Ripoff: Packages without Prices," Consumer Federation of America, Washington D.C.

T F 3. Those individuals who do not have children are not affected by all medicine lids being "childproof."

T F 4. If there are external benefits present from an exchange of a good, some individual(s) would be willing to pay to have more of the good produced.

T F 5. A person very averse to risk would be differentially benefited by the universal adoption of a safety standard, if all individuals shared equally in the cost of enforcing that standard.

T F 6. The term *caveat emptor* means "let the producer beware" and implies that sellers take their chances when they produce a good or service.

T F 7. Market-supporting regulation is government regulation of the kind that replaces the market system.

T F 8. Market-supplanting regulation is government regulation in which government replaces the workings of market supply and demand.

T F 9. Product liability laws establish who is responsible for the quality and safety of a product.

T F 10. Consumer sovereignty means that the consumer in the market is primarily responsible for the kinds of goods and services that producers provide.

Multiple-choice

The graph in Figure 13-1 reflects a competitive market demand and supply situation for steel in terms of private costs and benefits. Answer each of the questions below based on the information presented in the graph.

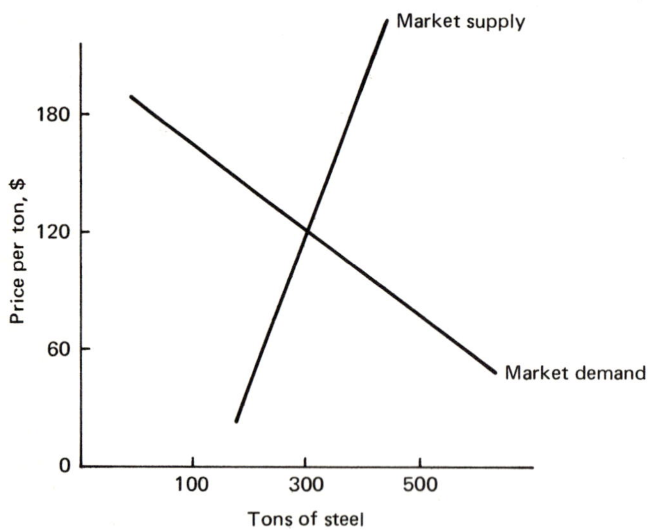

FIGURE 13-1 Competitive market demand and supply conditions for steel (billions of tons)

1 The free-market solution would tend toward a production of steel up to
- (a) 100 units
- (b) 200 units
- (c) 300 units
- (d) None of the above

2 At the free-market solution, for the last unit produced
- (a) Marginal cost is less than marginal benefit
- (b) Marginal cost is equal to marginal benefit
- (c) Marginal cost is greater than marginal benefit
- (d) Society could be better off by purchasing more steel at the prevailing price

3 Suppose that all members of the society suffer from polluted air as a result of the production in the steel industry. These costs take the form of increased medical care, shorter life expectancy, and higher laundry costs. If Figure 13-1 were adjusted to take these costs into effect,
- (a) The supply curve would shift upward to the left
- (b) The supply curve would shift downward to the right
- (c) The demand curve would shift downward to the right
- (d) None of the above

4 Given the information in question 3, the presence of social costs leads to
- (a) The overproduction of steel by the private sector
- (b) The optimal amount of steel
- (c) Not enough steel being produced in the short run
- (d) None of the above

14

The Demand for Resources

The production of goods and services is something like a magician's hat: you put in a scarf and out pops a rabbit. Certain things that are not goods and services are somehow combined to become the commodities that consumers desire. Inputs in the production process are all the components that go into the completion of a final good. These inputs are commonly called *factors of production.* Literally thousands of factors go into the production of any single good, but for the sake of simplifying the discussion we generally lump all factors into four groups. Land, labor, capital, and entrepreneurial ability are the most common factor classes. The resources that are directly provided by nature (minerals, fisheries, forests, and land, for example) are called *land. Labor* refers to the physical as well as mental skills of people. *Capital* services are all the resources that are fabricated aids to production, and *entrepreneurial ability* is the special class of labor that has the capacity to combine the other resources to produce goods and services.

Unlike final goods and services which are demanded for their direct, want-satisfying characteristics, the demand for factors of production depends upon their usefulness in the production process. The demand for factor services changes with the demand for the final goods with which they are associated. Thus, the demand is *derived.* For example, you may demand typing paper, not because it can satisfy a particular want but because your professor requires a term paper. If you wish to pass the course, you must write the paper (the paper is the final product). If the term paper were not a course requirement, then your demand for typing paper would be zero. In this case, your demand for typing paper is derived from the demand for term papers.

One of the main problems in studying the demand for factor services is that many inputs are used to produce a single product In the case of the term paper, how much of the value of the term paper should be attributed to the 100 percent rag bond paper, how much to the electric typewriter, and how much to your efforts in composing the paper? All these factors, and more, went into the production of the term paper. It seems clear that the term paper was produced by a joint effort of all the factors of production. Thus, the demand for any particular input depends not only upon its price, but upon the price of all other inputs. As the price of typing services increases, for example, you may alter your mix of factor services. You could reduce the number of pages in the paper, reduce the quality of the bond paper, or type the paper yourself to save the typist fees (if you consider typing the paper yourself, don't forget to consider the opportunity costs of your time in your production decision).

If the production process is characterized by the jointness of inputs in determining output, then how does a producer of a final good know what inputs to hire? Further, how does the producer know how much of any single input to use? One way a producer can attempt to solve this problem is to try to single out the contribution of the resources to output. For example, suppose you are a farmer and you add one more worker in your potato field; as a result, 5 additional bushels of potatoes are produced. The contribution of the one additional worker was 5 additional bushels of potatoes. Suppose potatoes sold for $3 a bushel; then your income went up by $15 when you hired that worker. How much did the additional worker add to your costs? Of course the answer depends upon the wage rate. If your labor costs went up by $10, then you are clearly better off as a result of your decision to hire the additional worker. Why? Your additional output (the marginal product) was 5 bushels, and you can sell each of these for $3, thus earning an additional $15 (this is called your "marginal revenue product"). Your additional costs (marginal resource cost) were only $10. Therefore, you added $5 to your profits. You would continue to hire potato workers until their salaries added more to your costs than their labor added to your revenues We will hypothesize that producers will employ all inputs by following much the same rule. The decision maker will hire a factor of production, at least up to the point where the addition to revenue equals or exceeds the costs incurred.

KEY CONCEPTS

Derived demand The demand for a factor of production that is based on the demand for the final good in which it is used.

Minimum wage standard Concept that implies that there should be some lower limit to the wage rate that exists in the market.

Wage rate differentials Difference that exists in the payment of factors employed in the same line of work.

Marginal product The change in the output level that can be directly attributed to hiring of one additional unit of input.

Marginal revenue product The change in the firm's total revenue that can be directly attributed to the hiring of one additional unit of input.

Marginal resource cost The change in the firm's total costs that can be directly attributed to the hiring of one additional unit of input.

CASE 14:
No Pix, No Profits[1]

Neighborhood movie theaters throughout the United States are currently facing one of the most serious crises since the introduction of television on the American entertainment scene—a shortage of movies. Events in recent years have contributed to a drastic reduction in the number of motion pictures produced by film makers in the United States and abroad. During the "Golden Age of Movies" in the 1940s, the production of films in any given year numbered between 400 and 500 by the major Hollywood studios. But those days have been over for some time; rising production costs, expensive epics that flopped, and dismal performance results culminated in a motion picture industry depression in the late 1960s and early 1970s. Out of this crisis came the consensus that making fewer films was the only way that the major Hollywood studios could survive. It now appears that Hollywood's annual production contribution is in the range of 100 to 125 features.

The drastic reduction in the production of films is by no means adequate to supply the demand by film exhibitors. The number of movie screens in the United States has increased from under 12,000 in the early 1960s to over 16,000 today. Thus, in the face of production declines, the growing demand has left many theater owners with little or no choice as to the films they exhibit. This problem is worsened by the very seasonal nature of demand by the film-going audience. The peak attendance periods at films center on the traditional holiday seasons—Christmas, New Year's, Easter, and Thanksgiving—accumulating to about 25 weeks per year. Hence, the film studios concentrate the release of their product to coincide with these peak demand periods. Thus the theater owner is left with about one-third of the year when films are not as readily available. The theaters do not disappear during these slack periods, and they must provide some product for the viewer if they are to remain in business.

QUESTIONS

1 One of the structural changes that has occurred in the theater industry has been the introduction of two or three small theaters in the same building with each theater sharing the projection room facilities. Why do you think theater owners have altered their product from one theater seating 600 persons to three theaters in the same building, each seating 200 persons? How has this structural change affected the demand for films?

[1] Facts in this case are reprinted with permission from A. D. Murphy, "Pinch Picture Playoff Patterns," *Variety*, March 17, 1976, pp. 1–34, and Joseph McBride, "The Shape of 1977 Pix Production," *Variety*, December 29, 1977, pp. 1–62.

2 In the past many individuals invested in movie production because they could receive special tax treatment on this investment relative to other kinds of investments. In 1976, the Internal Revenue Service laws were changed, and this tax benefit was eliminated. Explain how the demand for investment funds to finance films (a derived demand) could be expected to affect the neighborhood theater owner? The Hollywood studio owner? The investor?

3 As a theater owner, what are the adjustments that you could be expected to make in the face of continued restriction in the supply of films from major Hollywood production centers? What would be expected to happen to the price for which films are leased and the number of copies of films produced?

4 Entry into the film exhibitor industry appears to be relatively free of non-economic barriers. Therefore, what would be the expected adjustment in the number of theaters in the United States in the face of this input restriction? In the long run, what would be expected to happen to the market share of the major Hollywood studios with respect to the total world production of films?

TEST YOURSELF

True—false

T F 1. Entrepreneurial ability refers to the final good produced by a single firm which is not a corporation.

T F 2. Marginal revenue product refers to the dollar value of the additional output produced from one added unit of input.

T F 3. A common characteristic of consumer goods is that many inputs must be jointly combined to produce a unit.

T F 4. A machine used to make shoes would be an example of a capital good.

T F 5. Producers of commodities will hire inputs only as long as they add 20 percent more to revenue than to costs.

T F 6. Derived demand refers to the fact that factor services do not have direct want-satisfying characteristics.

T F 7. Outputs are another name for factors of production.

T F 8. If the demand for a good is not derived, then it must of necessity be a consumer good.

T F 9. Marginal product refers to the output changes that occur when an input level is varied by a single unit.

T F 10. Marginal cost is the cost associated with the total production of goods and services.

Multiple-choice

In any one week firm Z can sell Z-bars (a delicious confectionary treat) for $1 a bar; the plant of the Z company is operational once the candy makers are secured. The table below shows the output, cost, and labor figures for a 1-week period.

Units of Candy Makers	Units of Z-Bars (*Q*)	Z-Bar Price (*P*)	Total Revenue (TR)	Marginal Product (MP)	Marginal Revenue Product (MRP)
0	0	$1.00	$ 0	46	$46
1	46	1.00	46	46	46
2	92	1.00	92	36	36
3	128	1.00	128	22	22
4	150	1.00	150	18	18
5	168	1.00	168	2	2
6	170	1.00	170		

1 If we assume that firm Z has as its production objective the maximization of profit (minimization of loss), then the firm's demand curve for candy makers is given by:

(a) The units of candy makers available
(b) The marginal physical product of candy makers
(c) The total revenue from the production of Z-bars
(d) The marginal revenue product of candy makers
(e) None of the above

2 If the weekly wage rate of candy makers is $100 per week, firm Z will find it most profitable to

(a) Employ more than six candy makers
(b) Employ only three candy makers
(c) Employ no candy makers at that wage rate
(d) Produce no Z-bars
(e) (c) and (d) only

3 Suppose that the weekly wage rate of candy makers falls to $30 per week. Firm Z will find it profitable to employ

(a) More than six candy makers
(b) At least three candy makers
(c) No candy makers at that wage rate
(d) Only two candy makers
(e) Not possible to determine

4 When making hiring decisions, profit-maximizing firms will compare the cost of a resource with its

(a) MRP
(b) MC
(c) MPP
(d) TR
(e) None of the above

5 Suppose that the market conditions under which firm Z operates change so that it finds it can no longer sell all the Z-bars produced in one week at a constant price of $1. Instead, as it brings more candy onto the market, it finds that it must lower the selling price in order to induce consumers to purchase the confection. In this circumstance, we would expect the employment of candy workers to

(a) Rise
(b) Remain the same
(c) Fall
(d) Be inversely related to the marginal physical product
(e) (c) and (d) only

6 Given the market change discussed in question 5, we would expect firm Z to

(a) Increase its production of Z-bars
(b) Decrease its production of Z-bars
(c) Alter its production in some unspecified manner
(d) Keep production levels constant since candy makers' costs have not changed
(e) None of the above

7 On the graph below, plot the implied demand curve for candy makers by firm Z under the market conditions specified in the table. Then indicate how the change in market circumstances outlined in question 5 would alter your implied demand curve.

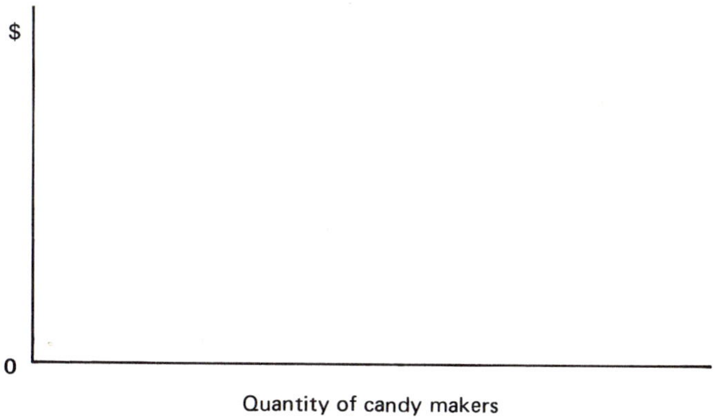

15

Power in the Market for Resources

All transactors (buyers and sellers) in all markets at all times are attempting to improve their market position by gaining additional power over the terms of trade. Thus, day laborers try to raise their wages relative to others at the same time as their employer is seeking to hold down the wage rate paid to day laborers. In attempting to achieve these conflicting ends, can we say anything about who is likely to win? Will the day laborer be successful in getting $5 an hour when workers with similar skills are being paid $4? Or will the employer be able to hire workers at a rate of $3 per hour when elsewhere similar workers are receiving $4?

The ability or power to receive more or pay less than the other transactors in the resource market clearly depends upon being protected from competition. For example, in the early 1900s the coal companies were the major employers of labor in many parts of West Virginia and Pennsylvania. These companies significantly affected the job market by their hiring practices. In many areas, either workers worked for the coal company or they left the area, for there was no alternative source of employment. Even in the extreme case of being the only buyer of labor in the market, the coal company's power was limited. The company could not force miners into the mines. An individual or firm who is in a position of being the sole *buyer* of a service, good, or resource is said to be a *monopsonist.* A firm or individual who is a dominant employer of a given type of labor is said to possess *monopsonistic power.* What impact does the presence of monopsony power have in the labor market? As the monopsonist, you can affect the market wage rate for workers when you alter your individual demand for labor.

On the sellers' side, resource owners will seek to reduce competition within their particular resource market. Thus if you are an automobile mechanic and provide repair services, you would prefer to be the only mechanic in town. This position would increase your power to sell your services at a higher than competitive price. If you are not the only mechanic, then when you set your price above the prices of other mechanics, buyers would go elsewhere. Therefore, in competitive markets where there are a large number of resource owners selling their particular service, the price one mechanic receives depends upon the price all others are willing to accept. Mechanics may be able to reduce their price interdependence if they can differentiate their product. If they provide the "friendliest," the "fastest," and the "most convenient" repair services, they *may* be able to charge a higher price. Another way that mechanics may raise their selling price is by restricting entry to their profession and reducing the supply of mechanics relative to demand. Labor unions, professional organizations, and occupational licensing laws are all examples of methods suppliers use to make their market less competitive.

KEY CONCEPTS

Monopsony A market where there is a single *buyer* of a good, service, or resource. (This is the buyer's equivalent to the case of a single seller, which we call monopoly.)

Monopsonistic power A *buyer* that has a significant enough influence in the market that his or her decisions alter the selling price of a good, service, or resource.

Monopsonistic marginal factor cost Marginal factor cost for the monopsonist is greater than the cost of buying *one additional unit* since all previous units purchased must now receive the higher price.

Unions and/or professional organizations Organizations of resource owners that seek to procure economic gains for the members. Unions may be organized around a specific skill held in common by all members (craft union) or organized on the basis of the particular manufacturing endeavor in which the workers are engaged (industrial unions).

Employers' associations Organizations of resource purchasers that band together with one of their purposes being to present a unified policy in labor negotiations.

CASE 15:
Special This Week: Divorce—$175 Plus Court Costs[1]

On January 18, 1977, the United States Supreme Court heard arguments on the question of whether the American Bar Association's (ABA) 68-year-old prohibition on advertising violates the First Amendment right of freedom of speech of lawyers and/or is invalid under the federal antitrust laws prohibiting restraints on competition.[2] On June 28, 1977, the Supreme Court ruled that lawyers can publish advertisements about the availability of routine services under the constitutional guarantee of free speech. That decision could change the very nature of the delivery of legal services in the United States. This case will summarize the arguments for and against the advertising ban.

POSITION OF BAN SUPPORTERS

The professional activity of lawyers has long come under the scrutiny and control of national and state bar associations which have long-established rules that delineate the manner in which lawyers may seek out clients. Expressly forbidden by the ABA's Code of Professional Responsibility is the distribution of information about fees and/or areas of legal specialization (e.g., criminal law or divorce law) by members of the bar. The continuation of the ban is supported by the various bar associations on the grounds that professional advertising is inherently deceptive. To allow professionals to advertise is "... an outright invitation to fraud and is incompatible with every element of a profession which makes a profession worthwhile as a calling, except money making."[3] In addition, opponents of advertising feel that the special nature of the services provided by lawyers is sufficiently beyond common understanding that buyers frequently can neither know what they truly want nor evaluate what they have received; therefore, price advertising would increase the probability of deception, since no common standard of evaluation would be available to the public. On the antitrust aspect of the advertising ban, the position of the bar is that this is a reasonable restraint given the unique nature of the service provided.

[1] Facts in this case are reprinted with permission from "To Advertise or Not to Advertise," *American Bar Association Journal,* vol. 63, pp. 341-345, March 1977.

[2] The specific case before the Court is *Bates v. State Bar of Arizona,* 555 p. 2d 640 (1976).

[3] State of Arizona brief.

POSITION OF BAN OPPONENTS

An individual's or group's right to freedom of speech can be limited by the state only if the state can prove that the restriction serves an extremely important state interest which outweighs the public interest in freedom of speech. Lawyers wishing to advertise their services and their fees argue that there exists no compelling reason for the state to limit their freedom of speech. In stating fees for specific services, it is argued that the seller would be providing the potential buyer with the most valuable type of economic information—who is producing what, at what price—for making a useful consumer decision. Lifting the ban would also be in accordance with the First Amendment right of potential clients to obtain legal services and the right to receive information. Opponents of the ban argue that the bar associations' attempt to protect the public really keeps the public in ignorance. Lawyers who wish to advertise argue that the ban is a classic anticompetitive device and that the consumers of legal services are just as entitled to the benefits of price competition as are the consumers of other services.

QUESTIONS

1 One of the primary ways that information is transferred between buyers and sellers in a market is via advertising. As a recent law school graduate just entering the legal profession, would the current ban on advertising harm or help you, relative to more established lawyers in the market?

2 As a consumer of legal services, you wish to purchase that package of services most closely fitting your needs relative to your income constraints. How does the current ban on advertising help you match your needs to the correct legal practitioner, and how might the ban harm you in achieving this goal?

3 Supporters of the current advertising ban argue that it prevents members of the profession from misleading the public and distorting information as to the nature of legal services. This view is in direct contrast with the position that advertising, by increasing the level of consumer information, makes the consumer more aware and less susceptible to unscrupulous sellers. How would your position with respect to advertising vary if you were a consumer? A judge? An individual charged with first-degree murder?

4 In 1976, the Supreme Court ruled that a Virginia law prohibiting pharmacists from advertising prices of prescription drugs was unconstitutional. Pharmacies may now advertise. If this ban were a means of maintaining monopoly power, what do you predict would happen to the prices of prescription drugs in the state of Virginia? Why?

TEST YOURSELF

True—false

T F 1. A monopsonist is a seller of a single product in a competitive market.

T F 2. As a seller of a service in a competitive market, you must compete with all other sellers of related products.

T F 3. Labor unions attempt to raise productivity of workers by restricting the supply of labor.

T F 4. The United Mine Workers would be an example of a buyers' organization that might attempt to reduce wage rates.

T F 5. In a monopsonistic market, the buyer of labor affects the wage rate for workers.

T F 6. Monopsonistic power means that a seller of a good can charge a higher than normal price.

T F 7. If all resource sellers get together, they can alter the supply of their resource.

T F 8. A group of individuals who join together with one of their goals being to work toward a reduction in the cost of labor is called a labor union.

T F 9. Craft unions are organizations that contain members having a particular skill or talent.

T F 10. The musicians' union would be an example of an industrial union.

Multiple-choice

Figure 15-1 represents the employment market for medical interns by hospitals in the United States for any given year. All hospitals that employ interns in the United States are accredited by the Council on Medical Education and Hospitals of the American Medical Association (AMA); they must pay interns a uniform wage established by the council or face losing their accreditation.

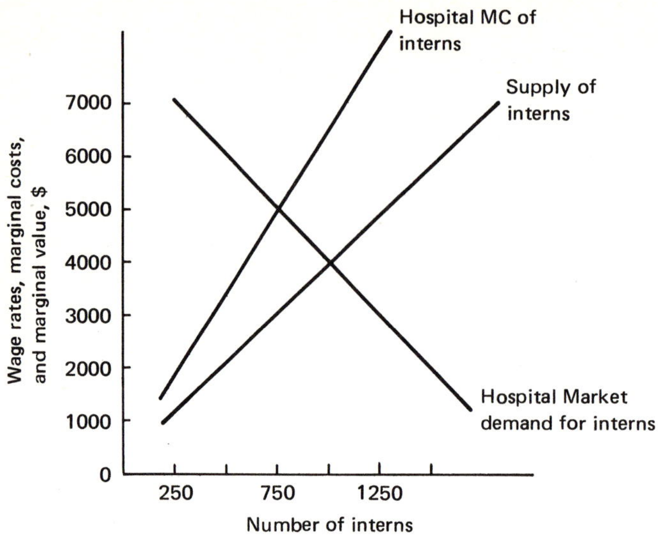

FIGURE 15-1 Employment market for medical interns for a one-year period

1 Under conditions where each hospital competed in an open market for its yearly supply of interns, the number of interns employed would tend toward

(a) 1000
(b) 500
(c) 750
(d) 1250
(e) None of the above

2 Under conditions that exist in the real world, the market for interns is cartelized by the hospitals. This fact would tend to change the outcome generated in question 1 by

(a) Increasing the number of interns employed to 750
(b) Increasing the number of interns employed to 1250
(c) Decreasing the number of interns employed to 500
(d) Decreasing the number of interns employed to 750
(e) None of the above

3 When all hospitals offer a uniform price for the services of interns established by an employers' cartel, the interns will

(a) Be faced with a wage below the free-market wage rate
(b) Be unable to compete the wage rate down if they possess inferior skills
(c) Get the same reward regardless of the level of training and skill they possess
(d) All the above
(e) (a) and (c) only

4 The hospital cartel will value the services of the last intern hired at

(a) $3000
(b) $5000

(c) $4000
(d) $1000
(e) Not possible to determine

5 The hospital cartel will establish the uniform wage rate for interns at

(a) $3000
(b) $5000
(c) $4000
(d) $1000
(e) Not possible to determine

6 Suppose that all interns in this market banded together to form a union, where they each agreed to withhold services from the hospitals and let the union bargain with the cartel for higher wages. What is the maximum wage that the hospital cartel would be willing to pay and still employ the same number of interns?

(a) $3000
(b) $5000
(c) $4000
(d) $6000
(e) Not possible to determine

7 By not allowing interns to form unions (this practice is specifically prohibited by the AMA), the hospital cartel during this one-year period can reduce its labor costs by

(a) $1,500,000
(b) $750,000
(c) $2,250,000
(d) $10,000
(e) Not possible to determine

16

International Trade and International Finance

The markets considered thus far have been domestic markets, where all goods and services could be purchased or sold using dollars. Many transactions are made across national borders, and in each case the money of both countries must be used. If you wanted to buy a car made in Germany, for example, the German firm would want marks. Although you could make this transaction through your bank, essentially you must convert your dollars into marks before the car could be purchased. But how many dollars are equal to the number of marks required to buy the car? In order to determine this, you must know the *exchange rate*.

In a free market for currency, the price of one currency in terms of another country's currency (which is our definition of exchange rate) is determined by the laws of supply and demand. If many United States citizens want to purchase German goods, the price of the mark will rise with respect to dollars. This situation describes a *freely fluctuating exchange rate*.

At times, governments have attempted to prevent their currencies from changing value constantly. It is believed by some that the amount of world trade depends on each person's knowing precisely in advance the value of his or her currency in terms of every other currency. To avoid exchange rate fluctuations from day to day, each government could set a rate of exchange and commit itself to buy foreign currency at this rate despite the supply and demand of that currency in world markets. This situation describes *fixed exchange rates*.

From time to time a country will attempt to spend and invest more abroad than that country earns by selling its products to foreigners. For example, if United States citizens and their government import lots of cars and clothing, travel abroad on foreign airlines, fight a war, and invest in overseas businesses, then the dollars leaving the country could exceed the foreign currency earned from exports, foreign travel in the United States, and Arab investment in United States industries. A financial statement that outlines precisely what one nation spends abroad and for what that nation receives foreign currency in return is called the *balance of payments*.

If the value of imports exceeds exports, the *balance of trade* section of the balance of payments is in deficit. And if the value of imports plus investment abroad exceeds the total amount of foreign currency abroad, then the balance of payments, in general, is in deficit. A country experiencing a deficit must ship gold abroad to buy back its own currency, hustle some loans from other governments or the International Monetary Fund, lower the value of its currency, or restrict its citizens' spending abroad. A balance-of-payments deficit may not continue indefinitely.

It is difficult, at first, to understand why lowering the value of its currency would help solve a balance-of-payments deficit. First, one must realize that if the value of the United States dollar declined, the amount of dollars needed to buy a German car would increase. Therefore, United States citizens might decide to buy a car produced in the United States, which would lower the total amount of United States dollars spent abroad. In addition, a German citizen would now have to spend fewer marks to get the dollars needed for a United States car. If the German citizen bought the United States car, the value of United States exports would increase. Reduced imports and expanded exports, resulting from the decreased exchange value of the dollar, would help correct the balance of payments. The reduction in the value of a currency under a fixed exchange rate system is called a *devaluation*. A *depreciation*, which occurs under a freely fluctuating exchange rate system, is a reduction in the value of a currency not because of government action but rather because banks and individuals refuse to buy the currency at a higher rate.

A government facing a balance-of-payments deficit will have difficulty maintaining a desired exchange rate because it does not have sufficient foreign currency. To avoid a *devaluation* or *depreciation*, the country will initiate exchange controls, which is precisely what the mythical country did in the following case.

Under an exchange control system, all purchases and sales of foreign exchange are handled by the government which allocates or rations the supply of foreign currencies to its citizens. Thus, the government can force a balance-of-payments equilibrium on the nation by restricting imports to the value of exports.

KEY CONCEPTS

Balance of payments An accounting statement, usually prepared by a designated national agency, of all the economic transactions between that nation and the rest of the world in a given year.

Balance of trade The difference in value between the goods that a nation exports and the goods that it imports.

Depreciation The reduction in the value of a currency due to less demand and/or increased supply.

Devaluation The reduction in the value of a currency due to an official decision not to buy or sell it at the previous rate.

Exchange controls A system of government regulation of foreign exchange. Under this system, all purchases and sales of foreign exchange are handled by the government.

Fixed exchange rate The value of a currency set by the government which agrees to buy and sell at that rate.

Freely fluctuating exchange rate The value of a currency determined by the market forces of supply and demand.

International Monetary Fund (IMF) An international financial institution affiliated with the United Nations which provides loans to its member nations experiencing balance-of-payments difficulties.

Tariff A tax on imports or exports levied by a government and payable when the item enters or leaves the area.

CASE 16:
The Attempts by One Nation to Support a Fixed Exchange Rate[1]

Armexil, a developing republic ruled by a five-member military junta, experienced severe difficulties maintaining its official exchange rates in the latter part of the 1960s. The official fixed exchange rate was 20 pesos per dollar, but on the street people would pay up to 200 pesos for a dollar.

The junta reasoned that they had three alternatives. First, they could abandon the fixed exchange rate system and the official rate. Left to market forces under a freely fluctuating exchange rate system, the peso would inevitably depreciate which would help correct the balance of trade. Second, the junta could maintain the fixed exchange rate system but devalue the peso to its black market rate.

Finally, they could initiate a system of exchange controls. All exporters would be required to forfeit their foreign exchange earnings to the government and accept in return the amount that the government was willing to pay them. The foreign exchange would then be allocated (i.e., sold) to importers in the amount and at the price the government saw fit.

The junta rejected depreciation and devaluation because they believed ostensibly that it would be inflationary. In addition, they doubted that exports would increase and imports decline significantly with a lowered value of the peso. Armexil then developed an elaborate system of exchange controls to force the balance of payments into equilibrium.

As indicated in the table, exporters were required to remit dollars earned to the government and accept a certain amount of pesos in return. Exporters of cocoa and

Exchange Rates under Exchange Controls

Multiple Exchange Rates	Pesos per Dollar Paid
Official Fixed Exchange Rate	20
Black Market Rate	200
To Cocoa and Coffee Exporters	80
To Processed Cocoa and Coffee Exporters	100
To All Other Exporters	200 (150 in cash)
By Newsprint Importers	100
By Raw Material, Equipment, and Some Consumer Goods Importers	220 approximately
By Other Importers	600 approximately

[1] Based, with the author's permission, on a paper by Maryann O. Keating, entitled "Speculation, Based on Three Alternative Theories, on the 'Effectiveness' of the Mexcian Devaluation," Radford College 1977.

coffee were given 80 pesos for every dollar they earned. Exporters of processed coffee and cocoa were given 100 pesos for every dollar they earned. All other exporters were given 200 pesos but immediate cash payment of 150 pesos was made, with the balance paid in 6-month notes on the Bank of Armexil.

Armexil's importers could not get their goods through customs unless they had an import license and bought their foreign exchange from the government. Newspaper printers could import newsprint for 100 pesos per dollar, but exchange for imports of most commodities had to be bought in auctions held separately for two categories of goods. The auction rate was about 220 pesos per dollar for raw materials, equipment, and some consumer goods. The rate for all remaining goods, considered to be "luxury" goods, was over 600 pesos per dollar. Payment had to be made immediately at these auctions but the foreign currency was generally not available for 150 days.

This system enabled the junta to determine the structure of Armexil's imports and exports as well as equate the flow of foreign currency into and out of the country.

QUESTIONS

1 Was the fear of a devaluation or depreciation justified? Explain your answer in terms of the elasticity of demand and supply for Armexil's imports and exports.

2 What was the intention of the junta in structuring the dollar payments to different types of exporters? Importers? On what basis do you think the junta granted preferential exchange rates to importers?

3 In what way are foreign exchange controls similar to tariff duties and subsidies?

True—false

Read the following statements and note whether each is true or false.

T F 1. Flexible exchange rates allow the forces of supply and demand to determine the value of one currency in terms of another currency.

T F 2. An exchange control system usually accompanies a fixed exchange rate.

T F 3. A country has a balance-of-payments surplus when it gains gold and/or foreign currencies and the amount of money held by foreigners decreases.

T F 4. The balance of trade is the difference in value between a country's imports and exports of goods and services.

T F 5. Exchange controls or freely fluctuating exchange rates cannot be used to eliminate balance-of-payments disequilibriums.

T F 6. The decision of a government to lower the value of its currency is called a "depreciation."

TEST YOURSELF

Multiple-choice

1 Assume that the rate of exchange for the British pound (£) is $2. An American can then buy with $100
- (a) £200
- (b) £50
- (c) £100
- (d) £400

2 If the value of the American dollar appreciates, this means that
- (a) Americans can now purchase less foreign currency with a dollar
- (b) Americans can now purchase more foreign currency with a dollar
- (c) Only intergovernmental transactions will be affected
- (d) The exchange rate will not change

3 The balance of payments is a relationship between a nation's
- (a) Exports and imports
- (b) Economic transactions and those of the rest of the world
- (c) Currency value and another nation's currency value
- (d) GNP and another nation's GNP

4 The balance of trade is
- (a) A relationship between a country's economic transactions and those of the rest of the world
- (b) The difference in value between a given country's exports and imports
- (c) The difference between the amount of gold given to one country by another country

5 When a country engages in using a fixed exchange rate,
- (a) It may be necessary to resort to exchange controls
- (b) The balance of payments automatically stays in balance
- (c) The balance of trade automatically stays in balance

6 When a country engages in using a flexible exchange rate,
- (a) Depreciations in the value of the currency never take place
- (b) The prices of foreign goods will usually increase
- (c) The value of that country's currency may fluctuate with respect to another country's currency

17

The Roles of Government

When we try to think of a society such as ours existing without any form of government, the organization seems difficult to comprehend. The impacts of local, state, regional, national, and international governments appear to be so pervasive that it is not possible to imagine how individuals would interact or behave in the absence of such entities. Governments are extremely important in affecting the environment in which we live, and their activities shape the way people interact in their private and collective activities. But what does the government do specifically that sets it apart from other organizations in our society? What role does the government perform to change our lives? While government performs many complex and varied functions in our society, it nonetheless seems possible to classify all government activities into two groups of actions. (1) The government is the producer and/or supplier of goods. (2) The government is the protector of rights and the enforcer of rules.

In pursuing their own self-interests individuals may discover that the market as a social organizer will not adequately provide them with certain kinds of goods and services they desire. Individuals may freely agree to transfer their ownership rights to private property to some collective group in return for an agreement to provide some bundle of public or collective goods. For example, in settling the American West, pioneers discovered that it was essential to survival to have some haven against enemy attack. However, no one individual was willing to provide and maintain a fort for all to use at a specified price. The problem was solved by each settler's giving up labor, land, and provisions to build and supply a fortification that was then available to all members of the community. In much the same way, our government undertakes the provision of national defense and other public goods in our society that have widespread benefits.

Goods, like the fort or national defense, that would not be provided by private firms or individuals in a market economy are nonetheless valuable. People derive benefits from being protected against the threat of foreign invasion; yet no firm can profitably sell national defense. Why? Once national defense is provided, it is available to all people regardless of whether they have paid for it or not. The cost of providing national defense for one person is exactly the same as providing it for 100 or 10,000 persons. Economists call goods with this characteristic *collective consumption* or *public goods*. Collective consumption goods are noncongestable. That is, adding another consumer does not reduce the value of the good to current users. For example, suppose that you are the only sunbather on the beach at Waikiki and one additional person comes to bask in the sun. That individual's consumption of sun does not diminish your consumption of sun; therefore, we could say that the cost of adding one more sunbather was zero. You are no worse off even though you are now sharing the consumption of the good (the sun) with someone else. Think how this is different from the case of a private good—a candy bar, for example. It seems clear that the range of zero marginal cost in consumption is limited for most collective consumption goods. If people continue to go to Waikiki beach to sunbathe so that 10,000 persons are now on the beach, the sun you previously enjoyed may well be blotted out. Not all goods that are provided by the government are collective consumption goods, such as national defense. The kinds of goods that are provided by government in our economy, however, will generally contain some "publicness" features.

For order to exist in a society of free and independent individuals, a system must emerge where the rights to action, property, and interaction are specified among the members of that society. A mechanism for the establishment and enforcement of individuals' rights is necessary for a society to function without anarchy. Government plays the role of ensuring that the "rules of the game," once freely agreed to by individuals, are enforced and that changes in the rules occur in a specified manner. The system of laws and rights thus established sets the boundaries within which social interaction can occur. To the extent that the rights of individuals and the rights of the collectivity are maintained, economic exchange is made easier.

KEY CONCEPTS

Government budget A statement of the expenditures and tax receipts of the collectivity.

Public interest The notion that there exists a unified set of government activities that will make everyone better off, when they are pursued.

The minimal state The least amount of collective activity consistent with protecting all citizens against violence, theft, and fraud, while providing enforcement of contracts.

Government intervention The use of coercive power by the collectivity to alter the voluntary or market arrangements into which individuals would otherwise enter. The intervention of government necessarily reduces the choice set of individuals.

Collective consumption goods Goods that can be consumed by everyone at no additional cost once they are produced.

CASE 17: The British Lighthouse System[1]

The present authority in charge of the building and maintenance of lighthouses for England and Wales is Trinity House, which was granted its charter in 1514 by Henry VIII. The first lighthouses built on the English coast by Trinity House were established in the early seventeenth century and were operated for the private betterment of this medieval seamen's guild. Private entrepreneurs were also in the business of erecting lighthouses in response to the demands of shipmasters, sailors and fishermen. The method used by the private entrepreneurs to avoid infringing on Trinity House's statutory authority was to obtain a patent from the Crown which empowered them to build a lighthouse and to collect a specified levy. The tolls were collected at the ports by agents who were commonly customs officials. The toll varied with the lighthouse, and ships paid a toll, varying with their size, for each lighthouse passed.

Throughout the seventeenth and eighteenth centuries, lighthouses on the English and Welsh coasts were provided by private individuals and organizations, as well as by Trinity House. In 1820, only 11 of the 46 lighthouses in existence had been built by Trinity House, with the remainder being provided by private individuals. However, by the 1830s there was increasing pressure on Trinity House from Parliament (British government) to purchase the privately owned lighthouses. The support for the consolidation of the lighthouse system under the reigns of Trinity House came mainly from the shipping industry. Shippers were attempting to get a reduction in light dues. The shippers wanted the lighthouses to be paid for and maintained out of the public treasury. By 1842, all lighthouses were consolidated under the control of Trinity House which had purchased the ownership rights to the private lighthouses.[2] The system of light dues was still in effect, although shippers were pressuring Parliament to restrict the net income Trinity House could earn from the operation of the lighthouse system. (All income earned was devoted to the support of retired sailors, their widows, and orphans.)

The use of the proceeds of the light dues for charitable purposes was abolished in 1853, with a corresponding decline in light dues. No longer were revenues above costs of operation permitted, even if those revenues were used for charitable purposes. In 1898, the system of setting lighthouse fees was altered to take into account changes in shipping routes that resulted from the introduction of the steam engine. The dues system was based on so much per net ton payable per voyage for all vessels arriving at, or departing from, ports in Britain.

[1] Facts in this case are reprinted with permission of Ronald H. Coase from his article "The Lighthouse in Economics," *Journal of Law and Economics,* 17(2), October, 1974, pp. 357-376.

[2] According to the Report of the Select Committee on Lighthouses of Parliament, 1845, sums of upward of 445,000 £ (equivalent to $7 to $10 million today) were paid to the owners of the private lighthouses.

The general character of the lighthouse finance system established in 1898 is still the present system in use today. Light dues, which are paid by shipowners into the General Lighthouse Fund, go to cover the likely expenditures of the British and Welsh lighthouse system. A Lights Advisory Committee, representing shipowners, underwriters, and shippers, reviews procedures and budgets of Trinity House and advises the Department of Trade as to the probable effects of new works or changes in the existing arrangements. This committee also serves in an advisory capacity for any proposed changes in the schedule of light dues.

QUESTIONS

1 What are the built-in incentives of the British system of lighthouse provisions that would tend to ensure that lighthouses would get built in the most needed locations and that the number of lighthouses would not be excessive? You may wish to contrast the operation of the British system with that of the United States where lighthouses are financed and maintained out of general tax revenues. (*Hint:* The British system is financed by user charges, therefore, shippers pay for additional lighthouses.)

2 Economists are often found arguing that in the case of lighthouse provision (or any other good whose marginal cost in consumption is zero) inefficiencies will occur if such goods are sold at a positive price. What would be the inefficiency generated by the British system of light dues?

3 If the description of the British lighthouse system is correct, it seems that it was quite possible for private individuals to make quite high returns by providing a commodity that is generally termed a *purely collective good*. Lighthouse light is indivisible—it is available to either all or none. It is characterized by MC = 0 in consumption—one additional ship steering by the light to avoid the rocky shore does not decrease in any way the use of the light by other ships. What seem to be some of the necessary conditions for such a good or service to be provided in the private market?

TEST YOURSELF

True—false

T F 1. Individuals may choose to be coerced by government and still be better off than in the absence of any government.

T F 2. Collective consumption goods are always produced by government.

T F 3. The expansion of government activities in recent years may be due to an ideological shift in the preferences of the members of society.

T F 4. Private property rights are necessary for the operation of a market economy.

T F 5. When markets fail, government production and/or control will of necessity be the only remedy to the resultant problem.

T F 6. External costs occur when an individual is able to shift some of the negative consequences of his or her actions to others without their consent.

T F 7. Goods vary to a great extent with respect to the character of "publicness."

T F 8. Government is expressly forbidden to produce those goods which can be classed as purely "private."

T F 9. The system of laws and courts that exists in the United States is an example of a "public good."

T F 10. For a good to be classified as a "pure public good," it must be available to the entire reference group if it is available to any one member.

18

The Ethics of Distribution

In a purely private market economy that operates within the broad confines of established property rights and rules of order, the income that any individual receives depends directly on his or her contribution to the production of goods and services. It is not sufficient to be willing to supply your talent or time to earn a reward in such a system; it is also necessary for someone else to desire your particular skills or talents. In such an economy, how will the "economic pie"—the goods and services produced—be distributed among the members of the society? First, we can note that those individuals who do not or cannot make some contribution that will be worth payment from others will have no claim on the output of the society. These individuals must depend upon charity to survive. What of those who compete in the marketplace and contribute to the production of goods? What will the distribution of shares look like for these individuals? Will everyone end up with a fraction of the output? Will 10 percent of the individuals get 80 percent of the product? Can we predict anything?

It seems virtually certain that the distribution of total income in this economy will be divided *unequally* among the members. A simple example should make this clear. Suppose that we have a world of ten individuals who each reach adulthood with equal economic opportunities. In pursuing his or her own best interest within the market system, each individual can be expected to choose from alternative activities. At some later time, we would expect that the individuals who worked the hardest, chose the "right" professions, took the greatest risks to gain the greatest amount, and were just "lucky" would have a greater share of the output than those individuals who chose leisure rather than work, made unprofitable investments, chose the "wrong" professions, or were generally "unlucky." In addition, in the real world the distribution of total income depends not only upon an individuals' productivity but also on his or her wealth position. In addition, inequalities will arise because different individuals possess varying endowments of property, income or talents. For example, if you inherit from your father a beautiful singing voice that is in great demand by others, you can use this talent to increase your income relative to the incomes of those who were not so fortunate. In the same manner, if you inherit from your father a stock of capital goods, your wealth position will differ from that of those who receive no inheritance.

In our society today, individuals have the right to make gifts of money or valuables to whomever they please. The voluntary exchange mechanism of the market is the primary means of social organization. Thus, we can be certain that the income shares will be distributed unequally among members of the society. Beyond that statement, can we make any judgment about the resulting distribution? Is it just? Is it good? Is it too equal? Is it too unequal? What does it mean to say that the distribution resulting from social interactions is just?

The notion of justice with regard to any distribution is not a clear-cut concept. It depends upon the standard chosen. For example, you may think income is distributed *justly* when you have 90 percent of all income and everyone else in society has 10 percent. More generally, however, when people talk about a just distribution of income, they are refering to the distribution's meeting a standard that all, or at least a majority of, individuals would agree on. For example, in a purely private market economy this rule might be stated as "to each according to what he/she and the resources he/she owns produce." Under such a rule, a just distribution would be one where everyone's share was based upon his or her productive effort. But what if a productive individual wished to share income with someone who was nonproductive—the aged, the infirm, or the sick? Would such charity be just? Not if the acquisition rule is just, because the charitable transfer would give a person income even though he or she did not contribute a productive activity. It seems reasonable that individuals, even in an economy that uses the market as its only social organizer, might wish to adopt another method of distributing income among its members.

What can we say about the distribution of income shares in the United States in the 1970s? What are the norms that our society uses to evaluate any given income distribution? Should government be used to alter the distribution? If so, how? These are questions for which there is no single or easy answer. Some members of our society see grave injustice in the unequal shares that characterize our present income distribution. They would use the coercive power of government to change individual income to create their idea of a just distribution. Others see the role of government as one of removing barriers to economic opportunities. Government should alleviate monopoly franchises, import quotas, and other market restrictions that artificially prevent individuals from achieving their maximum potential income. They do not feel it is just for government to coercively redistribute individual income. Still others view a just distribution as one which is generated by the operation of a voluntary exchange economy with government playing no active role. The ethics of any distribution clearly depend upon your view of the roles of the individual and the state.

KEY CONCEPTS

Distribution of income The manner in which the economic output of the society is divided among the members of that society.

Economic efficiency The process of organizing the productive resources of a society so that the output of goods and services is maximized.

Just distribution A division of output among the members of the society that satisfies some *subjective* requirements.

Social justice The assigning of rights and duties to the basic institutions in the society so that the outcome generated by the interaction of individuals satisfies some *subjective* requirement.

Acquisition rule An accepted manner or behavior by which individuals acquire rights to property, income, wealth, or other assets within the society.

Distributive justice An allocation of the economic pie to members of the society in accordance with some subjective requirement.

CASE 18:
How Liberty Upsets Patterned Principles of Distributive Justice *or* If It's Just, Must the World End?[1]

If a distribution of income among the members of society is felt to be unjust, do you think they will agree to this distribution for long periods? Do people in society want the outcome of social and economic exchanges to be and to look just? If we agree that the concept of a just distribution of income is a goal of any free society, then we can ask some of the following questions about the way that members of the society view justice. Does society's vision of economic and social justice depend upon the *pattern of distribution* of the economic pie? Or is justice dependent upon the *principles that generate a distribution*? Let us explore two alternative criteria for just distribution and their implications for a society.

PATTERNED CRITERION FOR DISTRIBUTIVE JUSTICE

Who owns what in any society? How did they get it? Is the ownership pattern just? One way that we might look at these questions is to focus on the actual distribution as compared with an ideal distribution based on some *structural* principle. This procedure would involve looking at the end product of a method of income distribution. If the ownership pattern were the same as that dictated by the principle of a just distribution, then the distribution would be just. For example, consider "to each according to his or her intelligence quotient (IQ)" as the distribution principle. This principle would require that the total income vary directly with IQ levels. No person should have a greater income than anyone whose IQ is greater. We could substitute any number of criteria for "intelligence quotient." For example, "distribute according to ethnic background," "distribute according to the level of education of the male parent," "distribute according to moral merit," or "distribute according to the weighted sum of all three of the above principles."

In each case, the actual distribution of income for the society would be compared with the distribution principle. When the end result matched the standard chosen as just, then the distribution of income would be considered just. We can call a *principle* of distribution *patterned* if it states that a distribution is to vary along with some specified criteria. We can say that a *distribution* is patterned if it agrees with some *patterned principle*.

[1]Adapted from Chapter 7, "Distributive Justice," in *Anarchy, State and Utopia* by Robert Nozick, © 1974 by Basic Books, Inc., Publishers, New York.

ENTITLEMENT CRITERION for DISTRIBUTIVE JUSTICE

An alternative view of justice and the ownership pattern for the society might focus on how that pattern occurred. It might say simply that a distribution is just if all people are *entitled* to the income they possess under the distribution. The question then becomes: How do you determine *just entitlement*? If you hold a car but got it by stealing from your neighbor, are you entitled to it? If your grandfather stole property from the American Indians, are you entitled to it now, a hundred years later? If your mother possessed a prized artistic talent which you inherited, are you entitled to it? This view of distributive justice would, of necessity, contain criteria to determine whether persons were entitled to own whatever they possess.

Such a view of distributive justice would set out a theory of justice in acquisition. For example, it might state that acquiring by force or stealing was unjust, but acquiring by the use of your own labor was just. Thus, the process (or processes) by which things are acquired is the focus of attention. It would be necessary to state the just manner for transfer of holdings. For example, the theory of justice in transfer might state that transfer by violence (murdering your father to gain his property) was unjust, but that transfer by voluntary accord (at the time of his natural death, your father agrees to turn over his holdings to you) was just. In this way distributive justice would depend upon the underlying principles of just acquisition and just transfer of holdings.

Under the entitlement criterion it would be possible to have a just distribution where some persons receive their marginal products, some win at gambling, some receive a share of their mate's income, some receive grants from foundations, some receive interest on loans, some receive gifts from admirers, some make for themselves much of what they have, some discover things, and so on. This principle of distributive justice would *not* be patterned. We can call this principle of distributive justice the *entitlement conception of justice in holdings.*

CRITERIA CONTRASTED

Now we can return to the question of whether justice resides in a pattern of distribution or in the framework that generated that distribution. What does each criterion imply for a society based upon voluntary exchange? We can illustrate the contrast in views with the use of an example. Let us suppose that the income distribution which exists in society at present conforms to a given patterned principle of justice. Any principle will do. Let us adopt the principle, "everyone has an equal share" as the just principle of distribution. This means that in our society everyone has the same amount of income. Now suppose that Wilt Chamberlain's basketball ability is in great demand. Assume he signs a one-year contract with a given team. One of the conditions of the contract is that he receive $0.25

of the purchase price of every ticket for each home game. When people choose to attend a basketball game in which Chamberlain's team plays, they buy their tickets and drop a separate $0.25 into a special box with Chamberlain's name on it.

Let us suppose that at the end of the season 1 million people have attended home games and that Wilt Chamberlain ends up with $250,000. This amount is a much larger sum than the average income of the society. In fact, it is larger than the income of anyone else. Is Chamberlain entitled to keep this income? Is this new distribution just or unjust? The beginning distribution of equal income was a just distribution according to our patterned principle. People voluntarily altered their income by transferring parts of their share to Chamberlain. Is the resultant distribution just or unjust? Equal income is no longer a characteristic of this society's income distribution. Should equality be restored? The general point of this illustration is that it does not appear possible to maintain an end state principle (distributional patterned principle) of justice without either continuous interference in people's lives or having the world stop once the principle is achieved.

QUESTIONS

1 The government in our society intervenes with the voluntary exchange process in a variety of ways that alter the distribution of income. On the basis of public policy statements, can you infer any patterned principles of distributive justice that these policies are seeking to achieve? [*Hint:* It may help you to think of specific programs and the justification for their existence, for example Aid to Families With Dependent Children (AFDC).]

2 We have discussed previously that the roles of government in a voluntary exchange economy are either a goods producer/supplier or a rules enforcer/rights protector. How does redistribution of income via the fiscal process fit into this concept of the collectivity? Can you think of any grounds whereby individuals would voluntarily agree to grant the government the power to redistribute the outcome achieved by the voluntary exchange process?

3 Economists primarily deal with the efficiency criterion when addressing questions of income distribution. That is, are resources being combined in such a way that the maximum output (income if measured in dollar terms) is generated? Is the question of the ethics of distribution a legitimate one for economists? Why or why not? Can you think of cases where the avoidance of addressing the ethics of a distribution would alter the evaluation of the distribution's "efficiency"?

TEST YOURSELF

True–false

T F 1. Your ability to consume goods and services in a purely private market economy would depend upon your productive capacity.

T F 2. A patterned principle of distributive justice would allow us to evaluate some outcome.

T F 3. Justice in the distribution of income among members of the society means that no one has been coerced into achieving that distribution.

T F 4. If an outcome is just, it must by definition receive unanimous consent by the participants.

T F 5. "To each according to his or her IQ" would not be a patterned principle of distribution.

T F 6. In a voluntary exchange economy, reasonable people can readily agree on what is just.

T F 7. The government in our society has a primary responsibility to see that "justice is done."

T F 8. The size of the economic pie is an efficiency question, not an ethical question.

T F 9. "Taxing the rich to feed the poor" would be a program that was just by everyone's standards.

T F 10. The entitlement theory of distributive justice would imply that if you had something, you were entitled to keep it.

19

The Organization of Collective Action

In many cases individuals find it advantageous to form political organizations to provide themselves with collective consumption goods and services. The rational individual must decide what is his or her most preferred *decision rule* for the initiation of political action. In our society the most common rule for making a political decision is simple majority. This is the rule we use to elect our Presidents, senators, representatives, and most other officials. We will assume that any individual in a political setting will act so as to minimize his or her expected *costs of social interdependence.* This means the costs of cooperation between and among individuals. We wish to examine, in a very general way, how an individual decides what activities he or she would agree to have collectivized and what activities should be left to the private sector. In an economy in which government is used to distribute some goods, any individual is faced with two differing sets of costs when he or she interacts with fellow citizens to determine the public-goods bundle. There are costs which the individual incurs from spending time and effort in reaching agreement with the other individuals *(decision-making costs)* and costs that arise from decisions made by the group that are contrary to our individual's best interest *(political externality costs).* We can explore the relationship of these interdependencies with the aid of a simple example of group behavior.

Let us assume that there exists some public good, argnots, that all ten members of a group positively value but that is not currently being provided by the voluntary exchange process of the market. Suppose that all ten individuals meet and decide that they want some argnots produced, and each is willing to organize the production by means of the political process. That is, the ten individuals will determine by voting how many argnots to produce and how the cost will be distributed among the members of the group. Let us focus on a single individual, Jay, and the costs that he expects to incur as a result of the actions of others. In this way we can isolate the decision-making rule that minimizes Jay's expected costs. Jay will note immediately that if he agrees to any decision rule that is short of unanimous consent, he may be exploited. That is, the possibility exists that the other nine individuals will decide to produce a level of argnots and/or to choose a tax level that he would not voluntarily agree to support. For example, if only four voters must agree, rather than all ten, on the argnot output level, then the level the group chooses is less likely to be Jay's preferred output level. The smaller the number of individuals that are required to take political actions, the greater the probability that Jay will have costs imposed upon him coercively. We can call the cost that Jay would incur when the political organization coerces him into participation in the production of argnots with which he does not agree, a *political externality cost.* This cost is obviously zero under the decision rule of unanimous consent, and the cost increases up to the rule that one of the ten may make a binding decision for the other nine. These relationships are depicted in Figure 19-1.

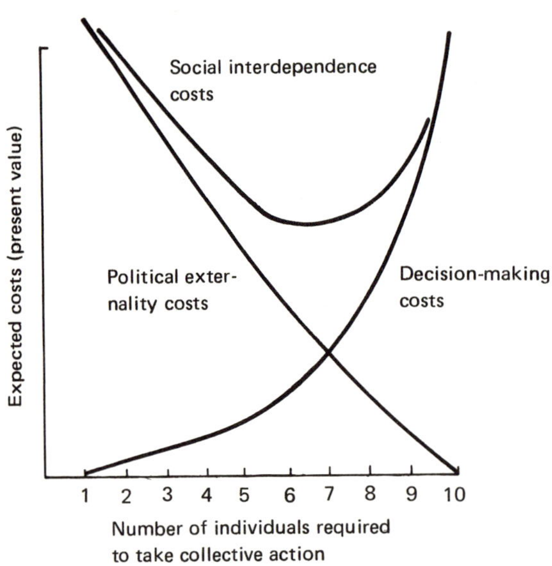

FIGURE 19-1 Jay's individual social interdependence costs

If the production of argnots is to be undertaken, however, someone must participate in the decision making. Any single individual, Jay, must incur some costs in reaching a decision; but if two or more individuals are required to reach a single decision, then time and effort of another sort are introduced, that is, the cost required to secure agreement. These costs increase as (1) the size of the group required to agree increases and/or (2) the opportunities for strategic bargaining increase. As the collective decision-making rule is changed to include more of the ten members, Jay's vote becomes more and more valuable as a way to extract gains from the others in the group. For example, if the decision rule is that *any* two individuals decide for the group, then if Jay asks for special favors in order to release his vote, the other members will try to get a positive vote from another member. However, with a unanimous decision rule, Jay's vote is a monopoly resource. These costs associated with the reaching of an agreement for collective action to be undertaken are called *decision-making costs.* These costs increase with the number of individuals included in the decision process. Figure 19-1 shows these costs for the individual Jay. To determine what decision rule is best in this case, Jay tries to minimize his costs. On the one hand, the larger the number needed to take action, the smaller his expected political externality costs, but the greater the expected decision-making costs. Therefore, he must find the decision rule that minimizes the sum of these costs. We call his summed costs from political decision making *social interdependence costs.* He will minimize his total costs of social action when a decision rule of 60 percent, or the agreement of six members, is adopted. He then expects to gain more from the political organization of argnot production than he would lose if this good were not provided for the group.

This decision of alternative decision-making rules assumes a framework within which individuals consider potential actions to be taken and then register their preferences in some manner, perhaps by voting. Even when the decision rule is agreed upon, it is still in the best interest of the individual to attempt to make sure that his preferences are dominant. Citizens at every level of government seek to influence their elected representatives to vote on issues in ways that will promote the citizens' best interests. For example, if as a student you contact your local state senator and seek her or his support for a bill that increases the level of state aid to higher education, you are a lobbyist.

KEY CONCEPTS

Median voter group The set of individuals who have views on a given issue that is in the middle of the political spectrum.

Voting rule An agreed-upon guide that determines the winning issue or candidate on the basis of a certain percentage of the votes cast.

Logrolling A process where individuals trade votes on issues in order to obtain a winning majority on their most desired political question.

Special interest group A subgroup of voters who share a common position on a political issue.

Federalism An organizational form of government where the powers of the collectivity are divided into many component units.

Social interdependence costs The costs of cooperation between and among individuals for their mutual benefit.

Decision-making costs The value of the effort, time, and expense (explicit and implicit) of reaching any decision.

Political externality costs The costs that an individual bears as a result of being in a minority position on any issue decided by the political process.

CASE 19:
Knowing the Influence Peddlers[1]

Since the political crisis of Watergate, Congress has focused more attention on making the political process more open. Toward the end of 1977, Congress once again considered the passage of legislation to tighten the loophole-ridden lobby registration rules. This attention to lobbying laws came at a time of widespread rumors and charges of corruption stemming from campaign contributions to members of Congress by the representatives of the Korean government. The federal campaign financing law required that contributors be identified by name, address, and occupation. The stated purpose of this disclosure law is to allow voters access to information that will aid them in determining the probable position of candidates on given issues.

Thousands of political action committees, corporations, labor unions and trade associations, lawyers, foreign agents, and political contributors pump millions of dollars each year into the electoral process to influence the outcome. If a citizen wanted to know what individual or group was providing financial support for his or her representative or senator, a directory published in 1975 would greatly aid in this task.

The *Washington Influence Directory* was compiled from public records on file with the Federal Election Commission covering campaign finance reports, from lobby registration forms filed with the Clerk of the House of Representatives, from foreign agent registrations filed with the U.S. Justice Department, and from witness lists of congressional committees. The directory works in this way: (1) if you have a contributor's name, the directory discloses his or her business affiliation; (2) if you have the name of a business, the directory will tell you its lobbying staff; and (3) in the case of lawyers and law firms, the directory will tell you for which clients they have lobbied within the last two years. For example, you can find out that the Good Government Fund, a political action committee, is run by Standard Oil of Indiana and that a group called Bipartisan Assistance for Local and National Candidates Election (BALANCE) is operated by the Bell-Aerospace Corporation. The directory has just short of 3000 such entries.

QUESTIONS

1 The key piece of information on the federal election disclosure forms would seem to be occupation, for if an individual is identified as a lobbyist, then he or she is known to represent some special interest group. It appears to be quite common

[1] Facts in this case are reprinted with permission from "Directory Identifies 2,800 Washington 'Influencers,'" *Editor and Publisher,* November 22, 1975, © 1975 *Editor and Publisher,* Inc.

for lawmakers, when filing disclosure reports, to identify lobbyists as executives and lawyers rather than to identify their special interest position. Why might members of Congress wish to hide the true identity of their contributors?

2 Assuming that Congress acts to shield the source of their financial support from the general voter, how would you assess the chances of their passing laws that would tighten the current federal campaign financing law?

3 It has been argued that a consequence of placing a dollar limit on the amount any individual or corporation can contribute to a given politician is to reduce the cost of "buying a political point of view" to the special interest groups. For example, it is argued that the gambling industry will still control the Nevada congressional delegation, but it will cost them less to do so. Evaluate this argument.

4 When the political process is used as the means of social organization to produce goods and services, is it not predictable that individuals and businesses would use economic persuasion to achieve their most preferred goods bundle? That is, couldn't you predict that Korean lobbyists would use dollars to try and persuade congressmen to vote for foreign aid to Korea? What, if any, should be the limits of this persuasion?

TEST YOURSELF

True—false

T F 1. It will become increasingly difficult to reach agreement on any single issue as the number of decision makers increases.

T F 2. Rational self-interest arguments would support the view that individuals will not try to swing public opinion in their favor.

T F 3. If the decision rule is one of unanimity, there can still be political externality costs for any given voter.

T F 4. Special interest groups work to pass laws favorable to their particular position.

T F 5. Nader's Raiders, Common Cause, and the National Association of Petroleum Importers would be examples of special interest groups.

T F 6. The most preferred voting rule for any individual will be at least a simple majority rule.

T F 7. Politicians, as the elected representatives of a particular group of individuals, will always act to pursue their constituents' best interests.

T F 8. In a democratic society, it is an easy matter for an elected official to find out what his or her constituents prefer.

T F 9. Influence peddling of all forms could be abolished by the passage of a new federal campaign financing law.

T F 10. Logrolling is a process where individuals trade votes on given issues to ensure passage of their most preferred single issue.

Matching

Select the term in the column at the left that best matches the statement in the column on the right. Not all the terms in the left column apply, and none is intended to be used twice.

A. Median voter
B. Special interest groups
C. Voting rules
D. Decision costs
E. External effects
F. Logrolling
G. Social interaction costs
H. Political externality costs
I. Democracy
J. Majority rule

___ 1. The value of the activity required to reach an agreement.

___ 2. A rule for decision making that states if an issue gets $(N/2 + 1)/N$ of the votes, it wins.

___ 3. Agreements that specify the conditions for taking political action.

___ 4. A class of individuals who have a particular bias on a given issue.

___ 5. Uncompensated interdependencies of action between individuals.

___ 6. The costs borne when the political organization coerces an individual to bear the costs of a position he or she does not support.

20

The Market for Local Public Goods

In private markets economic efficiency is achieved when an individual's marginal benefits from the consumption of goods and services equal the price and marginal cost of production. In the market for collective consumption goods, we know that price and quantity cannot generally be equal at the margin because of the nature of these goods and the problems of "free riding." Nevertheless, these concepts are still useful in describing characteristics that would be desirable in the organization of the local public sector. In the ideal unit of local government, the group of citizens benefiting from the public good would be those whose preferences were taken into account in the decision to provide that good *and* would be the group who paid for the good. This characteristic of a public-goods sharing group has come to be called *fiscal equivalence*.

What are the mechanisms or institutional structures, if any, that promote fiscal equivalence in the local government market? It is relatively easy to point out the features of public goods that make them difficult to be provided by private markets, but it is much more difficult to organize government so that demanded goods are provided efficiently. A major problem, of course, comes on the demand side. When citizens state their demands for goods in the public sector, it is done in the political arena. You *vote* on a budget which represents a bundle of public goods such as public schools, police protection, fire protection, and garbage collection.

You do not go out and purchase so many units of each service. Only if your preferences for the bundle of goods are identical to the preferences of the majority of the individuals in your community will you receive your preferred output level. If a government provides only one service, this will allow the taxpayer/voter to more closely state his or her preferences with respect to the given public good.

Equally difficult problems exist on the supply side of the local government market. In the vast majority of cases, the government is the monopoly supplier of a given public good whose output, costs, and benefits are virtually impossible to measure. For example, most cities provide for their residents the only fire protection services that the citizens consume (this does not mean that people do not buy fire extinguishers or alarms, only that they depend upon the local government for preventing or extinguishing fires in the community). Even if the citizen wants to know whether he or she is getting the best possible fire protection services for his or her tax dollars, it may be impossible to find out. Why? In order to evaluate the performance of any producer, public or private, there must be some basis for comparison. In the case of the fire department in your city, there are no competitors. Surely there are other cities, but they do not provide services to your property.

We know that if private producers are able to obtain monopoly franchises, then the output/pricing decisions will vary from those produced in the competitive market. However, resources will still be combined efficiently because these monopoly firms are still profit maximizers. We cannot infer the same efficiency condition for local government monopoly suppliers because they are *not* profit maximizers. It is argued that managers of city, county, or special district units of government will make the government's budget as large as possible in order to maximize their own income. However, under certain conditions the institutional structure of local government may reduce this monopoly power.

When there are many units of local government in an area, the taxpayer/citizen can "vote" against a unit of government by moving to a city whose goods bundle more closely approximates his or her preferences. If local government units are sufficiently fragmented in a metropolitan area, for example, the individual consumer can choose to reside in any of several cities without greatly affecting community costs. Competitive pressures would tend to force government managers to combine inputs in a least-cost manner and to provide the services that the majority of the residents desire. This result would occur because people would not choose initially, or would move out of, a city that had very high public-good costs relative to those of neighboring towns. For example, suppose the manager of city A combined inputs inefficiently and as a result fire services in city A were twice as costly, in terms of taxes levied, as those in city B. If everything else were the same in the two communities, people would leave city A and move to city B. In the extreme, if the city manager did not change his or her performance, he or she would lose the job because there would be no city. In addition, the citizen may alter the goods bundle by using the political process to remove city managers who do not provide the desired bundle of goods and services. Still another type of constraint that can be placed on the monopoly power of local government would involve alternative sources of services. When the city fire department is performing inadequately, according to your preferences, it is possible for you (and your neighbors) to hire private fire services to protect your property.

KEY CONCEPTS

Bureaucracy Subsections of government which are staffed by nonelected personnel.

Voting with one's feet The notion that an individual will change his or her place of residence in response to alternative policies of local government units.

Budget maximization The behavioral hypothesis that nonprofit managers seek to obtain the largest budget possible in order to maximize their personal gain.

Size maximization The behavioral hypothesis that nonprofit managers seek to make the size of their agency as large as possible as a way of increasing their personal gain.

Interjurisdictional spillovers The positive or negative external effects that a single unit of government bears as a result of an action taken by another unit of government.

Governmental fragmentation Many units of governments in a given territory with each unit providing services for its residents.

Governmental overlapping Many different levels of government may be providing the same types of service to a resident of a given community.

CASE 20:
Closing the Market for Local Government Units[1]

In 1963, the California legislature, acting for "... the discouragement of urban sprawl and the encouragement of the orderly formation and development of local government ...,"[2] radically altered the process by which new communities are formed. Prior to this time, California could have been characterized as a state with relatively free entry into the local government market. The 1963 Knox-Nisbet Act established the formation of Local Agency Formation Commissions (LAFCOs) in each California county and instructed these agencies to act so as to make the local government market more orderly by regulating entry into the "industry." The impact of the Knox-Nisbet Act was to grant to the existing units of government a complete veto power over new entrants into this market.

The central issue behind the enactment of this law is: What is the best pattern of local government for California? The proponents of the legislation argue that restricting entry will make local governments more efficient. Why? It is argued that the organization of local government, especially in metropolitan areas, prevents solutions in addition to causing problems. If we look at government units in metropolitan areas, we observe that many independent entities each provide services to their residents (this is called *fragmentation* of governments). In addition, alternative services are supplied by different units of government (this is termed *overlapping* of governments). For example, in Los Angeles County there are 76 cities, each providing unique government services to their residents, and at the same time services are being provided by Los Angeles County to residents of each city.

Supporters of the Knox-Nisbet Act feel that the fragmentation and overlapping structure of local government lead to a misallocation of resources in the public sector. This occurs because (1) services provided by one government are often enjoyed by residents of another city without their paying for the cost of provision (e.g., parks, zoos, museums), (2) cities are too small to take advantage of economies of scale, and (3) high information costs occur because residents must make decisions dealing with many government units. This suggests that a decrease in the number of units of government will allow the remaining governments to operate more efficiently, leading to decreases in spending levels.[3] One way to achieve this end is to decrease the establishment of new cities and expand the power of existing cities to increase in size (annexation of new territory).

[1] Facts in this case are reprinted with permission of Profs. Dolores T. Martin and Richard E. Wagner from their article "The Institutional Framework for Municipal Incorporation: An Economic Analysis of Local Agency Formation Commissions in California."

[2] Annotated California Code, § 54774.

[3] This prediction is based on actual evidence which suggests that the elasticity of demand for local public goods is less than 1 in absolute value.

An alternative view of the intertwining, overlapping, fragmented character of metropolitan area government is that this structure evolved in response to individual needs. The desires and preferences of individuals with respect to public as well as private goods vary greatly. Therefore, we could expect diversity in the units of government that respond to those needs. For example, elderly individuals may wish government to provide senior citizen centers and no public schools. Other groups could be expected to have different and perhaps conflicting desires for public goods. If diversity in services and units is a desirable feature of local governments, then what is the anticipated effect of making it much more costly to form a government to meet individual preferences? Suppose public sector managers behave the same as private sector entrepreneurs. In that case, the increased entry barriers will allow public sector managers to form a market-sharing cartel. (In terms of job description, there does not seem to be much difference between the tasks performed by the manager of a privately owned telephone company and those of a publicly owned electric power company.)

Public managers cannot take home any profits that arise in their operation of a city department. So how are they better off as a result of restricting entry to the local government market? The ability of the public sector manager to increase the power, prestige, and salary level of the office depends to a large extent upon the size of the budget he or she controls. The city manager of Chicago earns a higher salary than the city manager of Plains, Georgia. If local government managers want to increase the budgets under their control because this increases their salary, then one way to do this is to reduce the number of cities in existence. Economists who see no difference between public and private sector managers would view the increased barriers to entry as monopoly-enhancing. They see the Knox-Nisbet Act as providing a mechanism to enforce the establishment of a market-sharing cartel. According to this view, the 1963 change would lead to increases in total spending.

The anticipated impact of restricting the entry of new "firms" into the local government industry is quite different depending upon which of the above views you hold. The two perspectives yield generally different predictions as to what will happen to spending as a result of the change in the law. This is, of course, a question subject to real world examination. What did happen to public spending at the local level after the passage of the Knox-Nisbet Act?

An investigation of the likely factors that caused cities to be formed in California for the years 1962 and 1967 was conducted by economists Martin and Wagner. They estimated that LAFCO formation had significantly altered the number of local government units established. They estimated that LAFCOs could be credited with a 56 percent reduction in the rate of new community formation. *Thus, the act was effective in closing the market*. With regard to expenditure levels pre- and post-LAFCO, their study estimated that the level of public spending in 1967 would have been approximately 17 percent *lower* than it actually was, if *no change* in the legal structure had occurred.

QUESTIONS

1 What group or groups of individuals do you suppose were proponents of the passage of the Knox-Nisbet Act in California? For example, how do you think the position of the Urban League would differ from that taken by the Taxpayers Union?

2 If the structure of legal arrangements matters to the public-goods bundle that individuals receive at the local government level, then how might they matter to the bundle that is received at the state or federal level of government?

3 If governments can be treated as similar in behavior to firms in an industry, then what kinds of structural reforms might be warranted to make the governmental market more competitive? List at least five such reforms and be prepared to discuss the impact of the changes.

4 As a city manager, you keep your job only if the individuals who are elected to the city council are pleased with your performance. That is, you are not directly elected by the individual taxpayer/resident. If it is correct to assume that most elected officials come from the middle- and upper-income classes, how might that fact alter the kinds of local goods and services you as city manager provide for the city as a whole?

5 As cities grow larger and larger, it is argued that the level of citizen satisfaction with government falls, as well as the control the citizen feels he or she can exert over government. What will be the impact of the Knox-Nisbet Act on California cities if this hypothesis is correct? Why might you argue for its veracity?

TEST YOURSELF

True—false

T F 1. If everyone in a city had the same preferences with respect to the level of fire protection services, then this service would be provided efficiently by the city.

T F 2. One of the serious difficulties in providing public goods is that all individuals must necessarily consume the same output.

T F 3. New York City has a territorial monopoly in the provision of specific public goods.

T F 4. Competition among units of government means that each unit must take into consideration that its citizens may leave town if more attractive alternatives are available.

T F 5. City managers in cities with 500,000 people generally receive a higher salary than city managers in cities of 10,000.

T F 6. Provision of a public good by government means that government is the producer of that good.

T F 7. When taxpayer/citizens of city A provide a nice park on the edge of town and citizens of city B drive over and use the facility, this is an interjurisdictional spillover.

T F 8. People who live in the suburbs and "bedroom" communities surrounding St. Louis may receive the benefit of many public services without paying the taxes that support those services.

T F 9. When two previously separate cities combine (consolidate), it will be no more difficult for any single resident to make his or her preferences known about a given public good.

T F 10. When residents of New York City in the mid-1970s found that their government was in essence "bankrupt," aid was sought from the federal government to "save the city." This aid is an example of a fiscal equivalence transfer.

Matching

Select the term in the left column that best matches the statement in the right column. Not all terms in the left column apply, and none is intended to be used twice.

A. Fiscal equivalence
B. Monopoly power
C. Interjurisdictional spillovers
D. Fragmented government
E. Overlapping government
F. Bureaucracy
G. Size maximization
H. Voting with one's feet
I. Free-rider problems
J. Budget maximization

___ 1. The ability to survive in a market without facing competition.
___ 2. Manager's actions that increase the scope of her or his agency's activities.
___ 3. A service of government being provided by many different units.
___ 4. Costs of public-goods provision that are borne by nonresidents.
___ 5. Receiving a good even if you do not pay the price of providing it.
___ 6. Making those who benefit from and desire a public good pay for it.

21

Creation of Money

One of the more important institutions in our economy was created by the Federal Reserve Act, signed by President Woodrow Wilson on December 23, 1913. The act established the Federal Reserve System (the Fed). The Fed was established as an answer to the many problems in the banking system which occurred in the late 1800s and early 1900s. The Fed is the central bank of the United States that roughly corresponds in its operations to the Bank of England or the Bank of France. The purposes cited in the original Federal Reserve Act for the creation of a central bank were, first, to provide the country with a currency flexible enough to meet its demands and, second, to supervise the system of banks. The Employment Act of 1946 in a way extended the powers of the Federal Reserve and required it to also pay close attention to the levels of employment, production, growth, and inflation in the economy. While the Employment Act of 1946 created the Council of Economic Advisors to aid the President in these four matters, the Federal Reserve is often called upon to scrutinize them as well.

In large part the gold discoveries in South Africa and Alaska in the late nineteenth century caused rapid expansions in the money supply in the United States and rather sharp increases in the rate of inflation. These disturbances in the financial markets often preceded periods of economic downturn. In the 100 years before the institution of the Federal Reserve, there were at least six major financial panics or business recessions (in 1819, 1837, 1857, 1873, 1884, and 1907). All these panics were characterized by the single feature that citizens of the United States desired to convert one form of money into another kind of money. At times it was a desire to convert bank notes into gold, and at other times it was a desire to exchange bank deposits for United States currency. Once many people simultaneously decided to change one form of money for another, the banks were unable to accommodate the demands and would often have to suspend either gold payments or United States currency payments. This action would produce a fall in the value of bank notes because individuals would trade the notes at a discount; thus, a reduction in the money supply and often a major economic recession would follow. After the panic of 1907, Congress passed the Currency Act of 1908, which established a National Monetary Commission to recommend to Congress some improvements in the financial markets. The outcome of the commission's findings was the Federal Reserve.

The Federal Reserve System is composed of twelve regional reserve banks and a board in Washington whose members are appointed by the President and confirmed by the Senate. The seven members of the Board of Governors serve 14-year terms, reside in Washington, and meet almost daily at the Board of Governors' building. They have full authority over all the principal monetary actions of the Fed.

The Federal Open Market Committee consists of the seven members of the Board of Governors and five of the presidents of the twelve regional reserve banks. The Federal Open Market Committee has the responsibility of formulating open market policy. *Open market operations* involve changing the dollar amount of bank reserves by buying and selling treasury securities. This committee meets every three or four weeks in Washington for an entire day during which the committee members are briefed on recent developments in financial markets, are given forecasts of future developments, and then are required to decide upon alternative monetary strategies. The committee sends a directive to the manager of the open market account, who is located in New York City and who has the daily responsibility of executing domestic securities transactions. The meetings of the Federal Open Market Committee and its directives to the manager of the open market account are private and confidential at the time they are taken. Summaries of the meetings and copies of the directive are published only 90 days after each meeting.

In addition to open market operations, the Federal Reserve System has two other tools which it commonly employs to manipulate the reserves of the banking system and the amount of demand deposits which they can support. The first of these tools is the *reserve requirement* for member banks; this reserve requirement is a percentage of the deposits which banks have on hand that must be held as legal reserves. Those items which are included as legal reserves by banks are specified clearly by the Federal Reserve System. The second tool which the Federal Reserve uses to manipulate the money supply is called *discounting*. Members banks may, at times, borrow from the Federal Reserve System. The interest rate which the system charges the member banks is called the *discount rate*. By raising or lowering the discount rate, the Federal Reserve may encourage or discourage member banks from borrowing. Clearly, raising either the reserve requirement or the discount rate would reduce the ability of banks to make new loans and thereby decrease the money supply. A lower discount rate or a lower reserve rate would make new loans more attractive to banks and thereby increase the money supply.

KEY CONCEPTS

Federal Reserve System The central bank of the United States. Its primary function is to create an efficient financial system to promote the goals of the economy.

Employment Act of 1946 The act which sets forth the goals of the economy as full employment, stable prices, economic growth, and equilibrium in the balance of payments.

FOMC (Federal Open Market Committee) This body is charged with all domestic and international security operations.

Reserve requirements The percentage of deposits which a bank must hold as a reserve against deposit liabilities. These reserves are normally held in the form of cash or as a deposit at the regional Federal Reserve bank.

Discount rate The percentage interest rate which the regional Federal Reserve bank charges member banks for temporarily borrowing reserves.

Open market operations The day-to-day buying and selling of government securities by the Fed in order to affect the reserves of the banking system.

Reserves Cash held in a bank's vault, plus the bank's deposit with the regional Federal Reserve bank.

Required reserves The smallest amount of reserves that a bank may keep to support its deposits.

Money Demand deposits (checking accounts) plus currency and coin in the hands of the public. *Note:* Some economists would include time deposits (savings accounts) as part of money.

CASE 21:
Want to Buy a Bank?[1]

The United States today has about 14,000 banks. Of these, about 6000 are members of the Federal Reserve System. Most of the remaining banks are chartered by the states in which they do business and are subject to state bank examinations. Both the members of the Federal Reserve System and the state-chartered banks are required to adhere to many of the rules and regulations of the Federal Reserve System. The Federal Reserve's open market operations, reserve requirement ratios, and discount rates affect in one way or another almost every one of the 14,000 or so banks in the United States.

When Congress instituted the Federal Reserve, it was not the first time that congressional action had been taken to ensure orderliness in the financial markets of the United States. In 1791, Congress chartered the First Bank of the United States. This bank was privately owned and was authorized to perform many of the duties which today are associated with the Federal Reserve System. It issued bank notes which circulated freely as money throughout the United States. For a number of reasons, including a fear of centralized power, Congress did not renew the bank's 20-year charter when it expired. In the early nineteenth century, many state banks generated large supplies of bank notes. Each of these notes issued by a single bank was often not accepted in areas which were geographically removed from the issuing bank. Indeed, counterfeiting of these bank notes and attempts to circulate the counterfeit bank notes outside the immediate geographical area of the issuing bank were not uncommon in the United States in the 1800s. A booming business was created which supplied banks with catalogs containing facsimiles of notes issued by all the banks in the United States. These books were used to match facsimiles and actual notes in order to protect against such counterfeiting. However, the system of competing bank notes grew rather cumbersome, and in 1816 Congress chartered the Second Bank of the United States.

This bank again introduced a standard currency which was acceptable throughout the entire country, and it curbed the rather rapid expansion of bank notes by routinely collecting such bank notes and presenting them for redemption to the issuing banks. In this way, the Second Bank of the United States rather effectively regulated the nation's money supply. The demise of the Second Bank of the United States, however, was near, and even though Congress voted to renew the bank's charter, President Jackson vetoed the bill for much the same reason as for the nonrenewal of charter of the First Bank of the United States.

[1] Facts in this case are used with the permission of *The Wall Street Journal*. See "You Have a Friend at the Leroy Bank—The Owner Himself," *The Wall Street Journal*, May 9, 1977, p. 1. Reprinted with permission of *The Wall Street Journal*,

In 1863 Congress passed the National Bank Act which provided for the chartering of national banks subject to minimum standards. These banks were given the power to issue standardized, national bank notes. At the same time, Congress levied a tax on the bank notes issued by other banks, again curtailing the rapid expansion of bank notes by independent, nonregulated banks. The National Bank Act of 1863, then, reintroduced a national currency. It did not, however, solve the problem which occurs when individuals want to transfer assets from one type of money into another type of money. The panic of 1907 was the result of a refusal by banks to convert deposits into currency on demand. Bank customers had defaulted on their loans, and a run on the banks developed. This time, in 1907, the desire was not so much to turn deposits into gold as it was in previous runs, but to acquire the national currency. Bank checks began circulating at much less than face value, and banks began to charge 100 percent interest daily on callable loans. A number of institutions failed, and the National Monetary Commission was convened to make recommendations for the improvement of the financial structure of the United States.

Today almost all banks are regulated by the Federal Reserve, by the Comptroller of the Currency, and/or by state banking authorities. A few banks, however (fourteen, to be exact), remain private banks. Four of these banks are located in Texas, and the other ten are in Iowa, Pennsylvania, Connecticut, and New York. Most of these banks are so small that the Federal Reserve System has indicated that it has never heard of them. The Leroy Bank in Leroy, Texas, is one of these private banks. It has never been audited by bank examiners, and it doesn't publish statements of its assets and liabilities as all state-chartered and federally chartered banks are required to do. It does not carry deposit insurance with the Federal Deposit Insurance Corporation, and if some modern-day Bonnie and Clyde should ever decide to rob the old, wooden building, the FBI would not investigate. The Leroy Bank is a private bank, and it underscores this status by calling itself Leroy Bank Unincorporated.

In addition to escaping the rigors of bank regulation, private banks do not have to pay premiums to the Federal Deposit Insurance Corporation to insure their depositors. The banks themselves are legally liable for the money left with them. You won't be seeing many more of these banks in the near future, however. Fifty of the private banks have closed down over the past decade, and every state now prohibits new private banks from opening. These banks are the holdovers from a bygone era.

While most of the private banks are rather small, there is at least one gigantic private bank, and this is New York's Brown Brothers, Harriman, and Co. with deposits of over $424 million. The treasurer of Brown Brothers, Harriman, and Co. has indicated that Federal Deposit Insurance Corporation coverage for its depositors would be rather nonsensical, because the FDIC insurance has a $40,000 limit, which would be miniscule compared to the size of most of the corporate deposits held by the bank. Brown Brothers feels it has an edge in the competition with other banks, because any one of its twenty-seven partners can approve a loan on the spot. It is unnecessary to work through committees to approve loans, and there aren't any shareholders to be responsible to, because the private bankers are lending their own money. Problems can arise, however, with these private banks, such as occurred in January 1977 with the Cain Banking Company in Winnsboro, Texas.

Melvin Cain, the president of the private Cain Banking Company, allowed many local businesses in Winnsboro, Texas, to make overdrafts totaling $2 million. These overdrafts could not be repaid, and so after apologizing to his customers and rewriting his will to make the bank his beneficiary, Cain committed suicide. In this particular situation, the 3500 depositors who had placed $4.5 million in the Cain Banking Company aren't likely to recover more than $0.50 on the dollar.

QUESTIONS

1 Most individuals today find the Federal Reserve System to be an unquestionably necessary form of government regulation. Current conventional wisdom is that control over the money supply is an important tool for "tuning" the economy. The task of generating the correct supply of money in the United States has been allocated to the government in the form of the Federal Reserve. How large should this money supply be? The simple answer is that we should have enough money so that we can buy all the goods and services that the economy is able to turn out. With too little money, we will have unemployment and idle machinery. With too much money, we will have rapid inflation and no more real goods and services. The correct money supply, then, is just enough money to generate enough spending so that we have full employment and stable prices. Could such a "correct" supply of money be generated without the use of a central bank, such as the Federal Reserve System, and alternatively could we rely on private banks alone?

2 During the era of the private banks, there were at least six major financial panics, or recessions, in the 1800s and another in 1907. Since the establishment of the Federal Reserve System in 1913, there has been only one *major* recession in the United States, that commonly called the Great Depression. One might be expected to conclude, then, from the evidence that private banks were not able to ensure the "correct" money supply in the economy, but that the Federal Reserve System has certainly done, if not a perfect, a better job than the private banks.

More than one economist has questioned this line of reasoning, pointing out that the Federal Reserve System decreased the money supply rather drastically during the Great Depression. This is the very period in which most economists would indicate that an increase in the money supply would be in order if the monetary authority wished to act countercyclically. These same economists point out that the bank panics of the nineteenth and early twentieth centuries, such as the panic of 1907, caused a suspension in the convertability of deposits into either currency or gold. This, they feel, was not necessarily such a bad thing to have happen at that time. It did prevent the failure of a few banks from producing runs on each of the other banks in the financial system. In a short time, after the situation had normalized, the suspension of convertability could be lifted, and a recovery could be initiated without the sort of monetary contraction which occurred in the 1930s during the Great Depression. Assume, then, that the banking system, as we now know it, is abolished. The Federal Reserve System is disbanded, and private banks, like the Leroy Bank and the Cain Banking Company, are once again allowed to be chartered in the United States. Would there be any reason to believe that such a private banking system, unregulated and uninsured by either federal or state governments, would be superior in its self-regulation of financial markets, relative to the Federal Reserve System?

3 Certainly, one of the more important problems with the private banks in the 1800s was that of counterfeit bank notes. Another problem, perhaps even more serious than counterfeiting, is exemplified by Melvin Cain's $2 million dollar overdraft allowance (the economic equivalent to counterfeiting). Since, in a private banking system, there is no fractional reserve requirement, such as the Federal Reserve has now, it is possible for banks to engage in the economic equivalent of counterfeiting. Would you expect counterfeiting, or the economic equivalent of counterfeiting, to be rampant if a private banking system were to exist today? Is there any reason to believe that the economic equivalent of counterfeiting (overdrafts) would be in some way self-limiting in the system?

4 The Federal Open Market Committee (FOMC) of the Federal Reserve System certainly exercises the most powerful of the monetary tools of the Fed. By buying and selling government securities, the FOMC is able to reduce or increase the reserves of banks almost instantaneously. In turn, these banks are forced to either increase or decrease the amounts of their deposits almost as quickly. In such a manner, the money supply can be altered in a rather short time. Would there be any flexibility in the money supply with a private banking system? Recall that one of the reasons stated in the Federal Reserve Act for the institution of the Federal Reserve System was to create an "elastic currency." An elastic currency is one which increases and decreases with the needs of the financial system.

5 The FOMC does not disclose its directives to the manager of the federal open market account, nor does it publish the minutes of its meetings until at least 90 days after the fact. This means that at any point analysts do not have a statement from this most powerful of Fed bodies, clearly and precisely indicating its desire to either increase or decrease the money supply by a given magnitude. The reason often given for this secrecy in Fed operations is that unscrupulous individuals could profit by foreknowledge of the Fed's actions.

Some economists, however, have indicated that the Fed should publish its intentions in the form of a monetary rule. This monetary rule would be stated as the percentage increase in the money supply which the Fed would execute each year. The Fed would then have no arbitrary power to alter the rate of change in the money supply, either up or down. Since this rule would be well publicized, all individuals, banks, and institutions would be aware that the money supply would increase at a constant rate for the foreseeable future. Could individuals or institutions profit from foreknowledge, given a monetary rule like that described above? What might be the advantage of such a monetary rule when compared to the arbitrary power of the Federal Reserve Open Market Committee to increase or decrease the money supply at will?

TEST YOURSELF

Multiple-choice

1 Each of the following is a tool used by the Fed to control the money supply *except*

(a) Open market operations
(b) The reserve requirement
(c) Collateral requirements
(d) The discount rate

2 The Federal Reserve System was originally instituted to

(a) Provide a monetary system which could expand and control
(b) Provide revenue for the Treasury
(c) Insure banks against robbery and natural disasters
(d) Offset government fiscal policy

3 The elasticity of the money supply prior to 1913 (when the Fed was created) depended largely upon

(a) The whims of the Treasury
(b) Gold discoveries
(c) The market rate of interest
(d) The rate of inflation

4 A panic (in the economic sense) may occur when

(a) Prices rise more quickly than incomes
(b) The money supply increases rapidly
(c) Banks cannot convert one form of money into another form
(d) The Fed engages in large open market operations

5 Which of the following is *not* considered to be part of the money supply?

(a) Federal Reserve notes in your pocket
(b) Quarters, dimes, and nickels in your pocket
(c) The balance in your checking account
(d) The amount you may charge on your Visa card

6 When the Fed reduces the reserve requirement for member banks,

(a) The banks may increase loans, thus increasing the money supply
(b) The banks may make fewer loans, thus decreasing the money supply
(c) The banks will most likely make no adjustments to loans outstanding

7 When the Federal Reserve Open Market Committee orders the manager of the open market account to sell government securities, it is probably trying to

(a) Reduce the money supply
(b) Increase the money supply
(c) Make money for the Treasury
(d) Prevent a bank panic

8 The discount rate is set by the Fed and refers to

(a) The rate at which member banks may make loans to their customers
(b) The rate at which the Fed lends to member banks
(c) The rate at which member banks make loans to the Fed
(d) The interest rate on government securities

9 Private banks are those which are not members of the Federal Reserve System and which are not subject to state banking regulations.

(a) The number of private banks is rapidly growing today.
(b) Private banks are among the most important financial institutions in the United States today.
(c) Private banking flourished in the 1800s in the United States.

Matching

Select the term in the left column that best matches the statement in the right column. Not all terms in the left column may apply, and none is intended to be used twice.

A. Money
B. FOMC
C. Federal Reserve System
D. Board of Governors
E. Reserves

___ 1. Is charged with creating orderly financial markets
___ 2. Cash in vault plus deposits at the Fed
___ 3. Coin, currency, and demand deposits
___ 4. Pinnacle of Fed hierarchy
___ 5. Buys and sells United States government securities

22

Inflation

Most individuals familiar with watching the evening news with Walter Cronkite or Harry Reasoner or whomever are used to hearing announcements that the cost of living has gone up by seven-tenths of a percent in the month of July or eight-tenths of a percent in the month of August, and so on. The cost of living is important to us all because yearly each of us purchases thousands of items and the cost of living is a measure of how much of our income we will have to expend for those items.

The commonly accepted way for an individual to follow changes in the cost of living is the Consumer Price Index (CPI). This statistic is produced by the Bureau of Labor Statistics, a part of the United States Department of Labor. It measures how the price level changes over time (*inflation* is the term used for generally *rising* prices). Businesses and workers pay particular attention to the Consumer Price Index because they realize that wage contracts asking for percentage increases smaller than the amount of inflation actually leave workers worse off than they were the previous year. If a worker receives an increase in income less than the rate of inflation, the worker's *real income* (that is, the income adjusted for inflation) is said to have gone down. Many companies these days provide *escalator* clauses in their contracts which provide for automatic changes in wage rates in accordance with changes in the Consumer Price Index.

The Bureau of Labor Statistics began computing "cost of living" indices in 1919. In more recent years the Bureau of Labor Statistics has sought help in computing various indices from the American Statistical Association and the National Bureau of Economic Research. The calculation of the CPI today begins with the definition of a "market basket" of goods and services. The Bureau of Labor Statistics obtains the cost of this market basket as of January 1968, and this represents the base for the Consumer Price Index. If the market basket of goods (which might include items such as milk, shoes, shirts, bread, etc.) cost $1000 in January 1968, this is considered to be the base. In each time period following January 1968, when the CPI is calculated, the Bureau of Labor Statistics again adds the prices of all those items in the market basket (note that the quantities and items in the market basket do not change radically over time) and compares this figure with the January 1968 figure.

For instance, if the market basket costs $1000 in January 1968 and by January 1970 that same market basket of goods costs $1020, the Consumer Price Index would be $1020 \div 1000 \times 100 = 102$ percent. Now the actual calculation of the Consumer Price Index by the Bureau of Labor Statistics is actually slightly more complicated since it deals with various localities in the United States, because market baskets of goods change slightly over time (men's pajamas, for instance, were recently taken out of the market basket of goods because it appears that men no longer wear pajamas in the United States) and because the CPI deals with a large population rather than a single consumer.

Inflation in the year 1974, as measured by change in the Consumer Price Index, reached the rather high level of 10.4 percent. In periods before 1974 and since 1974, the rate of inflation has gone both up and down. Since 1974 prices have continued to rise, but the *rate* of increase accelerates and decelerates; that is, the rate of inflation has both increased and decreased in various months since 1974. It is this variation in the rate of inflation which causes so many individuals difficulty in coping with inflation. Most people find it rather difficult to spend money or make investments when they have no idea what the rate of inflation is going to be for the foreseeable future. One economist has likened the inflation situation to individuals playing a chess game where the rules at the beginning of the game are the standard rules for any chess game. After the first five moves are played, however, a referee steps onto the scene and changes the rules. For instance, the referee might say, "From now on rooks will be allowed to move as bishops and knights will be allowed to move as pawns." The players then continue playing the game for another five moves, at which point the referee steps in again and says that for the rest of the game kings will be able to move as queens and pawns will be able to move as rooks. Arbitrarily changing the rules of a game like chess places the players in roughly the same situation as consumers and investors in an economy where the rate of inflation is changing both up and down and rather unpredictably.

In periods of unanticipated inflation, for instance, investors may be induced to place their money in rather speculative ventures because these may be the only investments available which will offer a high enough return to guarantee the investors a profit, should the rate of inflation be rather high. In the absence of inflation or in the absence of unanticipated inflation, investors may have chosen much less risky projects. Unanticipated inflation, then, distorts the way in which investors might invest. In much the same way, unanticipated inflation may distort the purchases of consumers. Consumers may also turn to rather speculative methods for holding their savings, and sometimes they are "taken to the cleaners" in the process. The recent consumer interest in gold, diamonds, and exotic cars might be attributed to this kind of savings by consumers.

The link present in most market economies between effort and reward is often severed, then, by unanticipated inflation. Investors may make distorted decisions, and consumers may make distorted decisions. The costs of inflation are the losses to the economy of making these, perhaps, very poor decisions. Serious inflation (that is, a rapidly rising price level) leaves investors and consumers like the players in the chess game—apprehensive, insecure, and unsure that anything in the future will significantly change the situation.

KEY CONCEPTS

Inflation A *general* rise in the prices of goods and services (note that not *every* price must increase for there to be inflation; some prices may actually *decrease* in periods of inflation).

Stagflation The existence of both inflation and unemployment at the same time.

Recession A small downturn (decrease) in output and employment.

Depression A large or prolonged downturn (decrease) in output and employment.

Unanticipated inflation A general rise in the prices of goods and services not expected by consumers and investors.

Real wages The amount of goods and services which can be purchased with the money earned *or* the money earned adjusted for the rate of inflation.

Money wages The nominal amount of money earned *or* the money earned unadjusted for inflation.

Consumer Price Index (CPI) A measure of the general level of prices calculated by purchasing a market basket of goods at specific points in time. The changes in the CPI are a measure of the rate of inflation.

Indexing Adjusting wages and salaries, terms of contracts, tax bills, etc., to the rate of inflation (e.g., if a wage contract specifies that wages would increase 10 percent when the CPI increased by 10 percent, the contract is said to be indexed).

Nominal Expressed without adjustment for inflation (e.g., nominal wages, nominal price, nominal spending, etc.).

CASE 22:
The Capitol Hill Babysitting Cooperative[1]

It is not only the Board of Governors of the Federal Reserve System in Washington, D.C., which is being blamed for inflation in the United States. Another one of Washington's splendid institutions, the Capitol Hill Babysitting Cooperative, is fighting its own battle against inflation. For some very simple reasons neither institution seems to be winning.

The Capitol Hill Babysitting Cooperative is an institution which allows members to trade time which they spend babysitting for the services of a babysitter at a different time. Each family which is a member of the babysitting cooperative receives a given amount of "scrip," which are pieces of heavy paper. This scrip, which is actually like money, buys babysitting time; and the price of babysitting is fixed by agreement at one unit ("dollar") of scrip money for every half-hour of babysitting.

A few years ago the cooperative had what could reasonably be called a recession. Very few people wanted to go out and use the services of a babysitter, but many people wanted to babysit and receive scrip payment. In the more recent past, the situation has been almost the opposite. Individuals who wish to go out and use the services of a babysitter have had great difficulty in locating individuals willing to babysit for scrip. This latter situation is the classic situation of inflationary pressure: too much money (scrip) chasing too few goods (babysitters).

During the recessionary period of the babysitting cooperative, it appears there was a shortage of scrip. There was so little scrip that people who held it didn't want to go out and spend it. Those people who wanted to go out but didn't have any scrip found it difficult to get babysitting jobs. Now, note that this is a special case of a recession because the scrip price of babysitting could not adjust because of the fixed-by-agreement price of one unit of scrip for every half-hour of babysitting. The only thing that could happen was that the shortage worsened. The shortage became so bad, in fact, that the cooperative was forced to pass a rule saying that everyone must go out at least once every 6 months and use the services of a babysitter. The reason for such a rule was that some members of the babysitting cooperative were shirking. That is, they were not going out enough, and thus other members of the babysitting cooperative who wanted to go out but could not earn scrip were forced to stay home. The management of the babysitting cooperative felt that this sort of behavior was antisocial, and hence the bylaws were changed to discourage hoarding of scrip by staying home.

It should not be too surprising to most individuals that this change in the bylaws did not really solve the problem. The babysitting cooperative was finally

[1] Facts in this case are reprinted with permission of Joan Sweeney and Richard James Sweeney from their article "Monetary Theory and the Great Capitol Hill Babysitting Coop Crisis," *Journal of Money, Credit and Banking,* pp. 87–89, February 1977.

forced to take another action. In fact, it was forced to engage in what economists would call *monetary policy.* Old members of the cooperative were given 10 more hours of scrip while new members were given 30 hours of scrip when they joined but were required to pay back only 20 when they left the cooperative. As many economists might predict, when the money supply was increased in this way, a balance was arrived at between those who wanted to go out and those who wanted to babysit. What the rule requiring everyone to go out at least every 6 months had failed to do, monetary policy did. This equilibrium, however, of those who wanted to go out and those who wanted to babysit did not last very long.

After a time the situation reverted back to the recession which the cooperative had faced in earlier years. That is, few people wanted to go out, but many people wanted to babysit. The reason the cooperative went from a period of balance to a period of recession lies in the intricacies of how the management was "paid." It seems that every family who was a member paid dues to the management of the cooperative in the sum of two scrip "dollars" per month. The individuals in the cooperative who acted as the management, however (these were actually "monthly secretaries" who rotated the job of trying to fill requests for babysitters), were actually paid in scrip *less* than the amount they were taking in as dues. This meant that *over time the amount of scrip in circulation was slowly decreasing.* As the amount of scrip slowly decreased, the cooperative worked itself into the situation at which it began, that of a recession (or too little scrip).

QUESTIONS

1 The Capitol Hill Babysitting Cooperative is actually an economy with its own money and a single product (babysitting services). If the monthly secretaries of the babysitting cooperative were paid by merely printing new scrip money rather than by forcing members to pay two scrip "dollars" per month, what might happen to the money supply in this small economy? Would this change in money supply have any effect on the number of families willing to babysit as opposed to the number of families who might want to go out?

2 In the Capitol Hill Babysitting Cooperative, the price of babysitting is fixed by agreement at one unit of scrip per half-hour of babysitting. This is essentially the same as a government price control in the real economy, such as the one instituted in August 1971 by President Nixon. The price control in the Capitol Hill Babysitting Cooperative could be expected to have roughly the same effect on that economy as the price controls set by President Nixon in August 1971 had on the United States economy. Consider that the amount of scrip in circulation in the babysitting cooperative increases rather rapidly in a short time. If prices are fixed (as they actually are in the Capitol Hill Babysitting Cooperative), what would you expect to be the likely result? Would this same result occur in the United States economy if prices were fixed and the money supply was increasing at a rather rapid rate? Explain.

3 Since the price of babysitting is fixed in the Capitol Hill Babysitting Cooperative and since the definition of inflation is generally rising prices, is it possible that there could ever be inflation in the Capitol Hill Babysitting Cooperative's economy? Explain.

4 In Chapter 11 price controls were seen at times to lead to black markets in an economy. Would there be any tendency in either the recessionary periods or inflationary periods experienced by the Capitol Hill Babysitting Cooperative toward the formation of a black market? If the black market were to form, what sort of "service" would you expect it to provide to members of the cooperative?

5 The Federal Reserve System conducts monetary policy for the United States economy and the management of the Capitol Hill Babysitting Cooperative conducts monetary policy for that small economy. Explain how monetary policy in these two different situations amounts to much the same thing.

6 The management of the Capitol Hill Babysitting Cooperative acts as the Federal Reserve does because it increases and decreases the amount of scrip (money) in circulation. This is not unlike the Federal Reserve's controlling monetary policy in the United States economy. Is there any reason to believe that the management of the Capitol Hill Babysitting Cooperative will engage in the "right" monetary policy for that small economy? Are there incentives which lead the management to make the "correct" monetary policy decisions? Is there any reason to believe that the Board of Governors of the Federal Reserve System of the United States will make the "correct" decisions of monetary policy?

TEST YOURSELF

Multiple-choice

1 Inflation is a situation in which (**a**) all prices are rising, (**b**) prices, in general, are rising, (**c**) wages are rising, (**d**) the money supply is increasing.

2 Real wages are (**a**) only earned wages, (**b**) wages adjusted for inflation, (**c**) wages less individual expenses.

3 A term describing a general decrease in output and employment is (**a**) recession, (**b**) crest, (**c**) trough, (**d**) boom.

4 Deflation is (**a**) a situation in which all prices are falling, (**b**) a drop in purchasing power, (**c**) a situation in which prices, in general, are falling, (**d**) a rise in prices.

True–false

Read the following statements and note whether each is true or false.

T F 1. Inflation inhibits investing.

T F 2. Deflation is a decrease in purchasing power.

T F 3. In a recession, unemployment is high.

T F 4. In a boom, unemployment is low.

T F 5. Price and wage controls effectively eliminate inflation.

T F 6. Monetary policy can be used to control inflation.

T F 7. If a person's nominal wages are increasing, his or her real income is also necessarily increasing.

T F 8. Voluntary wage and price controls (guidelines) are very effective.

T F 9. If the Consumer Price Index is at 150, the purchasing power of $1 in the base year is $0.48.

T F 10. A recession can be caused by too little money in circulation.

23

Unemployment

In Chapter 22 we examined a measure of total (called *aggregate* by economists) performance for the economy, inflation. *Macro*economists, who study the *entire* economy, are also interested in another measure of total economy performance—the unemployment rate. Along with the rate of inflation, the unemployment rate is commonly quoted as a measure of the "health" of the national economy.

In this chapter we'll discuss unemployment to see how it is calculated and what it means. In terms of the individual, unemployment can mean hardship for the worker and his or her family. On the national level, large numbers of unemployed individuals mean that many resources (not just people) are being underused or left idle—and it means that the economy as a whole may be suffering.

When economists study unemployment, they distinguish between three different types of unemployment: structural unemployment, frictional unemployment, and cyclical unemployment.

Structural unemployment occurs because individual workers do not "fit" the available jobs in the economy. As an economy changes over time, certain skills will become more valuable, new skills will be needed, and some skills may become obsolete. Any shift in the skills needed in the economy will most likely result in some individuals being structurally unemployed. That is, too few jobs will be available for workers with certain skills. Many blacksmiths had to find new jobs as the Model

T became popular and widespread. Structural unemployment, in the sense that it is caused by the rules set up by society, may also be caused by laws which government imposes on the labor market, such as the minimum wage law. With a minimum wage law, some businesses which would otherwise hire employees at wages below the minimum may curtail employment.

Frictional unemployment is a consequence of incomplete information in a labor market. Often workers will not be aware of jobs presently available, or employers will not be aware of individuals seeking jobs. In such a situation, individuals may remain out of work for short periods while they search for the openings which are available in the economy. Frictionally unemployed workers may be thought of as being "between jobs."

Cyclical unemployment derives its name from business cycles. Business cycles may be thought of as patterns of upward and downward movement in the level of economic activity in an economy. As an economy decreases its level of activity, it can be thought of as moving down in terms of aggregate demand for goods and services. In such a situation, businesses might be expected to lay off or fire some workers; thus unemployment would rise. Cyclical unemployment is different from structural or frictional unemployment. Workers who are cyclically unemployed are unable to find jobs, not because they lack complete information or because they do not have the requisite skills, but because the demand for labor has declined.

The actual calculation of the unemployment rate is made from the Census Bureau's monthly survey of approximately 50,000 households. In official language, the term *unemployed* refers to anyone who is not working currently but who has actively looked for a job sometime in the preceding 4 weeks. An employed individual is anyone who is a paid employee, excluding the institutional population of the inmates in mental hospitals and prisons. The unemployment rate is always quoted by the government as a percentage of the labor force. The labor force includes all individuals in the noninstitutional population who are 16 years of age and older who are either working or actively looking for jobs. Thus the labor force equals the sum of employed individuals and unemployed persons (labor force = employed + unemployed and seeking work). Another important consideration concerning unemployment is the official definition of participation rate. The percentage of the entire adult population, that is, noninstitutionalized individuals 16 years or older who are in the labor force, is called the *participation rate*.

Although full employment would theoretically be 100 percent employment of the labor force, the employment statistics have never actually recorded the situation where 100 percent of the labor force was employed. In fact, since World War II in only a few periods has the unemployment rate dropped below 4 percent. In no period since World War II has the unemployment rate reached a figure lower than 3 percent.

It is not overly simplistic to say that economists have different views about the causes and cures for unemployment. One view of unemployment indicates that it results from insufficient aggregate demand, and thus the solution to unemployment is to stimulate aggregate demand which will in turn increase employment. Alternatively, another viewpoint of unemployment hinges on an analysis of the microeconomics of unemployment. This view indicates that long-run unemployment is a result of peculiarities in the various labor markets. These peculiarities prevent real wage rates from falling to their equilibrium levels, where the number of workers demanded by employers would equal the number of individuals willing to work. This view states that examples of such peculiarities are minimum wage laws and union contracts. Both these peculiarities inhibit wage rates from falling in general. Lack of information in the labor market is also cited as a reason why wage rates tend not to fall.

KEY CONCEPTS

Unemployment rate The percentage of the labor force actively seeking but unable to find employment.

Labor force All individuals 16 years or older who are working or actively seeking work.

Participation rate Percentage of the adult population which is part of the labor force.

Aggregate demand The sum of demand (or planned spending) in the four sectors of the economy (i.e., consumer, business, government, and foreign).

Structural unemployment Unemployment caused by workers' skills not matching those skills required for available jobs.

Frictional unemployment Unemployment caused by workers changing positions or because of incomplete information.

Cyclical unemployment Unemployment caused by too little aggregate demand.

CASE 23:
It Pays to Be Unemployed[1]

In Great Britain between World War I and World War II, that is, between 1921 and 1939, unemployment never declined below 9.5 percent. It is also true that since World War II the unemployment rate in Great Britain has never been as high as 9.5 percent. For a number of years, economists have been ill at ease to define the reasons why the unemployment rate for Great Britain was so high before World War II and why it has never reached such high rates since World War II. Most of the reasons purported by economists to explain this apparent anomaly have centered on the fact that Great Britain was a strong adherent of the gold standard. This line of thinking held that at times between the world wars the money supply in Britain fell as a result of Britain's being on the gold standard, this in turn causing output to decline and the unemployment rate to climb to over 22 percent in 1932.

Recent work done by economists Daniel Benjamin and Levis Kochin, however, suggests that the unemployment rate in Britain between World War I and World War II might have had little to do with the gold standard and much more to do with unemployment benefits. Benjamin and Kochin demonstrated that lowering the cost of an activity will increase the incidence of that activity. The particular activity which they were studying was unemployment. Before World War I in Great Britain the only public assistance available to unemployed individuals was locally financed and administered. It was not until 1911 that a sort of centrally administered unemployment insurance compensation was made available to some of the workers. By 1920, the weekly benefits had increased substantially, and the coverage had been extended to a wide range of the population.

Unemployment compensation benefits were paid during the interwar period of Great Britain for spells of unemployment as short as one day. The maximum period for which benefits could be collected in 1921 was 26 weeks per year. Because of the average length of unemployment in the years shortly after 1921, many individuals would have quickly exhausted their insurance benefits if the government had not moved to supplement the unemployment insurance with additional forms of unemployment assistance. The additional forms of assistance were to aid individuals who had exhausted their rights to regular unemployment insurance benefits. By 1925, a worker who had made thirty weekly contributions to the unemployment compensation scheme during his or her working life could draw full benefits for unemployment for an unlimited time.

Benjamin and Kochin have calculated what the unemployment rate would have been in interwar Britain if the unemployment compensation had been maintained at its 1913 level. The results of their calculations are shown in Table 23-1.

[1] Facts in this case are used by permission of Daniel K. Benjamin and Levis A. Kochin from their paper "Searching for an Explanation of Unemployment in Interwar Britain," Discussion Paper 76-14, Institute for Economic Research, University of Washington.

Table 23-1

Year	Actual Unemployment in Great Britain (%)	Calculated Unemployment, Using 1913 Compensation Benefits (%)
1920	3.9	5.1
1921	16.8	17.4
1922	14.3	12.3
1923	11.7	9.1
1924	10.3	7.3
1925	11.3	7.1
1926	12.5	6.5
1927	9.7	6.5
1928	10.8	7.2
1929	10.4	6.8
1930	16.1	10.9
1931	21.3	15.9
1932	22.1	17.5
1933	19.9	15.1
1934	16.7	11.7
1935	15.5	9.8
1936	13.1	7.1
1937	10.8	5.0
1938	12.9	7.1

Source: Daniel K. Benjamin and Levis A. Kochin, "Searching for an Explanation of Unemployment in Inter-war Britain," University of Washington Discussion Paper No. 76-14.

QUESTIONS

1 The second column of Table 23-1 shows the calculated unemployment assuming that compensation benefits in Great Britain had been held at the 1913 level. Assume for a moment that no compensation benefits were paid between 1920 and 1938. Would you then expect the calculated unemployment between 1920 and 1938 to equal zero percent? Is it true that for an economy to be operating efficiently it must have zero percent unemployment?

2 Is it clear from the data on Great Britain that the presence of unemployment assistance affected the utilization and unemployment of labor? Would the presence of unemployment assistance also affect the utilization and employment of resources other than labor?

3 *Search unemployment* is the term economists use to describe individuals who are currently unemployed and are remaining so to aid them in their search for a new (and perhaps better) employment opportunity. Would you expect search unemployment to rise in response to an increase in unemployment benefits? Would the calculated unemployment rate change in any way?

4 If unemployment benefits are instituted in an economy where previously there were none, would you expect that vacations might be relabeled as layoffs and/or that some individuals would sign up for benefits even though they had no

intention of returning to work? Might it not also be the case that some individuals would reap a subsidy by engaging in "part-time" employment, that is, employment of only a few days per week or a few months per year? Would these individuals be behaving rationally in an economic sense? What would be the effect on the calculated unemployment rate of an individual acting in the above manners?

5 In many industries, inputs other than labor are substituted for labor. If laborers are induced to become unemployed as a result of unemployment benefits, will industry be induced to increase the utilization of other inputs?

6 One view of unemployment holds that unemployment is due in large part to deficient aggregate demand. Would it be possible for an economy to suffer from deficient aggregate demand and at the same time incur some unemployment as a result of relatively high unemployment assistance benefits?

7 In late 1976 there was much discussion in Washington, D.C., over the Humphrey-Hawkins bill. One of the purposes of this proposed legislation was to provide the right to productive employment at "fair" rates of compensation for every adult American able to, willing to, and seeking work. The bill sought to establish supplementary employment policies to be used, as required by economic conditions, to ensure full employment. If the government were to employ large numbers of the unemployed at "market" wages, would it be possible for a shift to take place from private to public employment? Would there be any incentives for individuals employed in a public job to look for a job in the private sector? Is it possible that the net impact on job creation of such a public service job program would be zero?

8 Would you expect that an increase in unemployment benefits would lead to an increase in the size of the labor force? What effect might this have on the calculated unemployment rate? (*Hint:* in addition to the labor force's changing as a result of an increase in unemployment benefits, would you also expect the participation rate to change?)

TEST YOURSELF

Multiple-choice

1 The unemployment rate is
- (a) The percentage of the United States population currently without a job
- (b) The percentage of the United States population actively seeking a job
- (c) The percentage of the labor force actively seeking a job but out of work
- (d) The number of people looking for jobs divided by the number of people who have jobs

2 The *labor force* is a government term meaning
- (a) All individuals over 16 years of age currently working
- (b) All individuals over 16 years of age currently working or actively seeking work
- (c) All individuals over 16 years of age who would like to work

3 In the actual calculation of the unemployment rate, the Census Bureau
   (a) Surveys a number of households, inquiring about their employment status
   (b) Uses Internal Revenue Service income tax forms to obtain data on work status
   (c) Performs extensive door-to-door interviews once a year with virtually every household in the United States

4 Minimum wage laws
   (a) Prevent unemployment by ensuring a decent wage to every worker
   (b) Increase unemployment by making workers more expensive to employers
   (c) Have little to do with rates of unemployment

5 Unemployment benefits seem to
   (a) Reduce the unemployment rate
   (b) Increase the participation rate
   (c) Have little to do with the size of the labor force

6 The unemployment rate never reaches zero percent because
   (a) Government is inefficient in alleviating unemployment
   (b) Some individuals will always be out of work but looking for new positions
   (c) Many individuals are lazy and refuse to work at all

7 The basic Keynesian solution to a high unemployment rate would be to
   (a) Increase unemployment benefits
   (b) Reduce the government deficit
   (c) Decrease the money supply
   (d) Increase aggregate demand

8 The basic monetarist solution to a high unemployment rate would be to
   (a) Repeal minimum wage laws and reduce unemployment benefits
   (b) Decrease the money supply
   (c) Increase aggregate demand
   (d) Reduce the government deficit

True–false

Read the following statements and note whether each is true or false.

T F 1. The labor force does not include unemployed individuals.

T F 2. The United States has never reached 100 percent employment of the labor force.

T F 3. Monetarists believe that changes in the minimum wage laws will have little effect on the unemployment rate.

T F 4. Keynesians would recommend increasing aggregate demand as a way of reducing the unemployment rate.

T F 5. Unemployment benefits may affect the labor force participation rate.

T F 6. Unemployment benefits may affect the unemployment rate.

T F 7. An individual who is unemployed but has not looked for work in a year is included in the unemployment rate.

T F 8. Each unemployed individual is questioned by the Census Bureau at least once a year.

24

The Classicists, the Keynesians, and the Monetarists View Unemployment and Inflation

Different economists hold differing views of the relationship of economic variables in determining the stability of the economic system. Therefore, economists would recommend different solutions to counteract the presence of such instabilities as unemployment and inflation. Briefly we will review what three alternative schools of thought see as the major cause of economic disturbances and the manner in which they can be remedied.

THE CLASSICISTS

Until the 1930s the prevailing view of a market system was that if an institutional structure which promoted competition in all levels of economic endeavor were operative, then the system would tend toward stable prices and full employment of resources. While varying widely on specific points, this so-called classical school of thought held that unemployment was a short-run condition. The market process held the keys to unlocking these problems in the form of flexible wages and prices.

For example, if because of a technological discovery resources in industry A were currently unemployed (buggy whip makers in the advent of the invention of the automobile), laborers would bid their wage down rather than go without working. At lower wage rates, employers can hire more workers for the same dollar outlay; thus, via price and wage flexibility, all laborers are again reemployed. The major causes of instabilities in this theory arise from innovations, technological changes, changes in preferences, and discoveries. The market system can adapt to these changes; therefore, the necessity of government interference in the adjustment process would be minimal. In the classical view, the primary role of government was to promote an environment (property rights protection, laws against fraud, theft, and murder) that would allow the competitive market process to promote fully the mutual gains from trade.

THE KEYNESIANS

With his book the *General Theory of Employment, Interest, and Money*, in 1936 J. M. Keynes attacked the classicists' view of the stability of a market economy. Keynes argued that falling prices led to falling incomes and thus a lower level of production of goods and services. Rather than helping the economy move toward full employment, falling wages and prices might well work to keep the system at levels far below full utilization of all resources. He pointed to the Great Depression, during which prices had fallen by 50 percent and still one-third of society's resources were unemployed, as proof of the inherent instability of markets.

Keynes theorized that the instability of a market system was caused by fluctuations in business investment in plant, machinery, and inventory. Business managers expanded their productive capacity in response to changes in consumer demand, but eventually capacity catches up with demand and investment declines; this decline causes a decrease in the demand for resources and a decline in aggregate demand, thus causing a further decline in the willingness to invest. Keynes argued that a market system could have unemployment and/or inflation in the short run and that there would be no "self-correcting" mechanism. Thus, government would have to step in to stimulate the aggregate spending in the economy and help it move toward full employment.

THE MONETARISTS

The school of thought that focuses on the level of, and changes in, the money stock of the society sees this economic variable as the major source of economic instability. The monetarists theorize that a direct link exists between the level of spending in the economy and the stock of money. They see no basic inability of a market system to generate full employment with stable prices. Rather they argue that it is the government's incorrectly altering the money stock that keeps the market economy from producing stability. When the money stock increases, individuals find they have excess money holdings; therefore, they will go out and purchase goods and services. This action stimulates producers to produce more goods by hiring more laborers. The full employment of laborers sets the limit on the amount of expansion in production (or real output) that can be achieved by increases in the money stock. If government increases the money stock in excess of this maximum amount, then the only result will be inflation. Likewise, if government contracts the money supply, it will have a recessionary impact on the economy. The monetarists point to the Great Depression as proof of the effect of contracting the money stock. Between 1929 and 1933, the money supply was reduced by one-third. Monetarists point out that when monetary authorities reversed the trend in the money stock in 1934, real income grew at a rate comparable to the increase in the money stock. Thus, the monetarists see the proper role of government as one of ensuring a stable, predictable level of long-run growth in the supply of money.

KEY CONCEPTS

Equilibrium income level Any level of income for which the circular flow of economic activity is stationary.

Stagnation An unsatisfactory rate of growth of real per capita output or income.

Economic stability A condition of high-level economic activity with an absence of severe cyclical fluctuations in production, employment, and prices.

Monetarists Economists who believe that fluctuations in economic activity are directly linked to variations in the money stock. The policy recommendations of this view focus on changing the money supply to achieve economic growth and stability.

Keynesians Economists who believe that the market economy is characterized by inherent instability and that government authorities have an obligation to use taxation, spending, and money stock changes to stabilize the economy.

Classicists Economists who believe that as long as markets operate to keep buyers and sellers informed as to changes in market forces, then the economic system will display long-run stability.

CASE 24A:
Price Levels from 975 to 1975; Does History Hold the Key to Understanding Stagflation?[1]

Nobel laureate economist Paul Samuelson has been quoted as saying, "No jury of expert economists can agree on a satisfactory solution for the modern diagnosis for the modern disease of 'stagflation.' " The number of cures offered is in no way limited by the number of conflicting economic theories. The monetarists blame growth in the money stock. The fiscalists (Keynesians) blame monetary policy. The business sector blames escalating wage demands. Labor claims capitalist greed is to blame. The "gold bugs" blame paper money. The conservatives blame government for "too much action." The liberals blame government for "too little action." One thing seems clear from the current exchanges of rhetoric: there is a lack of consensus as to the *cause* of the stagflation problem. Prior to enacting corrective surgery, it is necessary to know not only the symptoms but the cause of the ailment. Here it seems that the surgeon will "cut" in different places, depending upon whether she or he is a monetarist, Keynesian, or whatever.

Although it is said that history never repeats itself, it has also said that "it is possible to learn from past mistakes." Can a historical review of price and economic growth provide some key to the economic problems that are faced in much of the world today? Thanks to the labors of British economic historians E. H. Phelps Brown and Sheila V. Hopkins of Oxford, it is now possible to trace price movements for necessities over the past 700 years. Brown and Hopkins constructed a rough market basket of essentials—food, fuel, and clothing for an English worker—and traced its cost from 1264, both in terms of money price and in terms of the purchasing power of the workingman's wages. They developed, in other words, a price index. Over the 700 years in England things changed considerably, but the basic concept of "essentials" was changed very little. Thus in the year 1300, the basket contained no fuel at all; by 1500 it had a little charcoal, by 1750 some coal; and by 1950 it included kerosene. There was no attempt to compare all prices over the period; rather this is a pure cost-of-*living* index. The Brown and Hopkins index has been extended backward 300 years and forward to 1974 (see Figure 24-1), looking for what Sir John Hicks calls "the shapes that repeat among the details that do not repeat."

A review of the peaks and valleys of the price index reveals that only *four* times in 1000 years has there been a great explosion in the money price of the Brown and Hopkins basket. Prices trend upward for 75, 100, even 125 years, more or less relentlessly; then *three* times the price level has settled at some new plateau and stayed there. The price explosion stopped, and regular cycles of rising and falling

[1]Reprinted by permission of *Forbes* magazine from the November 15, 1976 issue, © 1976 *Forbes,* Inc.

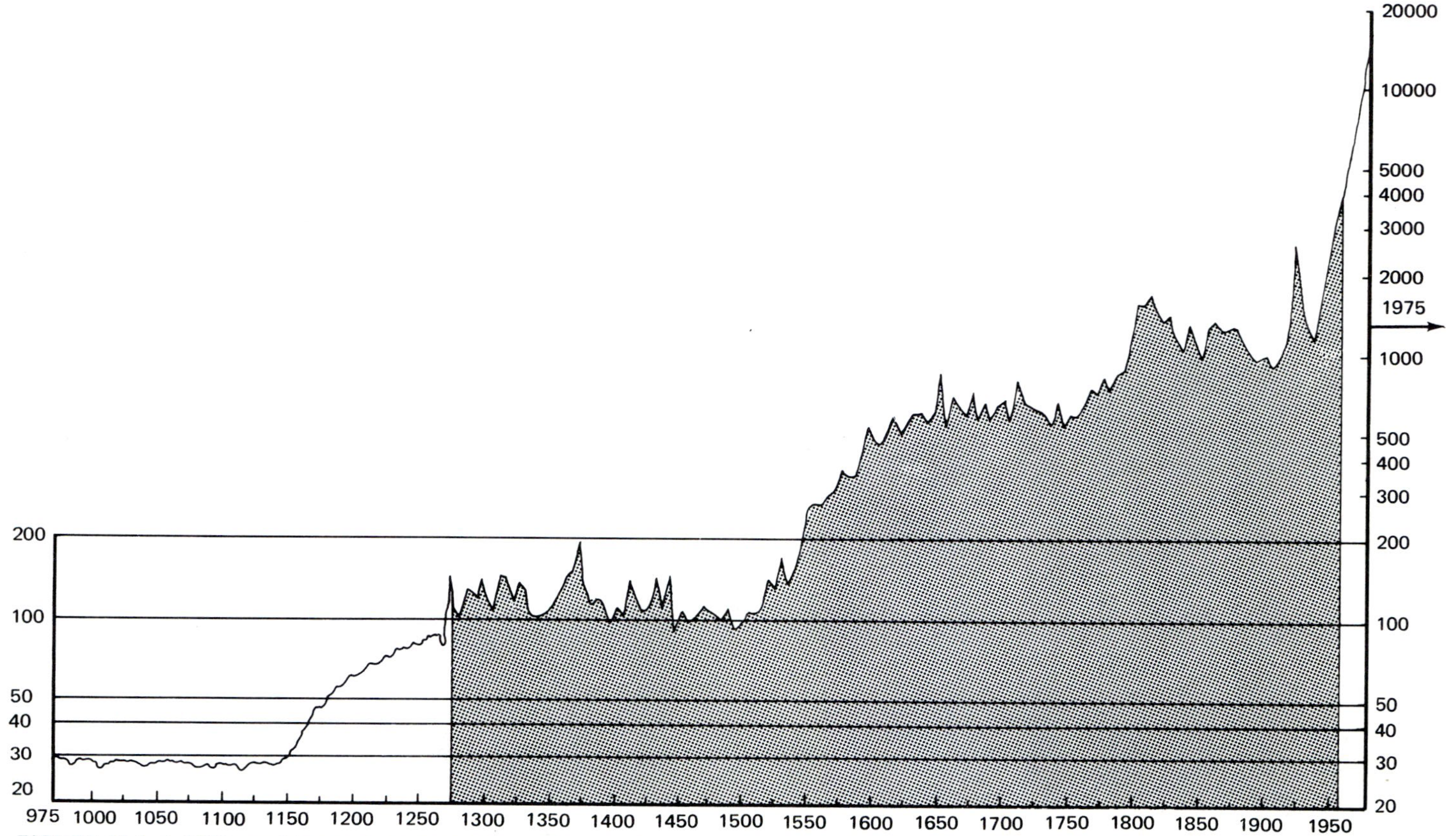

FIGURE 24-1 A 1000-year history of the price of a simple market basket of human needs. (*Reprinted with permission of Peter DiGeorge.*)

prices took over again. The explosions seem to be irreversible events, quite different from the ups and downs. The *fourth* explosion began in the 1960s, and it has not yet stopped.

Historians can identify three of the great historical price revolutions not in terms of inflation but in terms of social revolutions. These were periods when the entire social fabric was altered—how people lived and thought of themselves and acted. Respectively, these were the commercial revolution of the Middle Ages, from 950 to 1350; the capitalist revolution, from 1520 to 1640; and the industrial revolution, from 1750 to 1850. What does economic theory say about these historical inflations? The monetarists can make a case of sorts by focusing on the money stock. In the first instance, it was the growth of a money economy itself; in the second, the discovery of gold and silver in the New World; and in the third, the huge explosion of credit by private bankers. The fourth, and present, instance is said to be attributable to central banking and the Federal Reserve System's monetary policies.

An alternative explanation can be found in population theories that have their roots in the works of Thomas Malthus. Each of the four periods has been associated with an explosion in the population. Population pressure would bid prices up, there would be less to go around, and people would starve. Since the proponents of each point of view have not been able to generate a consensus, could there be another explanation of these price revolutions?

If we consider these periods in social terms, rather than in terms of supply and demand or money, we note that they all have a common element. In each period a new sector, a distinctive part of the economy, grew up, and with it came a new way of doing things. In the commercial revolution, it was the merchants and artisans; in the capitalist revolution, it was that incredibly diverse mix of occupations that Marx dubbed the bourgeoisie; and in the industrial revolution, it was the industrial sector itself. And the fourth price revolution? Our own? What new sector has sprung up since the 1950s that has altered our way of doing things? One suggestion is the public sector. Our age may come to be known as the time when the common people learned to depend on government for something besides pomp and protection. Perhaps when enough time has passed to make a historical perspective possible, our age will be known as the *public revolution* and be ranked with those other great socioeconomic upheavals. What may be needed in economics is not more refinement of the classical, neoclassical, Keynesian, or monetarist theories but rather a new theory to help us to understand our own public revolution.

QUESTIONS

1 In response to the monetarists who would argue for their interpretation of the four "price revolutions," it has been said that this is like arguing that growing crops makes the sun shine. How would the monetarist respond to this criticism?

2 The historical view of the four price revolutions might argue that inflation is just a consequence of fundamental changes in the fabric of society, not the cause of

the alteration. From this perspective, money supply changes don't explain anything—they are a result of changes. For example, it was people's ability to reach the gold and silver in the New World that caused the price explosion of the sixteenth century. Evaluate this view of economic theory.

3 If the current general rise in prices is, in fact, a result of a shift in individuals' view of the role of government and the growth of public sector goods and services, how would you assess the chances of bringing rising prices under control?

4 One of the most difficult problems in developing a theory to explain and predict economic outcomes is that, of necessity, this theory must attempt to predict and explain human behavior. Under such circumstances, should it come as a surprise that "no group of economists is in general agreement on economic policy"? Why or why not?

5 In terms of the Keynesian theoretical framework, what would be the causes of each of the four price revolutions, and what should be done concerning the present inflation in the United States?

CASE 24B:
Deficits, Prosperity, and Unemployment[2]

John Maynard Keynes was an English economist, but it may be that Keynesian economics is no longer practiced in Great Britain. In 1976 Prime Minister James Callaghan, then leader of the Labor Party government in Great Britain, disavowed Keynesian economics in the following way.

> We used to think that you could spend your way out of a recession and increase employment by cutting taxes and boosting government spending. I tell you, in all candor, that that option no longer exists, and that in so far as it ever did exist, it only worked by injecting bigger doses of inflation into the economy followed by higher levels of unemployment as the next step. That is the history of the past twenty years.

At the time Prime Minister Callaghan was speaking, Great Britain was suffering from high levels of unemployment as well as rapid inflation. Callaghan was referring to the theories of Keynes often called the "new economics" or "Keynesian economics," which proposed that an economy in recession may be "stimulated" by injecting large amounts of government spending (public works, government jobs, etc.) into the economy.

It is certainly the case that budget deficits stimulate demand and, in turn, employment. These government deficits are thought to be subject to a multiplier effect which boosts GNP by more than the amount of the original government deficit. The following figures, however, may contradict this theory. It would appear from the data in Tables 24-1 and 24-2 that what many believe about deficits and their effect on employment may be tacitly incorrect. It is difficult to draw from the tables the conclusion that government deficits lead to growth, prosperity, and accompanying high employment. There is no strong correlation shown in the tables for average annual rates of growth and average deficits as a percentage of GNP. *The Wall Street Journal*, which published the tables, found that most Americans were amazed to learn that *not* all governments run deficits all the time. It is clear from Table 24-1 that some governments in the period 1965 to 1974 had an average surplus rather than an average deficit. On the whole, these countries (with average surpluses) seem not to have done significantly more poorly than those countries which ran rather large deficits as a percentage of GNP.

Was Keynes actually wrong? Could it be that there is no relationship between government deficits and the rate of unemployment and economic growth? Keynes knew that when the government ran a deficit, either it had to print the money

[2] Facts in this case are used with the permission of *The Wall Street Journal*. See "Keynes Is Dead," *The Wall Street Journal*, January 31, 1977, p. 12. Reprinted with permission of *The Wall Street Journal*,

Table 24-1 Deficits and Growth, 1965 to 1974

	Average Deficit (Surplus +), % GNP	Growth (Average Annual), %
Italy	-4.04	4.7
Ireland	-3.42	3.9
United Kingdom	-1.19	2.5
United States	-0.76	3.3
Netherlands	-0.32	4.9
West Germany	-0.30	4.1
France	+0.34	5.3
Canada	+0.78	5.2
Portugal	+0.79	6.8
Japan	+1.39	8.7
Australia	+1.43	5.2
Luxembourg	+1.95	3.7
Norway	+3.43	4.5
Finland	+3.54	5.0
Sweden	+4.08	3.5

Source: "Keynes Is Dead," *The Wall Street Journal*, January 31, 1977, p. 12. Reprinted with permission of *The Wall Street Journal*,

Table 24-2 Public Spending and Growth, 1962 to 1971

	Government Expenditures (Except Transfers), % GNP	Growth (Average Annual), %
Sweden	25.6	3.7
Denmark	23.8	4.7
United States	23.2	4.4
Canada	22.4	5.5
United Kingdom	20.7	2.5
West Germany	20.4	4.5
Finland	18.6	4.9
Belgium	16.5	4.8
Italy	16.0	4.8
Australia	14.9	5.4
France	14.0	5.8
Switzerland	12.9	4.1
Spain	12.3	6.9
Japan	10.4	10.1

Source: "Keynes Is Dead," *The Wall Street Journal*, January 31, 1977, p. 12. Reprinted with permission of *The Wall Street Journal*,

which it was spending or it had to borrow the money. Keynes believed that the money could be borrowed without causing a corresponding decrease in spending in the private market. This was because Keynes believed that there were "speculative cash balances" available in the economy; that is, he believed individuals and businesses were holding cash balances idly and it would be possible for the government to tap these balances and inject them into the spending stream to stimulate the economy. Of course, the important question is, Are there idle balances in today's inflationary economy?

QUESTIONS

1 Assume that in an inflationary economy there are no idle cash balances but that the federal government wishes to engage in a program of economic stimulation. This government has decided to borrow from the public to finance the program of economic stimulation by issuing bonds. Since there are no idle cash balances in this economy, what would you expect to happen to the sales of private corporation bonds?

2 Carrying the assumptions from question 1, would it be possible that the government bonds might perfectly "crowd out" the corporate bonds? Assuming perfect "crowding out" took place, what would be the effect on aggregate demand?

3 Monetarists believe that crowding out as a result of government bond sales has the effect of lowering capital investment. Explain why this might be the case and indicate why it might lead to slower economic growth.

4 Is it reasonable to assume there are substantial speculative cash balances in an inflationary economy? With less inflation, would there be a propensity to hold more or less speculative cash balances? What do speculative cash balances have to do with unemployment?

TEST YOURSELF

True--false

T F 1. The monetarists argue that government can adjust the money stock to counteract cyclical changes in economic activity.

T F 2. The classical economists theorize that the market economy could achieve full employment with stable prices if government helped by stimulating demand.

T F 3. The Keynesians believe that a market economy is inherently unstable.

T F 4. Both the monetarists and the Keynesians point to the 1930s as proof of their theories.

T F 5. Price and wage flexibility is a key factor in the monetarists' arguments.

T F 6. Business makes long-term plans about plant, machinery, and inventory levels and then does not vary these plans in light of the performance of the economy.

T F 7. When government increases the money stock, this effects the rate of interest in the Keynesian view.

T F 8. Workers are generally able to find jobs by offering to work for less money.

T F 9. During the Great Depression, the price level remained stable.

T F 10. Monetarists believe that changes in the money supply will first affect the rate of interest and then spending.

MATCHING

Select the term in the left column that best matches the statement in the right column. Not all terms in the left column apply, and none is intended to be used twice.

A. Keynesians
B. Neo-Keynesians
C. Monetarists
D. Classicists
E. Price and wage flexibility
F. Money stock
G. Inflation
H. Stagflation
I. Economic stability
J. Stagnation

___ 1. A continuing increase in the general level of prices.

___ 2. A low level or a negative level of economic growth.

___ 3. The notion that factor and commodity prices change in response to supply and demand.

___ 4. The total amount of dollars in circulation.

___ 5. A period with constant prices at or near full employment of all resources.

___ 6. Economists who view investment as the major source of economic instability.

25

Information Problems and the Keynesian Model

Of all the consequences of the "Keynesian revolution" in economics, the most striking is the change in the role of government in our economic system. In 1929, government purchases of goods and services were 8.2 percent of gross national product; by 1977 this figure was just under 30 percent. The Keynesian policy recommendations for a market economy call for government to actively intervene to alter the outcome generated by the voluntary change process. The key variable that triggers government action is aggregate demand, the total private and public demand for goods and services in the economy. Macropolicy planners attempt to manage aggregate demand in such a way that the economic system maintains *full employment of its resources at stable prices.* The critical questions for the policy makers are when to intervene and how to do it.

A unique feature of a market economy is that there is no one decision maker (or group of decision makers) that sets output levels, prices, and resource use; but rather these variables are determined by the interaction of millions of independent individual decisions. Each individual decision maker acts to secure his or her most preferred outcome. It is an extremely difficult task to know how these interactions are related for a single market process, let alone for all exchanges in the system.

For example, let us look at the aerospace industry. Suppose it is known that as a result of President Carter's decision in 1977 to scrap the B-1 bomber, 6000 employees of North American Rockwell have lost their jobs. What is the appropriate macropolicy, if any, to counter this increase in unemployment? Clearly, the answer depends upon what the policy planner thinks is likely to happen in the future. Will these individuals be permanently unable to find other jobs? Will they be rapidly rehired by other aerospace producers? Will the reduction in employment at Rockwell's California plants severely damage the local economy? How will the electronics, steel, and rubber industries be affected by this decrease in employment? The questions go on and on.

To formulate a policy directed at altering some economic consequence, the policy maker is faced with the problem of first finding out what is currently going on and then constructing a hypothesis about what is likely to occur in the future. It seems clear that even for a single market process this is a difficult task; when all market interactions are considered simultaneously, it is infinitely more complex. What does an unemployment rate of 6 percent mean? What is going on in all the submarkets of the system, and is it likely to continue? How much time must pass before consequences of independent decisions as to output and employment can be recognized by the policy makers? These are the first set of problems that the aggregate demand managers must face.

Then, if we can make the heroic assumption that the first set of answers can be known, an equally difficult set of problems arises. What are the likely consequences of alternative policy actions? How are they distributed over time? How do they work themselves out to alter the independent decision making of individuals? Again, let us focus on the aerospace industry, and assume it is known that the 6000 laid-off workers will not find work anywhere in the private sector for at least the next two years. What policies, if any, should government initiate to alter this outcome? Will it be "best" to: hire these workers at federal government jobs; lower the tax rate of aerospace producers; give dollars to local governments to retain these workers for jobs that are currently available in the market; extend the unemployment benefit coverage of these workers to two years; reduce interest rates and hope to stimulate investment in the aerospace industry; expand the money supply and hope to increase aggregate demand and thus employment; or use any combination of these or other policies? Even if the planners knew the necessary relationships for this single market, the policy prescription recommended would not necessarily work for any other market in the economy. The unemployed workers from the B-1 project surely have different skills and talents than the unemployed youths in American inner cities.

Once a decision on policy is made, this does not end the difficulties, for the impacts on the economic system are not instantaneous. If policy planners decide that it will be most advantageous to the laid-off workers to grant low-cost loans to the aerospace industry to stimulate production, this decision must still be enacted. The President must be convinced of the appropriateness of the plan; then it must be sent to Congress for consideration. There are considerable time lags in this process. For example, in late 1973 the economy began experiencing a business downturn (we now know this from looking at performance records of the system), but it was not until March 1975 that Congress passed an antirecessionary tax cut, which by past standards was very speedy action.

The problem doesn't end with the time lag between decision and action—there exist considerable time lags once a policy is put into effect. Economists do not know the exact (or even approximate) length of time it takes a specific monetary or fiscal policy action to have an effect on the economy; however, the range seems to be somewhere between 4 and 20 months depending on the kind of action. That is, if in our example Congress acted today to appropriate funds for loans to the aerospace industry, it might be two years before this action registered an impact on employment. It is critical to know the future before macropolicy planners can hope to stabilize and coordinate actions. The distinct possibility exists that by the time the policy impact works its way through the economic system, the actual result will be the reverse of the desired one. For example, if government takes action to stimulate aggregate demand on the belief that a recession is ahead when, in fact, two years hence the economy is expanding, then the government "fuels the fires of inflation" and amplifies the business cycle.

KEY CONCEPTS

Economic forecasts Predictions of how key economic variables such as output, prices, unemployment, and investment will change in some future period.

Discretionary macroeconomic policy The use of expenditures, taxes, and the money stock for the express purpose of altering the performance of the economy.

Real GNP The economy's output of goods and services over some specific time, measured in terms of constant dollars.

Council of Economic Advisors An advisory board established by the Employment Act of 1946 to recommend economic policies to the President.

Recognition lag The time that elapses between a change in the performance of the economy and the realization by macropolicy planners that a change has occurred.

Decision lag The period that elapses between recognition of a change and the reaching of a policy prescription to deal with the problem.

Execution lag The time that elapses between reaching a policy decision with respect to some problem and the impact of that policy on the economic system.

Fiscal policy The determination of expenditure and/or taxation levels of government for some specific period of time.

CASE 25:
Evaluating CEA Forecasts[1]

When President Carter sent his 1977–1978 budget message to Congress, the majority of the spending and taxation proposals that it contained were based on the expected performance of the economy within the next 12 to 15 months. Predictions as to the economy's performance are contained in the Annual Report of the Council of Economic Advisors (CEA) to the President. For example, the CEA forecast for 1977 calls for an unemployment rate of 7.3 percent (down from 7.7 percent in 1976); a rate of inflation of 5 to 6 percent, but a decline in the Consumer Price Index from last year's 5.7 percent to a predicted 5.1 percent; and an increase of business inventories of 15 percent. The CEA predicts a moderate rise in the real GNP of the United States of 5.2 percent from 1976 to 1977.

As members of Congress consider action on the budget and the business and the household sectors contemplate saving, investment, and spending decisions, the critical question is: Just how good is the CEA forecasting record? A comparison of the predicted and actual values of economic variables leads to the conclusion that the forecasts are not very good. Since it began predictions in 1962, the CEA has generally underestimated the rate of inflation and generally overestimated the real economic growth rate. For example, examining the forecast record of the CEA for the last 15 years with respect to price movements, we find that in 11 of those years, the CEA understated the increase in prices. In estimating the direction of change from one year to the next, the CEA did no better than one could have done by "flipping a coin." Over the entire 15-year period, *on average* the CEA underestimated the *rate* of inflation by 0.8 percentage points. If we assume that 1977's price forecast is subject to the average error of the last 15 years, the actual rate of inflation would be 6.4 percent.

In forecasting real growth, the record of the CEA is better; in 11 of the last 15 years the direction of the change in the rate of real economic growth was correctly predicted. However, the forecasts have been overly optimistic in 9 of the 15 years, with the average overestimation of the rate of growth of real GNP over the entire 15-year period being 0.4 percentage points. This appears to be a very small error, but keep in mind that it is not the absolute level of GNP or prices that is being forecasted but the growth *rate.* For example, real GNP grew on average 3.5 percent during the 15-year period; therefore an average overestimation in the growth rate of 1 percent means that the forecast would be off by 33 percent in predicting the growth of real GNP.

[1]Facts in this case are reprinted with permission from Stephen K. McNees, "An Evaluation of Economic Forecasts: Extension and Update," *New England Economic Review,* pp. 30–44, September/October 1976, and "An Assessment of the Council of Economic Advisors' Forecast of 1977," *New England Bank Review,* pp. 3–7, March/April 1977.

In comparing the CEA's "track record" with that of a group of prominent private forecasters, there do not appear to be significant differences in forecasting skill. The CEA's record is inferior to that of private forecasters in predicting real GNP and just as accurate (or inaccurate) in forecasting inflation and unemployment. After looking at the record, praising the forecasters is, as Arthur Okun, former chairman of the CEA, puts it, "like saying that the Titanic had a good trip except for that iceberg."

QUESTIONS

1 Congress and the President in 1977 enacted into law a "jobs" bill, worked toward increasing the average duration of unemployment benefits paid by states by providing supplemental funding, considered and rejected a $50 tax rebate for each citizen, as well as passing numerous other pieces of legislation that reflect their view of the economic situation currently and in the near future. What assumptions about future economic activity must have been made by these policy makers in light of the kinds of programs that have been enacted?

2 A comparison of the forecasting accuracy of highly sophisticated mathematical models using economic variables (for example, the model used by the CEA or the famous Wharton model of the University of Pennsylvania) with informal judgmental models (the most famous of these is the General Electric Company model whose forecasts are the outcome of an iterative process in which provisional values are obtained from economic relationships but the final results are strongly influenced by the experience, "feel," and intuition of the business economists) reveals that judgmental economic forecasts continue to outperform mechanical approaches to predict economic activity. Is this result surprising, disturbing? Why or why not?

3 If we accept the notion that one of the primary functions of government in a mixed economy is to ensure a stable full employment level of growth through the use of fiscal and monetary policy changes, then what, of necessity, does this view imply about political relationships? Does this view of "government" (remember that government is simply a group of individuals who enact policies at the direction of mandates initiated by the political process, while at the same time pursuing their own self-interest) assume a conception of human interests and abilities in the political sphere that the economist would find unacceptable in the economic sphere? Illustrate your answer with at least two examples.

4 Stabilization policy calls for government injections when the economy is characterized by insufficient aggregate demand and government withdrawals when the economy is "overheated" (aggregate demand exceeds aggregate supply of goods). Economists are not in general agreement as to the length of the lags associated with specific monetary and fiscal policy tools; however, they are in agreement that such lags do exist. How do the existence of time lags and the apparent inability to accurately predict the level of important economic variables such as

unemployment and inflation rates affect the usefulness of stabilization as a policy goal of government? Why would you suppose that many economists argue for fixed policies rather than flexible policy decisions in response to economic conditions?

TEST YOURSELF

True—false

T F 1. Macropolicy refers to the independent decisions made by individuals and how they affect unemployment and taxes.

T F 2. Aggregate demand is a critical variable in the Keynesian economic model.

T F 3. Knowing that the economic system is headed for an inflation or a recession is a relatively easy matter, now that economists have developed mathematical models.

T F 4. Assuming that the government knows what to do to achieve full employment with stable prices is like assuming that the future is the present.

T F 5. Policy decisions can be carried out rapidly in the public sector.

T F 6. A decision lag refers to the passage of time needed to formulate a decision rule.

T F 7. Once the unemployment rate is known, a uniform policy to deal with it can be worked out.

T F 8. Predicting the future on the basis of past actions implies that relationships are stable over time.

T F 9. Taxes and spending are solely used by government to provide collective goods for society.

T F 10. All that is needed to more correctly forecast the performance of the economy is more information.

Matching

Select the term in the left column that best matches the statement in the right column. Not all terms in the left column apply, and none is intended to be used twice.

A. Council of Economic Advisors
B. Open Market Committee
C. Unemployment rate
D. Inflation rate
E. Fiscal policy
F. Execution lag
G. Economic forecasts
H. Real GNP
I. Decision lag
J. Recognition lag

___ 1. The time that passes between a change in the economy and knowing that it changed.

___ 2. Total production measured in constant dollars.

___ 3. Predicting what the economy will do in the future.

___ 4. The three-member advisory board to the President on economic affairs.

___ 5. The time it takes for a specific policy to have an effect on the system after it is enacted.

___ 6. The determination of the tax and spending levels of government.

26

National Planning

When most people hear the terms *central planning* or *centrally planned economy,* they immediately think of the Soviet Union as the prime example in our everyday world. Central economic planning did indeed come into being in the Soviet Union during the 1920s shortly after the Bolshevik Revolution. After the revolution, the destruction of private enterprise in the Soviet Union and the taking over of industry and finance by the government were the order of the day. The details, however, about what was to be done once capitalism was indeed overthrown were nonexistent. Some coordinating mechanism was needed in the Soviet Union, and the government lapsed into a system of devising short- and long-range plans linking actions in the different economic sectors.[1]

In order to understand central economic planning as it exists in the Soviet Union today, it is helpful to think of a line with a point on either end. The points on either end of the line will represent the two different ways of coordinating an economy. On one end of the line, the point may refer to an economic system which resorts to central economic planning. The point on the opposite end of the line may refer to an economic system which is organized entirely through

[1]Some facts in this chapter are reprinted with permission of the American Enterprise Institute for Public Policy Research, Washington, D.C., from their booklet, "Central Economic Planning: The Visible Hand" by G. Warren Nutter, 1976.

private contractual agreements. In the centrally planned economy, the society is run solely by authority. Everything is done as a result of commands passed from superiors in the economy to subordinates. Every individual in the economy must accept the authority of the supreme commander (except, of course, the supreme commander who has no boss).

On the other end of the line is the imaginary society which is organized solely through private contracts. The purest form of this sort of economy would be a perfectly competitive market where individuals freely exchange their goods and services for mutual benefit.

The Soviet Union is predominately a centrally planned economy while the United States is predominately a contractual economy. It is possible to see, however, some elements of what we might call central planning in the United States, while it is also possible to see some elements of what we might call perfect competition in the Soviet Union. Neither economy exists in the pure forms which we are imagining here. We have spent some time examining the competitive market in Chapters 7 and 8. Why, however, would some Americans prefer a centrally planned economy, and exactly what is a centrally planned economy?

Planning in the broadest sense is merely a systematic way of looking ahead, establishing procedures for filling particular goals, and then seeing that these goals, once defined, are carried out. You as an individual engage in planning every day of your life. When you get out of bed in the morning, you must plan what your next move will be. Will you turn on the radio and listen to the news, or will you run to the kitchen to examine the prospects for your long-awaited breakfast? Corporations in the United States also engage in planning. If the demand for automobiles is rising, a corporation may plan to build a new plant within the next year to meet the rising demand. Central economic planning, however, is the grandest of all planning schemes. The 5-year plan of the Soviets may be thought of as a large, empty box which is built to correspond to what the central planners feel the economy can do within the 5-year period. Once the 5-year box is constructed, the next step is to fit successively smaller boxes inside it, each applying to successively smaller time periods. Thus the yearly boxes would be placed inside the 5-year box, the quarterly boxes would be placed inside the yearly boxes, and so on until the schedules of day-to-day activities are carefully articulated. While this image of central economic planning as merely an extension of personal planning or corporate planning may make a great deal of sense in the abstract, it has little resemblance to the way things really work.

In periods of bad times and social crisis Americans are drawn toward this concept of central economic planning in hopes of finding it as the road to some kind of better coordination than might take place in our market economy. We change our minds from time to time about what areas of the economy we would like to see centrally planned, but the American fascination with central economic planning in one form or another has been around for many years. The important fallacy lying behind the concept of central economic planning which causes problems in actual practice can be seen in a fable told by Michael Polanyi.

Consider the situation of a potato farmer who has a sack of potatoes and wants to make it as compact as possible. Now one way of doing this is to contemplate the general shape of the potato and devise a scheme for measuring its dimensions. Measure every potato in the sack, put the measurements in a computer, and through some sort of program try to find to the closest packing arrangement which will fit the potatoes together such that they take up the smallest space. Since potatoes are rather oddly shaped, anyone familiar with advanced mathematics will see that this is a problem of rather gigantic complexity. In fact, it would be rather silly to grind out an optimum solution using this scheme.

Another way for the farmer to solve the problem is to put all the potatoes in the sack and give the sack a couple of shakes and let the potatoes settle in by themselves.

The important lesson to learn from this parable is that efficiency requires economizing in the use of knowledge. Knowledge is a costly resource. One of the most important advantages of a market economy over a centrally planned economy is that the market economy mobilizes knowledge for the benefit of society much more cheaply and effectively than any conscious effort can. This point can be more clearly seen by paraphrasing a story told by Nobel Prize-winning economist Friedrich A. Hayek.

Assume that somewhere in the world a new use has been found for tin, or alternately assume that some of the sources of tin in the world have been eliminated. To tell the story, it does not matter which of the two assumptions we choose. It is important, moreover, that it does not matter which of the two assumptions we choose. Each of these two assumptions will make tin more scarce. All that the users of tin need to know is that the resource they employ can be more profitably used now somewhere else and so they must economize in the use of tin. There really isn't any reason for the users of tin to know what the new use of tin is or why the supply of tin might have fallen. The effects of either of our assumptions will rapidly spread throughout the entire economic system and influence every one of the users of tin and all the substitutes of tin and all the substitutes of the substitutes of tin, and so on. All this will take place without the great majority of actors in the economy knowing anything at all about the original cause of these changes. The mere fact that there is one price for the commodity tin brings about the solution which might also have been arrived at in much less effective fashion by some central economic planning scheme.

CASE 26:

National Economic Planning[2]

Nothing more dramatically captured the onset of bourgeois acquisitiveness during my years than the belated Soviet romance with the private car. To provide an incentive for the elite and the growing middle class of engineers, technocrats, and middle-managers, the Soviet leadership invested about $15 billion to build up its automotive industry from 1965–75 (a large chunk of that went for truck factories and a fair share of the eventual auto output was slated for export at cut-rate prices). Automobiles, once ridiculed by Khrushchev as "foul-smelling armchairs on wheels," were making it in Soviet society at last.

The West might be struggling to divorce itself from the pollution, congestion and fuel problems born of its early marriage with the internal combustion engine, but in the Russia of the early Seventies there was a giddy, newlywed excitement about cars. A Western ambassador told me that his wife had stopped one day for a red light in their imported Lincoln Continental and a swarthy pedestrian, evidently from Soviet Georgia, motioned her to lower the window and then offered her 30,000 rubles ($40,000) for the car. When I was traveling in Armenia, a factory director proudly gestured to a couple of dozen cars parked in the lot outside his 5500-worker plant and boasted to me, "Those are the private cars of our workers." An engineer whom I knew felt positively liberated by his car (until it had a breakdown) and talked ecstatically about the pleasures of "traveling wild" (that is, not bound by organized groups, bus routes, or set-package itineraries for vacation). In the warm summer and early fall, the woods and fields around Moscow were sprinkled with the boxy little Zhigulis (Soviet-made Fiats) of people escaping the city.

During my three years in Moscow, the number of private cars in the Soviet Union rose from 1.8 to 3 million (compared to nearly 100 million in America). Still, the private car remained well beyond the means of the average factory worker (who earns $187 a month). For the Soviet auto industry offered four makes and eight models, ranging from the little Zaporozhets-968, a European mini-car that putts along on 43 horsepower and sells for 3500 rubles ($4665), to the Volga M-124, a five-seater that looks like a medium-sized Plymouth but costs 9150 rubles ($12,200). The popular Zhiguli runs about $10,000. And there is no financing to help out; it's cash on the line. Russian friends told me that if the buyer is not fortunate enough to be on one of the special lists for the privileged class, the wait for a car can run from one to five years. I knew a journalist who had waited six years for a Volga and predicted, "It will be another five years before I get it." Actually, through connections, he landed one within the next several months. Those who have to wait normal rotation on the one, citywide public waiting list,

[2]Reprinted by permission of Quadrangle/The New York Times Book Co. from *The Russians* by Hedrick Smith, Copyright © 1976 by Hedrick Smith.

get little choice of color or extras when their number comes up. But this seems to bother no one. Russians are delighted with whatever is available.

QUESTIONS

1 According to Hedrick Smith, the Russians built up their automotive industry between 1965 and 1975 in order to "provide an incentive for the elite and growing middle class of engineers, technocrats, and middle-managers." Why has the United States economy built up its far larger and more productive automotive industry? Explain how your answer illustrates one of the basic differences between a command economy and a free-market system.

2 Apparently a large part of the automotive expansion in the late 1960s and early 1970s in Russia was geared toward producing automobiles for export at cut-rate prices. The Russians were able to purchase a Fiat factory from the Italians to produce Fiat 128s because the Italians were certain that the Russians would *not* export the automobiles and thus ruin Italy's foreign markets. Why do you suppose the Italians were sure that Russia would not export Fiat 128s (which were one of the most popular cars in Western Europe at the time)? Were the Russians able to export cheap Fiat 128s because they could produce them more efficiently than the Italian company? Explain. Would you buy a Russian-built Fiat 128 (some were actually placed on sale in the United States, and one automotive enthusiast magazine actually ran a road test on one)?

3 Why would a Western ambassador be offered such a ridiculous price ($40,000) for his Lincoln Continental? Could this be an indication of a "shortage" of Lincoln Continentals in Russia? Is the high bid price for the car an indication that more of them "should" be marketed in Russia?

4 The Soviet automotive industry offered eight models to consumers in the early 1970s. Ford Motor Company alone offers Americans significantly more than a modest eight models. Is it "efficient" to offer fewer models to consumers (perhaps Americans are "too" frivolous in their appetite for gaudy cars)? What would you consider to be the appropriate number of models for production in the United States?

5 When you buy a new Ford or General Motors product in the United States, the General Motors Acceptance Corporation or Ford Motor Credit stand ready to finance your purchase over 12, 24, or 36 months. Downpayments on new cars are small or even nonexistent in some localities. Why do the Soviets require cash on the line? Couldn't more cars be sold with proper financing? Explain.

KEY CONCEPTS

Central economic planning A systematic way of establishing goals, setting a procedure for fulfillment of those goals, and actually carrying out those procedures.

Command economy An economy characterized by central economic planning.

Capitalistic economy An economy characterized by decentralized decision making and free markets.

Gosplan A state committee of the Soviet Union charged with preparing current and longer-range plans.

Socialism A hybrid economy characterized by private ownership of the means of production but resource allocation by means of central planning.

TEST YOURSELF

Multiple-choice

1 Which of the following statements about the Soviet economy is true? (**a**) The Soviet economy is characterized by private ownership of the means of production. (**b**) The Soviet economy operates in large part as a centrally planned economy with centralized decision making. (**c**) The Soviet economy is characterized by competitive markets and decentralized decision making. (**d**) None of the above.

2 Business firms in the Soviet Union (**a**) arrive at production and pricing decisions by mutual consent, (**b**) receive instructions from the central planning authority concerning quantity and price, (**c**) are more efficient than United States producers because they manufacture fewer types of goods, (**d**) are controlled by worker cooperatives which make all decisions.

3 Which of the following is not a characteristic of the Soviet economy? (**a**) Centrally planned decisions, (**b**) lack of inflationary pressures as a result of fixed prices and wages, (**c**) government ownership of most of the means of production, (**d**) none of the above.

4 Central economic planning often fails in practice because (**a**) few individuals have mastered its intricacies, (**b**) it has always been administered by shortsighted leaders, (**c**) it fails to economize on knowledge, (**d**) most workers don't understand it.

5 Economies characterized by central economic planning are said to be command economies because (**a**) few commands are necessary in such economies, (**b**) government must often "persuade" firms to achieve objectives, (**c**) consumers command the means of production for their own purposes, (**d**) none of the above.

True–false

T F 1. The Gosplan is the Soviet Union's 20-year plan

T F 2. Command economies are better at economizing on knowledge than free-market economies.

T F 3. Central economic planning has only recently (in the last 10 years) been tried.

T F 4. Price acts as a rationing mechanism in the Soviet Union.

T F 5. A consumer in the Soviet Union "votes" with his or her ruble in much the way an American "votes" with the dollar.

T F 6. The profit incentive is difficult to use in a command economy.

T F 7. The United States is a perfect example of a purely contractual economy.

T F 8. Shortages are a common phenomenon in a command economy.

T F 9. Since no one person decides in a free-market (contractual) economy what to produce, the result is bound to be chaotic.

T F 10. Economic plans in the Soviet Union are not coercive but rather suggestions for output.

27

The Environment

Often in real-world situations when two people enter into an agreement, it is not only the people entering into the agreement who either benefit or suffer as a consequence of the agreement. Suppose that your neighbor contracts with a painter to have his or her house repainted. After examining all the available colors and their various costs, your neighbor decides to paint the house a vivid gold with dark blue trim. The neighbor contracts with a painter who is more than willing to accept the money to paint the house, and the house is painted the following day. Now your neighbor has paid for the services of the painter, and the painter has provided the service of painting the house for the neighbor. Both are happy with the bargain that they made, and each is confident that he or she will benefit from the bargain. The difficulty lies in the fact that you are not particularly fond of vivid gold houses with dark blue trim. This appears to be a color scheme much more suited for wear by football players on bright, sunny fall afternoons. Unfortunately, you had no way of expressing your opinion at the time of the transaction, but you are affected by the outcome of the transaction. (See Chapter 5.)

As long as one person who is affected by the bargain is left out of the transaction, there is what economists call an *externality.* An externality is an outcome of an action which influences the individuals left out of the action. The externality or outcome may be either positive or negative depending upon whether the third parties are harmed or benefited. In the case of the gold and blue house, you felt that you were harmed, and therefore we may consider the externality to be a negative one. The classical case of an externality described by many an economist is that of a smoking factory. Suppose that in a particular isolated area there is one factory and beside the factory there is a single house. The factory is run by a single individual, and one person lives in the house. The factory emits a great deal of smoke, and the smoke has the effect of peeling the paint off the house which is located next door to the factory.

Suppose that the law indicates that factories may make as much smoke as they want regardless of the consequences of that smoke. In this situation we might expect the houseowner to have an incentive to bribe the factory owner to reduce the emission of smoke. With the law so clearly stated and with the disadvantage that the house must constantly be repainted, it seems reasonable that the homeowner will attempt to strike a bargain with the factory owner. The factory owner, of course, has an incentive to listen to all such bargains since by receiving some payment from the homeowner and reducing the emissions slightly, the factory owner may be better off than at present.

Consider a second situation in which the law provides that a factory may not emit any smoke without the permission of surrounding homeowners. We might expect then that the factory owner would have an incentive to bribe the homeowner for permission to emit.smoke. Actually, it matters very little whether the law is stated such that factories have no right to emit smoke or that factories may emit as much smoke as they like. In either case, there is an incentive to bargain for both parties, and we might anticipate that the same smoke-emitting arrangements (in terms of smoke emitted) would be arrived at by the factory owner and the homeowner in either situation.

The homewoner in the situation just described is subjected to an externality by the factory owner, and the two solutions which we have suggested as making both the factory owner and the homeowner better off were examples of government intervention. Both the law which allows factories to emit as much smoke as they like and the law which allows factories to emit no smoke subject to homeowners' discretion are examples of government intervention in a market system. As long as parties are able to alter the initial assignment of rights then the possibility exists to make *both* parties better off. The simple case described of the smoky factory with its home-owning neighbor has many of the essential characteristics of environmental problems in the real world. The story, however, is a carefully selected abstraction which, when filled in with detail, makes the complexity of real world environmental problems apparent.

Suppose that the case is complicated by the fact that there are many homeowners surrounding the smoky factory. Some of these homeowners live very close to the factory while other homeowners live in distant regions not often affected by the smoke of the factory. With differing meteorological conditions some homeowners would be affected more on some days than others, and many homeowners might be only rarely affected. Another simple complication to the story would be the case where there are many factories as well as many homeowners. In this situation it might be extremely difficult to learn which factory is emitting smoke at a particular time. It may even be the case that the factories are emitting different "kinds" of smoke which combine in such a way to produce more harm than a single "kind" of smoke. A third complication which is commonly found in the real world would be to consider the type of government which made the laws we assumed in the example above. If the government which makes the laws has geographical boundaries which just exactly match the geographical boundaries of smoke damage, we might expect laws passed like those above. On the other hand, the more natural case would be that the government's geographical boundaries, whether it be a local or state government, do not exactly match the boundaries of the smoke damage.

With each of these three rather common complications, difficulties arise with the setting of laws and bargaining such that an optimal solution to the environmental problem may be extremely difficult or impossible to reach.

For example, if many homeowners now surround the single factory and if the law clearly states that factories may emit as much smoke as they wish, it is unclear exactly what the solution to the externality may be. How can the factory owner bargain with each of the homeowners such that each homeowner is allowed to purchase the exact amount of smoke reduction desired?

To take a second example where an optimal solution may be difficult to reach, consider the case where there are many factories but only a single homeowner, and the law once again states that factories may emit as much smoke as they like. How can the homeowner bargain with the many factory owners to receive the exact amount of smoke reduction which he or she is willing to pay for. In the third case where the geographical limits of the government do not match the geographical limits of smoke damage, the situation is perhaps most difficult of all. It may now be the case that some people who are damaged by smoke from the factory or factories may not be voters in the government which controls most of the smoke-riddled area. By the same token, some people living close to the factory who vote in the government may not be subject to smoke damage (they may be upwind, for instance). In this last case it is unclear which freely chosen rules one could decide might make everyone, including the factory owner or owners, better off.

The very important point to remember about externalities and environmental problems is that *the government may not be able to produce a better outcome than the market will produce when left to itself.* In many cases government "solutions" to environmental problems will not be optimal or perfect outcomes. In these cases it is reasonable to ask whether some situations, while nonoptimal, might be better off with no government intervention at all. On the other hand, it should be clear from the simplest smoky factory example above that some government intervention may produce a better outcome than the free-market solution.

CASE 27:
The Delaware River Estuary[1]

The estuary of a river is its wide mouth where the current of the river meets the tide of the ocean into which the river flows. The Delaware River estuary is an 86-mile stretch of the Delaware River from Trenton, New Jersey, to Liston Point, Delaware. This 86 miles of the Delaware is a densely populated area of concentrated industrial activity. While the Delaware River Basin is small by standards of great American river basins, the area holds a population of over 6 million. Some areas of the Delaware River Basin are among the most highly industrialized and densely populated regions in the entire world.

For many years, even after the heavy industrial concentration along the Delaware River, water quality problems were entirely overlooked. In 1936, however, the Interstate Commission on the Delaware River Basin (INCODEL) was formed, and under its control the states in the basin signed a reciprocal agreement on water quality control. This agreement provided the legal basis for the construction of water treatment plants by cities shortly after World War II. Unfortunately the standards of treatment were not rigorous, and on the average not much more was done than the removal of the largest solids. During the warm summer months of the early 1950s dissolved oxygen levels fell extremely low or became totally exhausted in some portions of the estuary from Philadelphia to the Pennsylvania-Delaware state line.

A study was made of the water quality in the Delaware estuary by the United States Public Health Service in 1957–1958. The water quality ratings were so bad that a comprehensive study was requested of the estuary under provisions of the Federal Water Pollution Control Act. The findings of this comprehensive study were published in the summer of 1966 by the Federal Water Pollution Control Administration. The title of the document was "Delaware Estuary Comprehensive Study: Preliminary Report and Findings." The study was an extensive effort to measure all the external costs as well as the cost of control for various water quality levels in the Delaware estuary.

Perhaps the greatest contribution of the estuary study, according to environmental economists Allen Kneese and Blair Bower, was the development of a rigorous, mathematical model of water quality in the Delaware River estuary. The model allowed researchers to examine the particular effects downstream of pouring in particular quantities and qualities of effluents upstream. For instance, if factory A, located in Trenton, New Jersey, were to dump X units of a particular effluent into the river at that point, the model would predict exactly what condition this might cause downstream in Liston Point, Delaware.

[1] Facts in this case are reprinted with permission of Allen V. Kneese and Blair T. Bower from their book, *Managing Water Quality: Economics, Technology, and Institutions* (Baltimore, Md., Johns Hopkins University Press, 1968).

The comprehensive study of the Delaware estuary made another contribution to solving environmental problems by broadening the range of benefits which were considered in water quality estimates. The estuary study included in the benefits of improved water quality recreational benefits of swimming, boating, and sport fishing. While the quantifications of these particular benefits may have been crude in the estuary study, the increase in the range of benefits considered would likely bring about more complete information on water quality.

Following the estuary study another study was undertaken, using the same models and data. This second study was to examine the benefits and costs of different methods of cleaning up the Delaware River estuary. Four different programs were analyzed by the study for cleaning up the estuary. The technological measure used for "cleanliness" of the estuary was the dissolved oxygen content of a given amount of water.

The first possible solution suggested by the study was the least-cost solution. This would use a mathematical programming technique to obtain the minimum cost distribution of waste removal. In order to use this program as a means of control, the government would be required to receive information on the cost of treating waste at each of the points along the estuary as well as information about the ultimate effect of each effluent discharged at each point along the estuary on the general level of water quality.

The second solution examined by the study was called the "uniform treatment solution." This solution would very simply require each waste discharger to remove a certain percentage of the wastes which were previously discharged into the river.

The third solution examined is called the "single effluent charge solution." This solution involved charging each waste discharger in the estuary the same price per unit of effluent discharged. The final solution examined by the study is called the "zone effluent charge solution." Under this solution waste emitters would be charged different effluent charges depending upon where in the estuary they were located. Presumably those waste dischargers located in the areas where discharges were extremely costly in terms of water quality would have to pay more than those dischargers located in parts of the estuary where discharges had little effect on water quality.

Considering all the costs of implementing each of these programs, the zone effluent charge solution appears to be the most efficient.

KEY CONCEPTS

Externality The outcome of an action which affects an individual not a party to the action.

Effluent charges A fee which a polluter must pay to the government for discharging waste.

QUESTIONS

1 Why do you suspect that the states along the Delaware River formed the Interstate Commission on the Delaware River Basin? Couldn't each state have treated its own part of the problem separately without interference from other states? Explain.

2 The Interstate Commission on the Delaware River Basin concentrated on building municipal water treatment plants as a solution to the water quality problem. Would polluters be affected in the amount of waste they emitted by the building of a large number of treatment plants? Wouldn't social pressure force the polluters to discontinue emitting because citizens (who paid for the treatment plants) clearly wanted to improve water quality? Explain your answers.

3 Could a model of pollution showing the causes and effects of various emissions, like the one constructed in the comprehensive study, be used as a basis for effluent charges in an *air* quality situation? Do you suppose that the pollution model constructed in the estuary study could have been constructed 50 years ago? Is there any indication that the "best" solution to environmental problems changes over time?

4 If you were a polluter located along the Delaware estuary and were subjected to an effluent charge of $50 per unit of effluent, would you have any incentive to reduce your emissions? To increase your emissions? *Could* effluent charges force you to reduce your emissions to zero? *Should* effluent charges force you to reduce your emissions to zero?

5 The least-cost programming solution studied for the Delaware estuary would have charged each polluter a different effluent charge depending upon how harmful the effluent was and the cost of cleaning up that effluent. Why do you suppose that this solution did not appear to be the most efficient (least-cost) solution? *(Hint:* Would there be any difficulties in implementing this system? Would the charges ever have to be revised? How often?)

6 The zone effluent charge solution also would charge polluters different charges. In each of three zones, the effluent charges would be different. Would some polluters move to the least-cost zones to pollute? Wouldn't this defeat the purposes of the effluent charges? Why might we want to charge polluters in different zones different effluent charges?

TEST YOURSELF

Multiple-choice

1 The externality of a smoky factory could be viewed as
- **(a)** a cost of production which the firm is not paying,
- **(b)** a cost of production which will be paid by consumers of the factory's product,
- **(c)** a cost of production which will be paid by the government,
- **(d)** all the above.

2 Effluent charges
   (a) are rarely used to decrease pollution in real world situations,
   (b) encourage polluters to reduce emissions,
   (c) are an ineffective way of reducing pollution in most instances,
   (d) are levied on companies based on their use of raw materials.

3 If an externality exists,
   (a) government intervention can always make each of the parties better off,
   (b) government intervention can never make each of the parties better off,
   (c) government intervention can sometimes make parties better off than if they had been left in a free-market situation.

4 Environmental problems involving externalities
   (a) will always require government intervention,
   (b) will never require government intervention,
   (c) may require government intervention,
   (d) none of the above.

True–false

T F 1. Effluent charges are payments by polluters for emissions.

T F 2. Externalities are negative outcomes to individuals not included in the transaction.

T F 3. Existence of externalities produces a clear case for government intervention.

T F 4. If an externality exists, it is because one party is trying to harm another.

T F 5. If many individuals are involved in an externality problem, agreement on a solution should be easy to attain.

T F 6. Effluent charges make little sense in terms of making everyone better off.

T F 7. Zero pollution may not be the most preferred solution for a society.

T F 8. Information about who is polluting is generally irrelevant to environmental problems in real world solutions.

T F 9. Information about who is being harmed is generally irrelevant to environmental problems in real world solutions.

T F 10. Monopolists will always have a tendency to pollute more than firms in competition.

28

Energy

For some reason the United States government considers the energy market to be an extremely peculiar animal in need of extensive repairing by regulations, subsidies, taxes, quotas, etc. The government has gone far beyond the rule-making function of the minimal state in the energy market—federal control of oil imports, natural gas prices, and exploration rights, to name a few areas, is overwhelming.

The members of the energy industry itself have often been among the most staunch supporters of regulation in this area. Neither the industry nor the government is willing to accept the direction of Adam Smith's invisible hand in this market. The industry has consistently lobbied for restrictions on fuel imports while, at the same time, requesting subsidies and exemptions from antitrust and full-disclosure laws. Most would-be reformers of the energy market today propose even *more* government regulation such as taxes on windfall profits or administratively determined prices.

All this outspoken need for regulation of the energy market stems from the feeling that energy is "too important" a commodity to let the free market allocate. The oil depletion allowance, for instance, is supposedly needed because, without it, many feel oil companies will not search for new deposits. Oil import quotas were supposedly needed to protect the employment, income, and production of domestic producers. Investment tax credits are supposedly needed to promote purchase of efficient capital equipment.

The "energy is too important" argument for regulation has two branches one commonly hears today. First, energy is "too important" because there is only a finite amount of it around; we are running out of it; therefore we desperately need to conserve what is left. There seems to be an easy solution to this energy shortage argument—simply raise the price. Each individual should be made to pay the full cost of the energy he or she is using.

The second branch of the "too important" argument involves national security. If we import energy, the argument goes, we become dependent on—at the mercy of—the energy producers (the bad guys are usually seen these days as the sheiks of OPEC). This argument may indeed carry some currency with you if you feel that a war is likely where large supplies of energy are needed over a long period. If that is true, we would presumably be willing to pay a price (perhaps a large one) for being self-sufficient in energy.

Economists of the recent past viewed this regulation as a set of decrees issued by politicians after intense discussion of its affect on general welfare. The regulations themselves were outside the domain of economics. This naive view of regulation, especially in the energy market, is hopelessly out of date today. The case which follows fosters an economic examination of what economist George Stigler has called "the largest public cartel in world history." He is referring to the governmentally supported oil import quota in effect from the 1950s until 1973.

CASE 29:

Oil Import Tickets[1]

For reasons vaguely reported to be "national defense considerations," the oil industry in the United States is seen by the government to be a "peculiar" industry requiring special treatment. The industry has been subjected to a constant stream of legislation from World War II to the present day—the oil import quota examined here is only one of a number of government intrusions on the energy industry.

In July 1954, then President Eisenhower established the Advisory Committee on Energy Supplies and Policy Resources. The committee recommended in February 1955 that a voluntary program of oil imports be instituted to reduce the level to the 1954 amount. The recommendation instantly received strong, sustained support through purposive campaigns engineered by the most importantly affected parties: domestic oil and coal producers. According to energy economists Yoram Barzel and Christopher Hall, the reason for the recommendation was presumably national defense. This line of reasoning held that if the United States continued to import cheap foreign crude oil, domestic producers would cut back their production; American dependence on foreign imports would increase, and eventually we might find our military forces themselves unable to operate without foreign oil. Putting our military preparedness in the hands of foreign oil producers was seen as rather foolish. By restricting imports with a quota, according to the domestic energy producers, American oil companies would have a clear profit incentive to increase production and reduce our reliance on foreign suppliers. Regardless of the validity of why the United States must be self-sufficient in oil, the interesting point is that the special interests strongly supported a quota (they could, for instance, have supported a tax on imports—a tariff—and used the very same argument).

The voluntary program was instituted, and the director of the Office of Defense Mobilization was placed in charge of keeping the oil companies in line. The voluntary program was a failure, and so another committee was formed to investigate the failure and make recommendations. They found that some oil companies like Delta Refining Company and Superior Oil felt they had volunteered enough and so began importing crude without obtaining voluntary allocations. Since the government could do little except bring the weight of public opinion to bear on them, the voluntary quota failed.

With a little help again from the domestic energy producers, the committee argued for a mandatory quota on oil imports. The new mandatory quota was

[1] Facts in this case are reprinted from Yoram Barzel and Christopher D. Hall's *The Political Economy of the Oil Import Quota*, with the permission of the publishers, Hoover Institution Press. Copyright © 1977 by the Board of Trustees of the Leland Stanford Junior University.

proclaimed by President Eisenhower in March 1959. Barzel and Hall explain how the import quota worked by postulating a simplified situation:

> Imagine, for instance, that an advertisement were to appear offering rights to import oil at a zero price, while they last, at your neighborhood Oil Import Administration Office. With one of these rights and two dollars you could have delivered to your home or refinery one barrel of first class Kuwait crude. Once delivered, this barrel of oil would sell for $1.25 more than you paid for it including the transportation charges from the Mideast. Due to limited supply, the ad goes on to say, the number of tickets will be allocated in books of ten tickets, via the first-come-stand-orderly-in-line method.[2]

Once you have an import ticket, you needn't actually import the oil—you could sell your ticket in what the government called a "swap" to anybody else wishing to import oil. Regardless of whether you actually imported the oil and sold it or swapped your ticket, you made money because the ticket originally cost you nothing (zero price). In actuality, the tickets were *not* handed out on a first-come, first-served basis but given (zero price) to firms which had been importing oil and to refiners who had been using foreign oil.

Not too surprisingly, attempts to "beat" the quota started about 30 seconds after the quota was conceived. At least three methods were used with varying success by various companies.

The first import-beating technique involved the way in which the quota was worded—in terms of barrels of "crude oil." Now everyone agreed that a barrel contains 42 U.S. gallons, but not everyone agreed on exactly what crude oil was. It seems crude oil is *not* a homogeneous commodity but varies in any number of ways from one barrel to the next. For instance, it may vary in specific gravity, sulfur content, amount of sediment, water content, etc. Realizing this, importers could vary the value of the imported crude oil allowed on their ticket by varying the contents of the barrel. Some importers even went further and imported "partially processed" oil (which they still called crude oil) which was treated to low-cost processing at the oil field.

A second method for "relaxing" the quota involved the special consideration given free-trade zones in quota regulations. Union Carbide requested permission to import 15,000 barrels per day to a plant to be constructed in Taft, Louisiana, in an area to be classified as a free-trade zone. While the request was never granted, it was rather innovative.

The most notorious technique is characterized by the infamous "Brownsville U turn" located in Brownsville, Texas. The quota regulations allowed Mexico and Canada special consideration in that oil brought overland into the United States was exempt from the quota. Oil was therefore shipped by tanker from Mexico to

[2] See Yoram Barzel and Christopher Hall, *The Political Economy of the Oil Import Quota* (Stanford, Calif.: Hoover Institution Press, 1977), p. 23.

Brownsville, loaded onto trucks, driven across the border into Mexico, and returned once again to Brownsville with the now quota-exempt oil.

The mandatory oil import quota was abandoned in 1973.

KEY CONCEPTS

Oil import ticket The right granted by the quota to import one barrel of crude oil.

Swaps An officially sanctioned method of cashing in one's oil import tickets.

Self-sufficiency The position that holds that the United States should be able to provide for all its energy needs through domestic production.

Oil depletion allowance Permits firms to deduct more than the actual costs of production in calculating taxable income. It supposedly promotes oil exploration.

Quota A limit on the quantity of a good which may be imported.

QUESTIONS

1 Why did the voluntary import quota fail? If you had been an oil refiner in 1955, would you have followed the rules of the quota? Explain.

2 The argument for energy self-sufficiency hinges on national defense considerations. Do you believe self-sufficiency is necessary in crude oil for an effective defense policy? Are there other commodities (other than energy) in which you feel we require self-sufficiency to have an effective defense posture?

3 Regardless of your answer to question 2, assume you are a domestic oil refiner. Would you rather see the mandatory import quota or a system of tariffs? Explain your answer in terms of your self-interest.

4 Some individuals feel the world is running out of energy resources. Would the oil import quota conserve or use up our domestic supplies more quickly?

5 Were there any costs to imposing the mandatory quota? If so, which individuals paid these costs? Were the benefits of the quota in excess of the costs?

6 Since the oil refiners and importers paid a zero price for their import tickets, did they incur any costs in obtaining import rights? Explain.

7 When the mandatory import quota was instituted, which way did the supply curve for crude oil (both domestic and foreign) shift? Would this have had any effect on crude oil prices in the domestic market?

TEST YOURSELF

True—false

T F 1. Voluntary quotas in the energy industry have worked rather well.

T F 2. Mandatory quotas in the energy industry have worked rather well.

T F 3. Oil producers and refiners did not lobby for a tariff on imported oil.

T F 4. Much energy legislation rests on the belief that the United States must be self-sufficient in energy.

T F 5. The energy market is one of the least regulated of the domestic markets.

T F 6. Energy regulations (i.e., quotas, tariffs, etc.) are a rather recent (1960s and 1970s) phenomenon.

T F 7. Crude oil is, like wheat, a homogeneous commodity.

T F 8. Special interest groups play a significant role in energy legislation.

T F 9. Energy is a "special" commodity because investment requires such a long lead time.

T F 10. Oil producers and refiners apparently would like less regulation.

ANSWERS TO TEST YOURSELF

CHAPTER 1. A WAY OF UNDERSTANDING THE SOCIAL ORDER

1. b
2. c
3. b
4. b
5. c

CHAPTER 2. THE FRAMEWORK OF ANALYSIS

1. b
2. c
3. b
4. a
5. b

CHAPTER 3. DEMAND AND PRICE ELASTICITY

1. -3, elastic
   -1.4, elastic
   -5/7, inelastic
2. Yes
3. -0.2
   -0.385
   -1.0
4. c
5. c
6. a
7. b
8. c

CHAPTER 4. THE LAW OF SUPPLY AND COSTS

1. See graphs on page 230
2. a
3. c
4. b
5. c
6. a
7. b
8. c

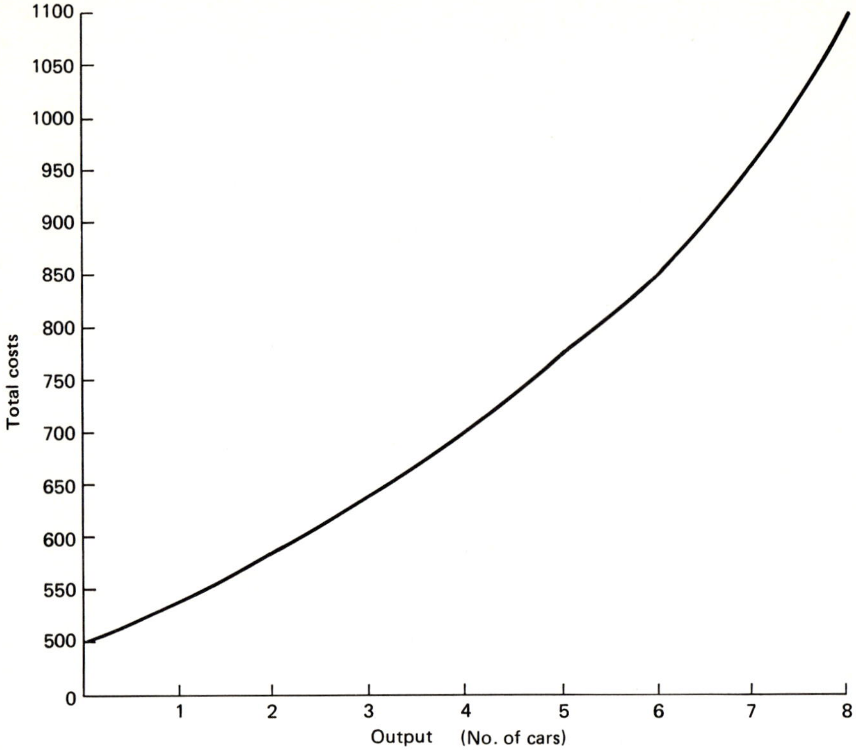

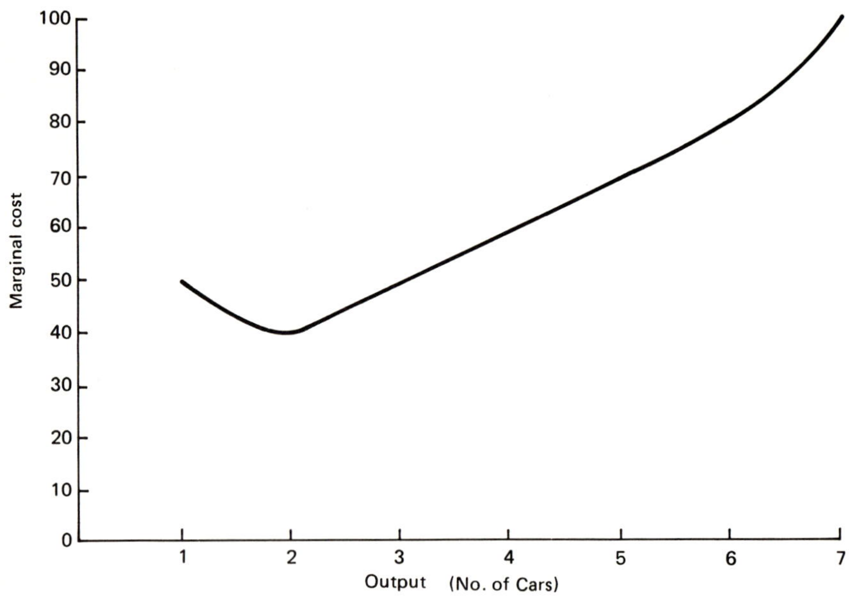

Question 1, Chapter 4

CHAPTER 5. PROPERTY RIGHTS AND SOCIAL ORDER

True–false

1. T
2. F
3. F
4. T
5. T

Multiple-choice

1. **c**
2. **c**
3. **d**
4. **a**
5. **d**

CHAPTER 6. THE LOGIC OF GROUP BEHAVIOR

True–false

1. T
2. T
3. T
4. F
5. T
6. T
7. T
8. T
9. F
10. F
11. F
12. T

CHAPTER 7. COMPETITION

Multiple-choice

1. **a**
2. **a**
3. **b**
4. **b**
5. **b**
6. **c**
7. **b**
8. **a**

True–false

1. T
2. F
3. T
4. T
5. F
6. T
7. F
8. T

CHAPTER 8. COMPETITION IN ACTION

True–false

1. T
2. F
3. F
4. T
5. F

Multiple-choice

1. a
2. b
3. c
4. b
5. a
6. e
7. e

CHAPTER 9. THE MARKET FOR FOOD

1. b
2. c
3. d
4. b
5. a
6. b
7. c
8. b

CHAPTER 10. MARKET PERFORMANCE AND MONOPOLY POWER

True–false

1. T
2. T
3. F
4. F
5. F

Multiple-choice

1. b
2. b
3. c
4. d
5. d
6. b
7. d
8. a

CHAPTER 11. PRICES: WHAT DO THEY TELL US?

True–false

1. F
2. T
3. T
4. F
5. F
6. T
7. T
8. F
9. T

Multiple-choice

1. a
2. c
3. c
4. c
5. a
6. b
7. a

CHAPTER 12. GOVERNMENT REGULATION OF PRIVATE MARKETS

True—false

1. T
2. T
3. T
4. F
5. F
6. T
7. T
8. T
9. F
10. T

Multiple-choice

1. a
2. a
3. e
4. c

CHAPTER 13. GOVERNMENT PROTECTION FOR THE CONSUMER

True—false

1. T
2. T
3. F
4. T
5. T
6. F
7. F
8. T
9. T
10. T

Multiple-choice

1. c
2. b
3. a
4. a

CHAPTER 14. THE DEMAND FOR RESOURCES

True–false

1. F
2. T
3. T
4. T
5. F
6. T
7. F
8. T
9. T
10. F

Multiple-choice

1. **d**
2. **e**
3. **b**
4. **a**
5. **c**
6. **b**
7.

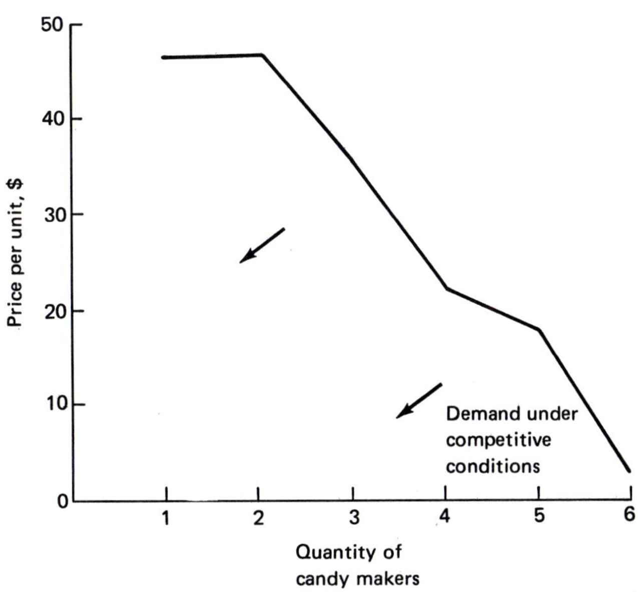

Figure 14-1 Demand curve for candy makers by firm Z.

CHAPTER 15. POWER IN THE MARKET FOR RESOURCES

True—false

1. F
2. T
3. F
4. F
5. T
6. F
7. T
8. F
9. T
10. F

Multiple-choice

1. **a**
2. **d**
3. **d**
4. **b**
5. **a**
6. **b**
7. **a**

CHAPTER 16. INTERNATIONAL TRADE AND INTERNATIONAL FINANCE

Multiple-choice

1. **b**
2. **b**
3. **b**
4. **b**
5. **a**
6. **c**

True--false

1. T
2. T
3. T
4. T
5. F

CHAPTER 17. THE ROLES OF GOVERNMENT

True—false

1. T
2. F
3. T
4. T
5. F
6. T
7. T
8. F
9. T
10. T

CHAPTER 18. THE ETHICS OF DISTRIBUTION

True—false

1. T
2. T
3. F
4. F
5. F
6. F
7. F
8. T
9. F
10. F

CHAPTER 19. THE ORGANIZATION OF COLLECTIVE ACTION

True—false

1. T
2. F
3. F
4. T
5. T
6. F
7. F
8. F

9. F
10. T

Matching

1. D
2. J
3. C
4. B
5. E
6. H

CHAPTER 20. THE MARKET FOR LOCAL PUBLIC GOODS

True—false

1. F
2. T
3. T
4. T
5. T
6. F
7. T
8. T
9. F
10. F

Matching

1. B
2. G
3. E
4. C
5. I
6. A

CHAPTER 21. CREATION OF MONEY

Multiple-choice

1. **c**
2. **a**

3. **b**
4. **c**
5. **d**
6. **a**
7. **a**
8. **b**
9. **c**

Matching

1. C
2. E
3. A
4. D
5. B

CHAPTER 22. INFLATION

Multiple-choice

1. **b**
2. **b**
3. **a**
4. **c**

True—false

1. T
2. F
3. T
4. T
5. F
6. T
7. F
8. F
9. F
10. T

CHAPTER 23. UNEMPLOYMENT

Multiple-choice

1. **c**
2. **b**
3. **a**
4. **b**
5. **b**
6. **b**
7. **d**
8. **a**

True—false

1. F
2. T
3. F
4. T
5. T
6. T
7. F
8. F

CHAPTER 24. THE CLASSICISTS, THE KEYNESIANS, AND THE MONETARISTS VIEW UNEMPLOYMENT AND INFLATION

True—false

1. F
2. F
3. T
4. T
5. T
6. F
7. T
8. F
9. F
10. F

Matching

1. G
2. J
3. E
4. F
5. I
6. A

CHAPTER 25. INFORMATION PROBLEMS AND THE KEYNESIAN MODEL

True—false

1. F
2. T
3. F
4. T
5. F
6. F
7. F
8. T
9. F
10. F

Matching

1. J
2. H
3. G
4. A
5. F
6. E

CHAPTER 26. NATIONAL PLANNING

Multiple-choice

1. **b**
2. **b**
3. **b**
4. **c**
5. **b**

True–false

1. F
2. F
3. F
4. F
5. F
6. T
7. F
8. T
9. F
10. F

CHAPTER 27. THE ENVIRONMENT

Multiple-choice

1. **a**
2. **b**
3. **c**
4. **c**

True–false

1. T
2. F
3. F
4. F
5. F
6. F
7. T
8. F
9. F
10. F

CHAPTER 28. ENERGY

True–false

1. F
2. F
3. T

4. T
5. F
6. F
7. F
8. T
9. F
10. F